⬧ W9-CMS-897

Whistle Blowing

LIBRARY

North Dakota State University

GIFT OF

Ralph Nader

_____

WITHDRAWN
NDSU

This book is printed on one hundred percent recycled paper.

Also available:

ACTION FOR A CHANGE: *A Student's Guide to Public Interest Organizing,* by Ralph Nader and Donald Ross

THE CHEMICAL FEAST: *Ralph Nader's Study Group Report on the Food and Drug Administration,* by James S. Turner

THE CLOSED ENTERPRISE SYSTEM: *Ralph Nader's Study Group Report on Antitrust Enforcement,* by Mark J. Green, with Beverly C. Moore, Jr., and Bruce Wasserstein

THE COMPANY STATE: *Ralph Nader's Study Group Report on DuPont in Delaware,* by James Phelan and Robert Pozen

THE INTERSTATE COMMERCE OMISSION: *Ralph Nader's Study Group on the Interstate Commerce Commission and Transportation,* by Robert C. Fellmeth

OLD AGE: THE LAST SEGREGATION: *Ralph Nader's Study Group Report on Nursing Homes,* Claire Townsend, Project Director

POLITICS OF LAND: *Ralph Nader's Study Group Report on Land Use in California,* Robert C. Fellmeth, Project Director

SMALL—ON SAFETY: *The Designed-in Dangers of the Volkswagen,* by the Center for Auto Safety

SOWING THE WIND: *A Report for Ralph Nader's Center for Study of Responsive Law on Food Safety and the Chemical Harvest*, by Harrison Wellford

UNSAFE AT ANY SPEED: *The Designed-in Dangers of the American Automobile* (expanded and updated, 1972), by Ralph Nader

VANISHING AIR: *Ralph Nader's Study Group Report on Air Pollution*, by John C. Esposito

THE WATER LORDS: *Ralph Nader's Study Group Report on Industry and Environmental Crisis in Savannah, Georgia*, by James M. Fallows

WATER WASTELAND: *Ralph Nader's Study Group Report on Water Pollution*, by David Zwick with Marcy Benstock

WHAT TO DO WITH YOUR BAD CAR: *An Action Manual for Lemon Owners*, by Ralph Nader, Lowell Dodge, and Ralf Hotchkiss

THE WORKERS: *Portraits of Nine American Jobholders*, by Kenneth Lasson

WHISTLE BLOWING

The Report of the Conference
on Professional Responsibility

edited by Ralph Nader,
Peter J. Petkas,
and Kate Blackwell

Grossman Publishers
New York 1972

Copyright © 1972 by Ralph Nader

All rights reserved

First published in 1972 by Grossman Publishers
625 Madison Avenue, New York, N.Y. 10022

Published simultaneously in Canada by
Fitzhenry and Whiteside, Ltd.

SBN 670–76224–5 (clothbound)

SBN 670–76225-3 (paperbound)

Library of Congress Catalogue Card Number: 74–170616

Printed in U.S.A.

HD
60.5
U5
C 68
1971
c. 2

Publisher's Preface

On January 30, 1971, the Conference on Professional Responsibility, held in Washington, D.C., brought together some of the leading exponents of "whistle blowing"—the act of a man or woman who, believing that the public interest overrides the interest of the organization he serves, publicly "blows the whistle" if the organization is involved in corrupt, illegal, fraudulent, or harmful activity—and some of the individuals who in different circumstances have felt compelled to speak out against the activities of their organizations. The conference was organized by Ralph Nader and his associate Peter Petkas, and sponsored by the Clearinghouse for Professional Responsibility. (The conference program and a list of its participants can be found in Appendix A.) This book is the report of that conference.

The proceedings began with four keynote speeches, which became the first four chapters of this book. Ralph Nader, who delivered the first, has uncovered and exposed abuses of the public interest by business and governmental groups since the publication of *Unsafe at Any Speed* in 1965. His efforts, in automobile safety, meat and poultry inspection, environmental quality, and other areas, have often been aided by whistle blowers, whose information and assistance have sometimes been rendered anonymously, sometimes publicly. It was a General Motors engineer, in fact, who first called his attention to the hazards of the Corvair. In the publication of the reports of study groups he has sponsored, in the creation of student Public Interest Research Groups, and in the establishment of the Clearinghouse for Professional Responsibility, he has both continued and broadened what he calls "full-time citizenship."

Wisconsin's Senator William Proxmire, the second keynote speaker, has served in the Upper Chamber since 1957. He has earned a reputation for speaking his mind to the public and to his colleagues, and is well known as a friend of the ordinary taxpayer and an opponent of those who would squander the public purse for private or parochial gain. He is perhaps best known as the nemesis of the defense establishment; a deeply patriotic man, he has not let the saber rattlers and the flagwavers daunt him in his efforts to curtail unnecessary expenditures and inefficient defense programs. Whistle blowers have made his work more effective, and he hopes to sew protections for them into the fabric of our laws.

Robert Townsend, author of the bestseller *Up the Organization!*, is an inside expert on how corporations operate. He has served as a director of Dun and Bradstreet, as head of investment and international banking for the American Express Company, as president and chief executive officer of an international rent-a-car company that is still number two, and chairman of the executive committee of a magazine and college textbook publishing company. Townsend, fifty-one, is now retired: he says he doesn't want any more money and that there's no job, public or private, that he would accept under any circumstances. Whatever he does, he says, he does for two reasons: first, because he loves the United States and thinks its leaders, public and private, have "gotten it into this mess," from which he would like to help the people extricate themselves; and second, because he enjoys it. Townsend believes that whistle blowing may be the only way left to save the free enterprise system.

Professor Arthur S. Miller of the National Law Center, George Washington University, is a specialist on constitutional law. He has written a number of wide-ranging articles on subjects at the frontier of constitutional development in civil rights and individual liberties and the relationship of individual citizens to various power centers within our society. His 1959 monograph for the Center for the Study of Democratic Institutions, *Private Governments and the Constitution,* was a milestone in advanced thinking on the role of the corporation in our constitutional system. Professor

Miller believes that present law must be changed in a number of areas before whistle blowers will have adequate protection from unfair and arbitrary treatment.

These keynote speakers were followed to the podium by several whistle blowers. In short presentations they described the nature of their actions, the pressures that led them to act, and the retaliation most of them faced; they also suggested, on the basis of their experiences, ethical and tactical guidelines for would-be whistle blowers. Their presentations formed the basis for the second part of this book, which recounts their experiences. Parts III and IV also evolved out of the whistle blowers' suggestions, as well as from the discussions that followed at the conference and from further research into corporate, legal, and government attitudes toward whistle blowing.

Contents

IV. Strategies for Whistle Blowers

"We complain about government and business, we stress the advantages of the free enterprise system, we complain about the totalitarian state, but in our individual organizations . . . we have created more or less of a totalitarian system in industry, particularly in large industry."

> —General Robert E. Wood,
> former chairman of the board.
> Sears, Roebuck & Company

I

Keynotes on Whistle Blowing

An Anatomy of Whistle Blowing

Ralph Nader

Americans believe that they have set for themselves and for the rest of the world a high example of individual freedom. That example inevitably refers to the struggle by a minority of aggrieved citizens against the royal tyranny of King George III. Out of the struggle that established this nation some chains were struck off and royal fiats abolished. Americans became a nation with the conviction that arbitrary government action should not restrict the freedom of individuals to follow their own consciences.

Today arbitrary treatment of citizens by powerful institutions has assumed a new form, no less insidious than that which prevailed in an earlier time. The "organization" has emerged and spread its invisible chains. Within the structure of the organization there has taken place an erosion of both human values and the broader value of human beings as the possibility of dissent within the hierarchy has become so restricted that common candor requires uncommon courage. The large organization is lord and manor, and most of its employees have been desensitized much as were medieval peasants who never knew they were serfs. It is true that often the immediate physical deprivations are far fewer, but the price of this fragile shield has been the dulling of the senses and perceptions of new perils and pressures of a far more embracing consequence.

Some of these perils may be glimpsed when it is realized that our society now has the numbing capacity to
destroy itself inadvertently by continuing the domestic
chemical and biological warfare against its citizens and
their environments. Our political economy has also developed an inverted genius that can combine an increase
in the gross national product with an increase in
the gross national misery. Increasingly, larger organizations—public and private—possess a Medea-like in-
tensity to paralyze conscience, initiative, and proper
concern for people outside the organization.

Until recently, all hopes for change in corporate and
government behavior have been focused on external
pressures on the organization, such as regulation, competition, litigation, and exposure to public opinion.
There was little attention given to the simple truth
that the adequacy of these external stimuli is very significantly dependent on the internal freedom of those
within the organization.

Corporate employees are among the first to know
about industrial dumping of mercury or fluoride sludge
into waterways, defectively designed automobiles, or
undisclosed adverse effects of prescription drugs and
pesticides. They are the first to grasp the technical capa-
bilities to prevent existing product or pollution hazards.
But they are very often the last to speak out, much less
to refuse to be recruited for acts of corporate or governmental negligence or predation. Staying silent in the
face of a professional duty has direct impact on the level
of consumer and environmental hazards. But this awareness has done little to upset the slavish adherence to
"following company orders."

Silence in the face of abuses may also be evaluated
in terms of the toll it takes on the individuals who in
doing so subvert their own consciences. For example,
the twenty-year collusion by the domestic automobile
companies against development and marketing of exhaust control systems is a tragedy, among other things,
for engineers who, minion-like, programmed the technical artifices of the industry's defiance. Settling the
antitrust case brought by the Justice Department against
such collusion did nothing to confront the question of
subverted engineering integrity.

The key question is, at what point should an employee resolve that allegiance to society (e.g., the public safety) must supersede allegiance to the organization's policies (e.g., the corporate profit), and then act on that resolve by informing outsiders or legal authorities? It is a question that involves basic issues of individual freedom, concentration of power, and information flow to the public. These issues in turn involve daily choices such as the following:

To report or not to report:

1) defective vehicles in the process of being marketed to unsuspecting consumers;

2) vast waste of government funds by private contractors;

3) the industrial dumping of mercury in waterways;

4) the connection between companies and campaign contributions;

5) a pattern of discrimination by age, race, or sex in a labor union or company;

6) mishandling the operation of a workers' pension fund;

7) willful deception in advertising a worthless or harmful product;

8) the sale of putrid or adulterated meats, chemically camouflaged in supermarkets;

9) the use of government power for private, corporate, or industry gain;

10) the knowing nonenforcement of laws being seriously violated, such as pesticide laws;

11) rank corruption in an agency or company;

12) the suppression of serious occupational disease data.

It is clear that hundreds and often thousands of people are privy to such information but choose to remain silent within their organizations. Some are conscience-stricken in so doing and want guidance. Actually, the general responsibility is made clear for the professional by codes of ethics. These codes invariably etch the primary allegiance to the public interest, while the Code of Ethics for United States Government Service does the same: "Put loyalty to the highest moral principles

and to country above loyalty to persons, party, or
Government department." The difficulty rests in the
judgment to be exercised by the individual and its implementation. Any potential whistle blower has to ask
and try to answer a number of questions:

1) Is my knowledge of the matter complete and
accurate?

2) What are the objectionable practices and what
public interests do they harm?

3) How far should I and can I go inside the
organization with my concern or objection?

4) Will I be violating any rules by contacting outside parties and, if so, is whistle blowing nevertheless
justified?

5) Will I be violating any laws or ethical duties by
not contacting external parties?

6) Once I have decided to act, what is the best
way to blow the whistle—anonymously, overtly, by
resignation prior to speaking out, or in some other
way?

7) What will be likely responses from various
sources—inside and outside the organization—to the
whistle blowing action?

8) What is expected to be achieved by whistle-
blowing in the particular situation?

In Part IV of this book we have developed a series
of possible strategies with these questions in mind and
in light of all the experiences presented in the inter-
vening pages. But the decision to act and the answers
to all of these questions are unique for every situation
and for every individual. Presently, certitudes are the
exception.

There is a great need to develop an ethic of whistle
blowing which can be practically applied in many con-
texts, especially within corporate and governmental bureaucracies. For this to occur, people must be permitted
to cultivate their own form of allegiance to their fellow
citizens and exercise it without having their professional
careers or employment opportunities destroyed. This
new ethic will develop if employees have the right to
due process within their organizations and if they have
at least some of the rights—such as the right to speak

freely—that now protect them from state power. In the past, as the balance of this book documents, whistle blowing has illuminated dark corners of our society, saved lives, prevented injuries and disease, and stopped corruption, economic waste, and material exploitation. Conversely, the absence of such professional and individual responsibility has perpetuated these conditions. In this context whistle blowing, if carefully defined and protected by law, can become another of those adaptive, self-implementing mechanisms which mark the relative difference between a free society that relies on free institutions and a closed society that depends on authoritarian institutions.

Indeed, the basic status of a citizen in a democracy underscores the themes implicit in a form of professional and individual responsibility that places responsibility to society over that to an illegal or negligent or unjust organizational policy or activity. These themes touch the right of free speech, the right to information, the citizen's right to participate in important public decisions, and the individual's obligation to avoid complicity in harmful, fraudulent, or corrupt activities. Obviously, as in the exercise of constitutional rights, abuses may occur. But this has long been considered an acceptable risk of free speech within very broad limits. Throughout this book, in the stories of whistle blowers and in the chapters advocating reform and spelling out strategies, we set out many of the risks and the necessary limitations on blowing the whistle in the public interest.

Still, the willingness and ability of insiders to blow the whistle is the last line of defense ordinary citizens have against the denial of their rights and the destruction of their interests by secretive and powerful institutions. As organizations penetrate deeper and deeper into the lives of people—from pollution to poverty to income erosion to privacy invasion—more of their rights and interests are adversely affected. This fact of contemporary life has generated an ever greater moral imperative for employees to be reasonably protected in upholding such rights regardless of their employers' policies. The corporation, the labor unions and professional societies to which its employees belong, the government in its ca-

pacity as employer, and the law must all change or be
changed to make protection of the responsible whistle
blower possible.

Each corporation should have a bill of rights for its
employees and a system of internal appeals to guarantee
these rights. As a condition of employment, workers at
every level in the corporate hierarchy should have the
right to express their reservations about the company's
activities and policies, and their views should be accorded a fair hearing. They should have the right to
"go public," and the corporation should expect them
to do so when internal channels of communication are
exhausted and the problem remains uncorrected.

Unions and professional societies should strengthen
their ethical codes—and adopt such codes if they do
not already have them. They should put teeth into mechanisms for implementing their codes and require that
they be observed not only by members but also by
organizations that employ their members. Unions should
move beyond the traditional "bread and butter" issues,
the societies should escape their preoccupation with ab-
stract professionalism, and both should apply their significant potential power to protecting members who
refuse to be automatons. Whistle blowers who belong
to labor unions have fared only slightly better than their
unorganized counterparts, except when public opinion
and the whistle blower's fellow workers are sufficiently
aroused. This is partly a result of the bureaucratized
cooptation of many labor leaders by management and
the suppression of rank and file dissent within the union
or local.

Government employees should be treated like public
servants if they are to be expected to behave like them.
Today, civil service laws and regulations serve two primary functions, each the exact opposite of those intended by Congress. First, they tend to reward or at
least shield incompetence and sloth. Second, they discourage creativity and diligence and undermine the
professional and individual responsibility of those who
serve. You might say that the speed of exit of a public
servant is almost directly proportional to his commitment to serve the public. The Civil Service Commission
itself is in need of major reform. Its clients are the

personnel managers of the various agencies, not the individual employees. Like other regulatory agencies it has been captured by the very group whose conduct it was created to regulate. A new administrative court should be created and invested with all the employee protection functions now given to the commission. Civil servants should be guaranteed the right to bring agency dereliction to public attention as a last resort. And they should have the right to go to court to protect themselves from harassment and discharge for doing their duty. To reduce the high cost of pursuing their lawful remedies, employees who challenge agency action against them should continue to receive their pay until all of their appeals are exhausted, and they should be permitted to recover the costs of their appeals from the government if they ultimately win.

All areas of the law touching upon the employee-employer relationship should be reexamined with an eye to modifying substantially the old rule that an employer can discharge an employee for acts of conscience without regard to the damage done to the employee. Existing laws that regulate industry should be amended to include provisions protecting employees who cooperate with authorities. The concept of trade secrecy is now used by business and government alike to suppress information that the public has a substantial need to know. A sharp distinction must be drawn between individual privacy and corporate secrecy, and the law of trade secrecy is a good place to begin. The Freedom of Information Act, which purports to establish public access to all but the most sensitive information in the hands of the federal government, can become a toothless perversion because civil servants who release information in the spirit of the act are punished while those who suppress it are rewarded.

Whistle blowing is encouraged actively by some laws and government administrators to assist in law enforcement. Under the recently rediscovered Refuse Act of 1899, for example, anyone who reports a polluter is entitled to one-half of any fine collected—even if the person making the report is an employee of the polluting company. And corporations constantly probe government agencies to locate whistle blowers on their

behalf. Consumers need routine mechanisms to encourage the increased flow of information that deals with
health, safety, environmental hazards, corruption, and
waste inside corporate and governmental institutions.
Whistle blowing can show the need for such systemic
affirmations of the public's right to know.

The Clearinghouse for Professional Responsibility,
P. O. Box 486, Washington, D.C. 20044, will assist in
the endeavor to establish such mechanisms and will
suggest alternative actions to sincere persons considering
blowing the whistle. Organization dissenters on matters
of important public interest should feel free to contact
the Clearinghouse with any information they believe
will help citizens protect themselves from the depreda-
tions of large organizations.

The rise in public consciousness among the young
and among minority groups has generated a sharper
concept of duty among many citizens, recalling Alfred
North Whitehead's dictum, "Duty arises from our potential control over the course of events." But loyalties
do not end at the boundaries of an organization. "Just
following orders" was an attitude that the United States
military tribunals rejected in judging others after World
War II at Nuremberg. And for those who set their behavior by the ethics of the great religions, with their
universal golden rule, the right to appeal to a higher
authority is the holiest of rights.

The whistle blowing ethic is not new; it simply has
to begin flowering responsibly in new fields where its
harvests will benefit people as citizens and consumers.
Once developed and defended as recommended by the
other participants in the Conference on Professional
Responsibility and by the final chapters of this book,
a most powerful lever for organizational responsibility
and accountability will be available. The realistic tendency of such an internal check within General Motors
or the Department of the Interior will be to assist traditional external checks to work more effectively in their
statutory or market-defined missions in the public interest.

This book presents a detailed excursion through the
pathways of courage and anguish that attend the exercise of professional and personal responsibility. We

hope by this method to provide a context of case studies from which a broader view of the overall phenomenon of internal dissent within larger organization can develop. The focus is the range of conditions for whistle blowing and the possibilities for understanding and defending whistle blowers. However, the exercise of ethical whistle blowing requires a broader, enabling environment for it to be effective. There must be those who listen and those whose potential or realized power can utilize the information for advancing justice. Thus, as with any democratic institutions, other links are necessary to secure the objective changes beyond the mere exposure of the abuses. The courts, professional and citizen groups, the media, the Congress, and honorable segments throughout our society are part of this enabling environment. They must comprehend that the tyranny of organizations, with their excessive security against accountability, must be prevented from trammeling a fortified conscience within their midst. Organizational power must be insecure to some degree if it is to be more responsible. A greater freedom of individual conviction within the organization can provide the needed deterrent—the creative insecurity which generates a more suitable climate of responsiveness to the public interest and public rights.

2

The Whistle Blower as Civil Servant

William Proxmire

Revolution, as President Nixon has reminded us, is as American as apple pie—and as the State of the Union Address. But how can we tell whether we are having an authentic revolution or a phony one? An invasion is termed an incursion. Air support is labeled interdiction. Military assistance is called "Food for Peace." There are countless ways to corrupt the English language and public policy.

But Mr. Nixon's point is well taken. The people are becoming more and more resentful of the concentration of power and are demanding change. The federal government is increasingly the object of this resentment because political power has historically tended to drift towards Washington. In the past there were good reasons for some of this drift. The Great Depression of the thirties and World War II presented problems that could only be handled by a strong central government. The trend has gone so far, however, that today the central government is, in many ways, the problem.

In 1969 Secretary of the Treasury Joseph Barr predicted a taxpayers' revolt. Barr was not wrong. The taxpayer was fed up with high taxes, with the burdens of war, with an already ominous inflation, and with the fact, Barr revealed, that twenty-two persons with incomes over $1 million each in a single year paid no income tax at all.

Today, the war goes on and appears to be widening; the inflationary spirals are still not under control; and despite the pump-priming effects of a bloated military budget, the nation is faced with a serious recession.

Unemployment is at a nine-year high. And make no mistake: unemployment has not increased because of the "painful transition" towards peace. There has been no transition to a peacetime economy.

The military budget was at a wartime level in 1969, and it is at a wartime level today. Despite strenuous efforts within the Congress, military spending has gone down by only a few billion dollars. In 1969, defense spending was $81 billion. Today it is hovering at about $77 billion, and the President is requesting $80 billion in new obligational authority. By no stretch of the imagination can $80 billion be considered a peacetime military budget. The six percent unemployment problem that we face today is wartime unemployment.

The President has called for a new revolution. I join him. But let's make it meaningful. I call for a peaceful professional revolution against the massive buildup of political and economic power in the executive branch of government, and specifically in the Department of Defense.

By peaceful, I mean nonviolent. Violence is clearly no answer to the critical situation that is before us. We want to render the Pentagon accountable to the Congress and the public for its actions. We want to eliminate waste and inefficiency. We want to slice the fat out of the budget. We want to make it smaller and more manageable. We want a strong defense program. But we want to remove it from areas and activities for which it is not suited and in which it has improperly insinuated itself: civilian surveillance, propaganda, foreign policy–making and international commitments, the purchase of weapons. Violence would be counterproductive.

By professional revolution I mean a reversal of the passive and acquiescent role played by the professional and managerial class of federal officials and private citizens without whom the corruption of the public trust could not be carried out.

Blowing the whistle, or raising a hue and cry, or

living up to the ethical standards that are already embodied in various codes of conduct is part of the antidote to the poisonous abuse of power that is infecting our society.

The bureaucrat, no less than the corporate employee, has to decide whether his primary allegiance is to his country and to his personal integrity or to his employer.

Do we live in a true society in which responsibilities are shared and the general welfare is a common goal, or is it every man for himself and the devil take the hindmost? It is a truism that the professional man—and every citizen, for that matter—has a higher responsibility than his own well-being or the well-being of his employer. But it has become a commonplace, I am sorry to say, for this responsibility to be ignored.

One of the reasons for this is the high risk involved in being ethical. What a tragic commentary it is that the price of being ethical is the loss of one's job, reduction in status, and personal ruin. At the very least, one's career is liable to be nipped in the bud.

Ernie Fitzgerald's case is only one of several that have surfaced in recent years. Innumerable others have occurred. Admiral Rickover, as well as Fitzgerald, has told in congressional testimony of the bureaucratic genius for retaliation against the wayward official who seeks to do his duty. Men are cut off from responsibility, isolated, transferred, demoted, suspended, ordered to take psychiatric tests, and subjected to the inscrutable and devious tactics of the personnel department.

There are laws on the books intended to prevent such abuses of authority. There are civil service regulations and a Civil Service Commission intended to protect the individual employee.

The laws, the regulations, and the Civil Service Commission have proven to be worthless. The reason for this is that rules of proper behavior need to be enforced in order to be effective, and they are not.

And the reason for this is equally clear. The Civil Service Commission and the Justice Department and the Pentagon are all agencies of the executive branch of the federal government. Is it likely for one agency of the executive branch to impartially investigate the wrongdoing of another agency of the executive branch? Apparently not.

The FBI has recently provided a diabolical variation of this theme. Who in the federal government would dare to investigate the excesses of the most powerful investigative bureau of all? Who investigates the investigators? The answer is, no one, if we remain within the confines of the executive branch.

Neither is it possible for the legislative branch to take it upon itself to correct all of the individual irregularities with respect to the treatment of executive employees. There are simply too many. The Congress is already overwhelmed with the task of living up to its own constitutional responsibility for managing the public purse.

The solution, in my judgment, is to seek a remedy outside of the executive or the legislative branches. I believe that every federal employee should have the right to file a civil action in a federal court against the federal government for damages that result from the unjust actions of his former superiors. This legal right of action should extend to those immediate superiors, bureau chiefs, and agency heads responsible for unlawful dismissals or other punitive acts.

I intend to introduce legislation along these lines in the current session of Congress and I welcome suggestions from those present while the language is in the drafting stage.

What I hope to accomplish with this bill is creation of a safety net for federal employees threatened with loss of job without just cause. If an official speaks out against waste or corruption within government he ought not be subjected to the kind of harassment and reprisals that now take place. A man ought not be punished for committing truth before a congressional committee.

My second suggestion is directed at the private sector, and the sponsor of this conference, among others. The rise of the public interest law firm and the consumer advocate over the past several years has been phenomenal. Some of the most constructive and effective criticism of public policy and government programs has emanated from such groups. Environmental pollution, tax policy, business regulation, food and drug controls, among other activities, have not escaped the investigation of the public interest organizations.

However, one area of political activity has remained seemingly immune from scrutiny. This is the area of national defense.

As I indicated earlier, the extravagance of the Pentagon, its uncontrollability, and its virtual sovereignty in military and foreign affairs, is responsible for much of what is wrong with America today.

Two of the men being honored today were formerly in the Department of Defense. But where are the public interest groups and the advocates who would seek to penetrate the mysteries of the Pentagon, to disclose irregularities, to dramatize bad policies, and to reveal the ways in which the public interest is not being served?

The fact that the President is asking for a large increase in defense spending gives no cause for comfort or for relaxing the new vigil over this area of political activity.

Let me cite an example of the hidden and furtive nature of the defense budget and the need to shed more light on it. Military foreign assistance has been limping along at the mere sum of $500 million to $600 million per year, or at least everyone thought it was until recently.

The 1970 federal budget estimated that $545 million would be spent in 1970 and $625 million in 1971. My Subcommittee on Economy in Government investigated the program and came up with these interesting facts:

The federal government has been spending not several hundred million dollars for military assistance, but several billion dollars.

No one really knows the precise amount that we are spending. Estimates range between $3 billion and $4 billion. The Army has actually kept no record of the hundreds of millions of dollars in weapons and ammunition given away to Thailand and South Vietnam. It doesn't know.

Part of the reason for the official ignorance is that the program was fractured into several parts at the outset of the Vietnam War and at various other times. Presently, a number of agencies have responsibilities for military assistance, including the State Department, the Agency for International Development (AID), the Defense Department, the Army, the Navy, the Air Force, and the Department of Agriculture. Most of the money is funneled through the Pentagon, but no one seems to be in charge of all of it.

The Food for Peace Program has been used to generate local currencies in foreign countries for military purposes. It is true that this use of Food for Peace appears to be within the letter of the law; however, it has never been publicly identified as part of military assistance. The public and the Congress were not aware of it. The highest officials in the State Department and the Defense Department were not aware of it until recently. The federal budget document has been positively misleading, referring to it in the most humanistic terms as a program to combat hunger and malnutrition, promote economic growth in developing nations, and develop and expand export markets for United States commodities.

Much of the aid that goes to foreign military establishments is classified. The country-by-country breakdown of recipients is classified. When I asked the Defense Department why this information should be kept secret from the American public, I was told that it would be embarrassing to the nations who receive the aid. The Pentagon feels no shame in hiding from the taxpayer the true costs of foreign military assistance, but the country-by-country breakdown has to be kept a secret because it would be embarrassing to the foreign governments.

The Lockheed situation is another case in point. This giant aerospace firm has filed claims in excess of $1 billion against the Defense Department based on four of its military contracts. The contract prices of the programs involved amount to several billion dollars. The claims are for sums over and above the contract prices. The reason for the claims, simply stated, is that Lockheed is spending far more on the contracts than the government originally agreed to pay. The question is, who picks up the tab for the cost overruns, the contractor who entered into binding commitments with the government, or the taxpayer?

The Deputy Secretary of Defense has recently indicated his preference. Under the proposal recently made public, Lockheed would be let off the hook on all of its contracts and would be paid sums totaling somewhere between $600 million and $1.4 billion. Typically, the Pentagon's public statement on the proposed settlement was too vague for anyone to completely understand.

Lockheed, meanwhile, has rejected part of the government's offer and is now acting as if it wants to go to court. Of course, it is also demanding that the government continue to underwrite the incredible cost overruns it is incurring on the C-5A program until the matter is finally settled.

Naturally, this corporation has the right to demand anything it wants to demand. But is it necessary, is it even legal or proper, for the Pentagon to accede to all of its demands?

The effect of all this is that Congress and the public are being whipsawed between the spineless and corporate-oriented behavior of the Department of Defense and the arrogant and greedy posture of its largest contractor.

The problem of the defense budget, the many programs that are hidden within it, the mismanagement, the waste, the inefficiency, and the excesses that go on under the shibboleth of national security are getting worse, not better. The contract system alone, whereby some $30 billion is spent for weapons each year, badly needs to be overhauled. What kind of a relationship do we have when the government allows and encourages its contractors to evade their contractual responsibility, to overrun the costs, to degrade the technical performance standards, and to delay delivery? The challenges that remain for all of us today are clear.

The fact is that the defense program gets away with budgetary murder each year. And we need more than just courageous individuals like Ernie Fitzgerald, John McGee, and the others who have spoken out to blow the whistle. We need private groups on the outside who will lend their professional expertise to the subject of miltary affairs, who will remain free and independent of ties to the Department of Defense or its contractors, and who will become voices for reform.

3

The Whistle Blower as Entrepreneur

Robert Townsend

When Ralph Nader mentioned the Whistle Blowers Conference to me, something went "click." The time seems right to test America and see what she deserves.

Are you happy with America? Content to see her continue in the direction she's going?

If about one-third of Americans answer "No," then we are about where we were in 1775, when about one-third were pro-British, one-third didn't know, and one-third were somewhere between opposed and violently opposed to the state and trends of the country. But who is the enemy today? Who's causing this winter of our discontent? Russians? Chinese? Domestic Communists? Long-haired kids? Military juggernauts? Lack of leadership?

In my opinion, the enemy is organizations. Big organizations. They accumulate large amounts of money and power, and if they're private corporations they chase narrow antisocial goals in the name of the almighty dollar.

Who are we going to look to, to make these giant organizations honest—to make them stop destroying the quality of all our lives (including theirs and their employees') for their own private interests?

The government? Union Carbide has all the know-how in chemistry, the government practically none; General Motors all the know-how in automobiles, the government just what they're allowed to know. And those government officials that can't be snowed can be bought. The military juggernaut owns John Stennis, body and soul.

The law? Union Camp, Inc., dictated the laws which enabled it to turn the Savannah River into an open sewer.

Corporate leaders? No, but why not? In my judgment, there are two reasons. First, we have a double legal standard in this country. If you—Peter Petkas, citizen—walk across the hall and kill your neighbor, you will probably be severely punished under the criminal law. If you—Peter Petkas, president of the Allison Division of General Motors—release a known defective airplane engine which causes the death of thirty-eight people, you won't be punished at all. Your company may be fined $7500 under the civil code. This they will deduct from taxes as a normal business expense. So corporate murder costs two hundred dollars a head before taxes and a hundred dollars a head after taxes. Standard Oil of California drew a million-dollar fine— the biggest in corporate history. It amounts to what they take in, in revenues, in two hours. If you earned $168 a week, the equivalent for you would be a two-dollar fine. So there's work to be done to eliminate the double legal standard and let the punishment fit the crime.

The second reason we can't expect leadership from our corporate moguls is that at the moment of assuming command we unfit them for the job. What we should do is tell them to take off their coat, go out among their people and their customers, and find out at first hand what the problems and opportunities are. What we do is give them two more secretaries, a private limousine, a private helicopter, a private elevator, a private dining room, a big increase in pay, and outside directorships. The result is that Lee Iacocca is never heard from again by his own people.

America became great in engineering and production because of its entrepreneurs. It was great at taking the calculated risk. Recently we've seen lawyers and accountants become chief executives. These people are trained in the elimination of risks—they know how to play it safe. Anybody who has been there knows that nine times out of ten the safe way is the surest way to

oblivion. Example: Here's what a few generations of
nonleadership has done to our great steel industry. On
January 26, 1971, in an article entitled, "Stumbling
Steel," the *Wall Street Journal* reports that the industry
is seeking federal help of several kinds, including (and
I translate into the language of the spoiled child):

   1) tighter restrictions on steel imports ("Mommy,
that bully is stronger than I am—hit him");
   2) relaxed antitrust attitudes on mergers ("Mommy, the naughty teacher won't let me cheat on my
tests—and how can I pass if I can't cheat?");
   3) more flexible enforcement of antipollution laws
("But Mommy, I want to break the neighbor's win-
dows—if it's illegal, then change the law");
   4) tax breaks ("Mommy, gimme some candy").

Unfortunately, this is typical of leadership in our
giant organizations.

This is why we need whistle blowers.

Whistle blowing has a long, distinguished corporate
tradition. Most companies today have an internal audit
operation, which goes around to the various offices and
branches and supposedly blows the whistle on wrongdoing. Most companies have certified public accountants (the financial equivalent of the family doctor) to
give them an annual checkup. Unfortunately, both these
operations wind up doing little more than counting the
petty cash. Nobody audits the decision to build an SST.

Every respectable practice has to have a father figure,
and I propose Dwight Eisenhower as the modern father
of whistle blowing. In his farewell address he warned
us to beware of the "military-industrial complex." In
retrospect, we should have paid much more attention.
He had been on the inside of the military, he was an
intimate of the corporate leaders of his day, and he had
seen the military-industrial complex at work from the
Oval Office in the White House. If we had only listened.

(Note: I don't regard the military-industrial complex
as a sinister conspiracy and I don't want to give that
impression. I think if we gave Billy Graham $85 billion
a year for a few years and then tried to take it away

from him he might destroy America in his efforts to hang onto it.)

When do we blow the whistle, Mr. Townsend? I think the answer to that is easy. Let's go back to some principles on which most Americans can agree: "Thou shalt not kill" (Exodus 20:13). "Thou shalt not steal" (Exodus 20:15). Example: A television or dental x-ray machine is released to the public with dangerous radiation. An automobile or airplane engine is released with a dangerous defect. A union leader blocks a major safety device.

Stealing can be polluting the air or water. Hypothetical case: Union Carbide is polluting the water. State, federal, and local governments start spending money and energy to get them to stop. Union Carbide starts spending large sums of money, first to pretend they're not polluting, and when that fails to stall for time. This is all done by paid liars who are normally called the public relations department. Meanwhile, two years ago one of their own scientists solved this particular pollution problem by inventing a process which turns the waste into a harmless substance. But because it costs a few dollars and didn't produce a profit, he couldn't get anybody's attention. Let him blow the whistle, and we'll make his process available, not only to his own company but to others as well.

Stealing can be Xerox Corporation avoiding the expenditure of five dollars per copy machine on a device which would reduce noise. By this omission it forces each customer to spend hundreds of dollars to isolate the machine.

Stealing can be claiming in advertising something for your product that it doesn't have, or offering services that you know you can't deliver.

If whistle blowing is going to help America, each whistle blower should ask himself "What's in it for me?" before he blows the whistle. And only blow it if you're clean. There is so much injustice and frustration in unions and corporations that the Clearinghouse could be overwhelmed with private grudges.

Also, before you blow the whistle see if your case is as complete as you can make it. Suppose you were King Solomon considering the case: would you be able to verify it, are there the necessary names, dates, and facts to substantiate it? Do you have enough information so that you would be able to render a judgment?

One question which I'm sure has crossed your mind is, "Mr. Townsend, won't this whistle blowing increase costs, reduce profits? And therefore isn't it bad for the free enterprise system?" It seems to me that the answer is clear: whistle blowing may save the free enterprise system—but if our system in fact depends on unpunished lying, stealing, and murder, then who wants to save it?

My twenty years in organizations have given me great faith in individuals and absolutely no faith in large institutions. Because the leaders of large organizations are distracted and corrupted by luxuries and the trappings of corporate success, they have no time to consider fundamental values like honesty, truth, and justice. They have no time to listen to the voices of their own people who know what's right and what's wrong with their products and services. Not knowing what's wrong, the leaders speak to the public only with the forked tongues of their public relations department.

On three totally separate occasions I set out to build honest organizations in which the goals were known, there was no secrecy, and a real effort was made to see that everybody got what they deserved. In each case, the results were electrifying—in human energy, in fun, and in profits. The reason for this is plain—everybody else working for a big organization is so disgusted, frustrated, or bored that he can barely deliver twenty percent of his energy toward the corporate goal if it has any. People from coast to coast are sick of the nauseating phoniness, triviality, and waste of big organizations. Give them a chance to work for a company which fires the paid liars, deals openly, tells the truth—in short, a company they can be proud of—and maybe you've started to save the free enterprise system.

4

Whistle Blowing and the Law

Arthur S. Miller

These remarks emphasize two main themes about whistle blowing:

1) The law at present provides very little protection to the person who would blow the whistle; in fact, it is more likely to assess him with criminal or civil penalties.

2) The law should provide, in its institutions and principles, protection in certain instances.

The first of these is a statement of "what is" and the second of "what ought to be."

Whistle blowing is sometimes actively encouraged by the government. The tax evasion informer, for example, when he snitches on someone, gets a portion of the money recovered. The same applies in customs matters and in at least one congressional statute concerning pollution—the Refuse Act of 1899. Those who turn in polluters supposedly can get monetary rewards—that is, if the statute is ever enforced, which at least until 1969 it had not been.

So, too, with the administration of the criminal law. Those who are caught would be far fewer in number were it not for a systematic use of stool pigeons by the police. The police need the active help of the citizenry if laws are to be enforced: we all remember Kitty Genovese and the three dozen people who heard her cries for help and who did nothing. When government has its interests threatened, it does not hesitate to ask for assistance.

SANCTIONS AGAINST THE WHISTLE BLOWER

It is one thing when government seeks the assistance of citizen against citizen in the enforcement of law; it is quite another when some person within government or within one of the private governments of industry or labor considers that he has a duty higher than to his immediate employer and who, accordingly, says "Hold on, enough" loud and long. (He will have to be heard and his views publicized, as we will note shortly.) When the person within one of the organizations of our hierarchically structured, bureaucratically organized society disapproves some action taken by that organization, he immediately runs the risk of severe adverse sanctions.

And sometimes many people would agree that the whistle blower deserved heavy sanctions. General MacArthur was sacked by President Truman for publicly disagreeing with his Commander in Chief. Otto Otepka got the deep freeze for squealing to a congressional committee. One should not think that all whistle blowing runs in one direction—that of "humane liberalism" or something similar. Quite the contrary. It can reach the depth of the unlamented Senator Joseph McCarthy, who said that he blew the whistle on subversives in the State Department. (He was greatly aided and abetted by the mass media, which swallowed his fantasies whole without bothering to check on them.) Indeed, the whistle blower is not liked. We have invidious terms for him: he is a "fink" or a "stool pigeon," a "squealer" or an "informer," or he "rats" on his employer. The preeminent virtue is loyalty, and the principle is "your organization, love it or leave it."

But there are some—far too few as yet—whose whistle blowing truly reflects both a higher loyalty and the public good—men who, in the words of the code of ethics for federal government employees, believe that "any person in government service should put loyalty to the highest moral principles and to country above loyalty to person, party, or government department." So some lawyers in the Justice Department publicly dissent from the administration's civil rights policies; Ernest Fitzgerald puts his job on the line by drawing attention to cost overruns on the C-5A airplane; Tamplin and Gofman draw the ire of the Atomic Energy Commission for daring to question radiation health standards set by the AEC; and FBI agent Shaw found himself suddenly transferred to Montana for daring to write a letter in partial criticism of J. Edgar Hoover.

PUBLIC GOVERNMENT

The employee of public government who snitches can often expect to be fired, cast into some obscure limbo, or criminally punished. Those who are not protected by civil service regulations — including political appointees and persons whose services are contracted to the government by corporations and consulting firms— are particularly vulnerable. Unfortunately, this category, since it includes many scientists and others with a reputation for independent initiative, covers those most likely to blow the whistle and to do so effectively. Job security for these whistle blowers is not great, as Walter Hickel learned.

If he is wrapped in the security of civil service regulations, he may be less vulnerable, since he cannot be dismissed without cause and without the benefit of minimum procedural rights, in some cases including a full hearing. A full hearing is what those who have the whistle blown on them least want—whether that hearing be a formal, judicial-type hearing or an informal hearing from which may come documents and exhibits subject to public scrutiny. The clever administrator can usually avoid all this by simply abolishing the job of the whistle blower.

In short, government officials, despite civil service rules and regulations, are second-class citizens within their organizations, deprived of a full First Amendment right to speak—a sentiment given classic expression by Oliver Wendell Holmes when he said in 1892, "The petitioner may have a constitutional right to talk politics, but he has no constitutional right to be a policeman." Fortunately, however, there has been some movement away from this position by the courts. The Supreme

Court, for example, held in 1968 that a high-school teacher could not be fired simply because he criticized his school board in a letter to the editor of a local newspaper.

There are other second-class citizens in government. The soldier is one, even one of those poor unfortunates who manage to get drafted in a country which provides ample ways of avoiding the draft. If he wants to speak out or march against the Vietnam "war," he very likely will find himself in trouble with his commanders. The organization exacts a loyalty higher than to one's ideals or to the highest moral principles of the country. How far the military can go in suppressing dissent in the ranks is, however, an unanswered constitutional question—one that is very much in flux, one that could result in the Supreme Court's making a lot of law in the next few years.

PRIVATE GOVERNMENT

Government in this country should be viewed not only from the narrow perspective of the visible institutions of public governance—federal, state, and local —but also from the point of view that social groups (corporations and labor unions, for example) are a part of a web of "invisible" *private* government. This statement appears in a recent issue of *Industry Week*: "Power is taking a corporate form all over the world. That may be the real what's happening of today. Managers in the near future will be inheriting more and more of the traditional acts and roles of politicians. Power is being pushed into corporate hands. . . . Is management ready to lead? Power, problems, planning—the responsibility is clear, that the future is too important to be left to the politicians. It's also too important to be left to the technicians. The future is left up to the corporations, the manager is moving to the world stage center."

"We are at the edge of a new renaissance, a new business age," writes David Secunda, vice president of the American Management Association, "and the corporation is the rolling force. Business corporations will probably influence our lives more than the government will." So we are governed by two sets of government

—one visible and public, one invisible and private— and industry spokesmen often candidly acknowledge this. So should Congress and the courts.

Those who toil in the private bureaucracies face problems at least as severe as those in public bureaucracies. Other than the universities, where academic freedom prevails and professors are at least as secure in their jobs as are federal judges in theirs, and possibly in industries where strong collective bargaining agreements protect the employees, sanctions of being fired, or being held civilly—or even criminally—liable for blowing the whistle are possible, even probable. The technical writer for the B. F. Goodrich Company who was ordered to falsify a qualification report for the A-7D aircraft had to resign in order to get the story told (and the practice stopped). A high executive for Bethlehem Steel who joined a local civil rights group found himself summarily fired — not an example of whistle blowing, to be sure, but illustrative of what can happen to the poor drones in industry.

An employee owes loyalty to his organization under the principles of law—contract or personal injury or agency law. The technical word is that he is in a fiduciary relationship. To breach it, he might be enjoined by a court or held liable in damages. Furthermore, if he discloses "trade secrets," he might, under the laws of some states, be punished criminally. Speaking generally, there is an obligation to keep a confidence if the person knows it is a confidential matter.

Under federal law, the National Stolen Property Act makes it a crime to steal anything *tangible* from an employer. This does not apply to intangibles, such as ideas, but there are bills pending in Congress to make it do so. Furthermore, it is a federal crime to peddle or sell information for profit.

That's the picture, and it is a glum one. A secrecy syndrome affects our public and private bureaucracies, backed by the law. That veil of secrecy is pierced now and then by the whistle blowers, either openly or covertly, and at times by enterprising investigative reporters who are able to sniff out shortcomings and wrongdoings.

By and large, however, the media and also the professional organizations are essentially establishment-oriented institutions. The press will pounce on the bizarre but tends to leave untouched much that goes on. Vice President Agnew to the contrary, the media, even those located in the northeastern United States, are house organs for the status quo, quite content—with some notable exceptions—blandly and blindly to repeat governmental or industry propaganda or hide the derelictions of our organizational society. Muckraking is at least faintly distasteful. "If you can't say something good about the United States, keep your mouth shut": that is the prevailing principle.

WHAT SHOULD THE LAW BE?

That the law needs changing seems to be self-evident. For those who are willing to put principle above job security, to blow the whistle when the magnitude of the harm and the degree of public danger require it, legal protections are needed.

However, one should be very careful about extending the principle of whistle blowing unduly. Surely it can be carried too far. Surely, too, an employee owes his employer enough loyalty to try to work, first of all, within the organization to attempt to effect change. Only when his way is blocked there, and only when the matter involves something more than mere trivia, should he put the whistle to his lips and blast away. There are no clear boundaries to how one might discern his duty in such instances. Each person must decide for himself, often with little external guidance, when he should say, "Enough is enough."

But the law can give, both in principle and institutionally, some external boundaries. To do so will take a combination of legislative, administrative, and judicial action.

The courts first: Due process could be accorded the employee, not only of public government, but also of private government. Already the Supreme Court has applied the Constitution to private corporations in more than one case: a company town in Alabama; a shopping center; political parties. It would take only a slight extension of present law to make the Constitution's due process principle applicable to the corporations and labor unions. That would mean that an employee would have a constitutional right to be treated fairly.

On a less lofty judicial plane, courts could allow for damage suits for "spite firings," much as the law traditionally has given protection against "spite fences" erected by feuding neighbors.

Neither of these would overly hamper the employer. Only those actions considered reasonable—not motivated by malice or ill will or based on false information—would be protected.

All of that could be done without legislation. Congress could, both for government and for those industries that fall within the expansive definition of interstate commerce, enact a "code of fair dealings" for employees. Indeed, it has already done so in part —in the labor laws that permit the unions to flourish and that protect employees against unfair labor practices, and also in the Civil Rights Act of 1964, which protects one against discrimination because of race, creed, or sex. The protection of the union, for many, will be enough, especially in those industries where union leaders have not crawled into bed with the corporate managers.

What is needed, however, is a legislative prescription for fair dealings—both for those who work for the government and those who work in industry.

Much, too, can be done administratively—by the executive branch and by the agencies who ostensibly regulate industry. As long ago as 1942, the President unilaterally inserted a "nondiscrimination in employment" clause in all federal contracts. That it was not enforced merely shows how far we have to go to make government govern adequately. And the powers of the agencies seem to be broad and flexible enough to allow them to issue rules that would protect the whistle blowers when they should be protected—by, for example, requiring that if an employee tips off the agency about an illegal act by his employer, the employer could not take sanctions against him if the allegations were proved.

All of this is predicated on one assumption: that Congress and the agencies, and indeed the courts, have a real sustained interest in doing something meaningful. The opposite may well be the case—as the several studies by Nader's Raiders indicate and as others have documented. The corporate state, American style, has not yet moved to that degree of protection of human liberty that is so necessary.

Another point needs underscoring: it will do little good for someone to blow the whistle unless he is heard. And he cannot be heard unless someone listens. The way that this can be done is through the communications media, aided by crusading members of Congress. This suggests two causes of action:

1) The Freedom of Information Act, enacted by Congress a few years ago, should be given full enforcement in letter and in spirit. As matters now stand, that act is rather a meaningless charade, the government not acting much differently from the way it did before enactment.

2) Some means of entry, of access, to the media must be established. My colleague Jerome Barron has argued for a constitutional right of access to the media, in order to make the "marketplace of ideas" foundation of the First Amendment truly effective. The law may be moving in that direction, however glacially, but over the strenuous opposition of the media barons.

A response is needed as well. It does no good to be heard or listened to unless there's a meaningful response and consideration is given. We all know the attitude of frontier days in this country: "Let's give the man a fair trial and hang him." You can't give the whistle blower a fair hearing and then say goodbye. The outside citizen should have an expanded way of blowing the whistle, of getting into court, or getting hearings.

A word, in conclusion, about the professional responsibility of the government lawyer. Who is his client? Is it true that, as recently stated in the *American Bar Association Journal,* the person who writes the legal opinions for the Department of Justice is "the president's lawyer?" Is he merely a legal mechanic, confined to grinding out legal justifications for proposed policies? If so, then I suggest that the lawyer in government is no longer a professional—the same may be true for his counterpart in private law firms and also in the house counsel of the corporations—and that we are faced with one of two choices: (a) either make him a true professional, one who sees beyond the immediate interests of his client (surely that is true for the government attorney), or (b) let us all drop the nonsense that the lawyer is a professional and call him a legal lackey. There may be a middle ground there, but not much of one.

There is much room for imaginative work by the bar associations and other organizations of professional lawyers. Why don't the lawyers blow the whistle on biased or incompetent judges? Can we rely on the American Bar Association? We cannot. The ABA Screening Committee had adverse information regarding Judge Carswell and failed to disclose it to the Senate committee. We cannot rely on them.

Let me emphasize that there are important, unresolved problems concerning whistle blowing. But if a society is to be built on the human scale, if we are not all to be immersed forever as nameless and faceless cogs in public and private bureaucracies, then we had better get on with the job, create some law protecting the whistle blower in proper instances, and also give hard, sustained thought to the type of society we want. Whistle blowing helps in pointing out shortcomings, but it is of no help at all in saying what *should* be done. Let our whistle blowers be joined by some hardheaded thinkers and doers, by those who will conceptualize the good society we all want. If the quality of life is to be improved, both are necessary.

II

The Whistle Blowers

Introduction

Who are the whistle blowers? Why do they decide to speak out? How can they be most effective when they do? What can they expect after they take action?

Nine men and women, all prominent whistle blowers in different areas of public concern, posed these questions at the Conference on Professional Responsibility. All emphasized that there is no formula for whistle blowing. The "how" and "when" of speaking out as a critic of a government or corporate employer depend on the issue itself and how it may best be developed, the various sources of support, the available means of getting the message to the public, and the possible repercussions to the individual. Because these nine whistle blowers and two others who came to the forefront after the conference represent a wide range of circumstances, their experiences as they reported them and as documented elsewhere are described in detail in the following chapters.

William Stieglitz resigned because of professional differences with his government employer and then spoke out about what he considered inadequate auto safety standards. Fumio Matsuda left the Japanese auto industry to become a full-time critic and defender of motorists outside the industry. Ralph Stein and his colleague Christopher Pyle took a similar route when they left the Army and went on to make dramatic disclosure of secret military surveillance of civilians. Dr. A. Dale Console resigned his job with a drug company and pondered for two years how he might speak out before he delivered his indictment of the drug industry before a congressional committee.

The most vulnerable whistle blowers are often those
who speak out from within their organizations—Edward Gregory at General Motors, Jacqueline Verrett
in the Food and Drug Administration, Drs. John Gofman and Arthur Tamplin within the Atomic Energy
Commission, Ernest Fitzgerald in the Defense Department, Charles Pettis of Brown and Root, and the workers at the Colt Firearms Division in Hartford, Connecticut. Gregory, Verrett, and the Colt workers have
remained with their organizations without serious difficulty. Drs. Gofman and Tamplin, who publicly questioned AEC safety standards, have undergone enormous
pressures, budget cuts, isolation, and personal recrim-
inations that may yet result in forcing them out.

These individuals testify to the fact that whistle
blowers may emerge in any profession or at any job
level. They may be of vastly different temperaments,
backgrounds, and skills. Among the conference participants, six were critics of the government agencies
for which they worked, three had criticized their corporate employers—as had Pettis and the Colt men,
three are scientists, three engineers, two students, and
one an auto quality control inspector. Pettis is also an
engineer, and the Colt workers are quality inspectors.
The whistle blowers range in age from twenty-eight
to sixty. Some were more successful than others in
accomplishing what they set out to do, and some were
better able than others to respond to the frustration
and the harassment.

They share, however, to a remarkable degree, a
common view of individual responsibility. None was
content, when conflict arose, to relinquish his professional standards or his personal self-esteem. They pose
a two-fold question: Can such integrity and candor
survive and grow in our corporate and governmental
hierarchies? And what will happen to the organizations
and their purposes if men and women like these are
totally suppressed?

5

A. Ernest Fitzgerald

*If enough well-intentioned, tough, and skillful people
take stands inside the Pentagon, the deterioration of
stewardship can be slowed, at least temporarily.*
— *Ernest Fitzgerald*

It was late in the morning and the hearings were drawing to a close. A few senators had already slipped from
the committee room, though most of the press remained
among their tangle of cameras and lights. Senator William Proxmire, chairman of the committee, paused a
moment, then said, "I am going to ask something unusual, but I think it will be most helpful. It would save
the time of the subcommittee and would perhaps save
your time, too, Mr. Secretary and gentlemen. I would
like to ask Mr. Fitzgerald to come forward and sit
next to Mr. Schedler at the witness stand here."[1]

From somewhere in the back of the room a man left
his seat and made his way to the witness table. There,
flanked by two assistant secretaries, sat the Secretary
of the Air Force, Robert C. Seamans, Jr. In comparison to the handsome, silver-haired Secretary, the
man who quietly made a fourth at the table was hardly
imposing. He was about five-foot-ten and slightly over-
weight. Ernie Fitzgerald was in fact a very average-
looking man. Nonetheless, he was responsible for the
fact that the Secretary of the Air Force had been sitting
before a congressional committee since early that
morning.

Just two weeks before the hearings, the four men at
that witness table were, at least nominally, as the Air
Force liked to say, "on the same team." Fitzgerald was

deputy for management systems in the Office of the
Assistant Secretary for Financial Management. His
specialty was cost control. One of the programs he
worked on was the C–5A, the giant cargo plane being
built for the Air Force by the Lockheed Aircraft Corporation. In November, 1968, Fitzgerald appeared
before Senator Proxmire's Joint Economic subcommittee and told them that the C–5A had a $2 billion
cost overrun, a fact revealed by Air Force analysts as
much as two years before but never reported by the
Pentagon. Proxmire's staff suspected the boondoggle;
Fitzgerald's testimony confirmed it. At that point, he
lost his status as a "team player." When the subcommittee convened a year later, the question was no
longer cost overruns but what happened to the man
who disclosed them.

"The Dismissal of A. Ernest Fitzgerald by the Department of Defense," the 216-page report that issued from
the hearings, is something of a classic in the annals of
whistle blowing. Rarely are such instances documented;
almost never so thoroughly. Describing the events that
led to his departure from the Pentagon, Fitzgerald
remarked, "The only thing that makes me unique at all
is that I have not gone away quietly, whereas most of
the others have."[2]

THE WHISTLE BLOWER

When he went to work for the Air Force in 1965,
Ernie Fitzgerald seemed cast from the same mold as
hundreds of other government employees. He was then
thirty-nine years old, was married, had three children
and a laconic drawl that came from Birmingham, Alabama. There was little in his background to indicate he
would not be a complying member of the Air Force
team. His boyhood in Birmingham featured the usual
hallmarks of Americana, the usual sandlot football
games and school days, as his mother told a reporter
later, when Fitzgerald's story was taken up by the
press. Later he acquired the common credentials for
adulthood: service with the Navy during World War II
and a degree in 1951 from the University of Alabama.
He married a classmate and went to work as an indus-

trial engineer for Hayes International, moving later to
Kaiser Aluminum. Eventually he became a management
consultant, founded·his own consulting company, and
developed a specialty in cost control. Among his clients
were the Air Force and the Navy. "My business was
reducing costs," he says, "and like any other consultant
I had many difficulties from time to time, was thrown
out of a place or two, but in general had good success
in reducing costs, and in particular I enjoyed and had
some success in reducing costs of weapons systems."[3]

His work was good enough for the Air Force to hire
him in 1965 as deputy for management systems in the
Office of the Assistant Secretary of the Air Force. He
was high in the ranks of Pentagon personnel, a GS–17
classification, a job that drew thirty-one thousand dollars a year. He and his family settled in a comfortable
house in a suburb of Washington. There was money,
security, and long weekends if he wanted them.

Among the hundreds of people who arrive daily at
the sprawling building on the south bank of the
Potomac, who make their way from the appropriate
parking lot to one of the numberless offices in the great
warren, Fitzgerald was perhaps unique in the wall
decoration he chose for his office. It was a framed
copy of the Code of Ethics for United States Government Service, the code approved by the Eighty-fifth
Congress. It begins:

"Any person in Government service should:

"Put loyalty to the highest moral principles and to
country above loyalty to persons, party, or Government department." Later the code admonishes: "Expose corruption wherever discovered."

As a wall decoration the code was highly acceptable
to the Pentagon, though it is probable that few people
noticed it and even fewer considered that the man at the
desk beneath it took seriously what it said.

Fitzgerald was a member of an elite group in the
Air Force, reporting directly, as one of three deputies,
to the Assistant Secretary of the Air Force for Financial
Management. The chain of command went directly up
to the Secretary of the Air Force and from there to the
Secretary of Defense. He was assigned to cost control
problems of the largest Air Force weapons systems,

including the F–111, Minuteman, SCRAM, and the C–5A. In February, 1966, after six months at the job, he was assigned "Outstanding" performance ratings. Again the following year, in February, 1967, his work was rated "Outstanding."

By that time, he had already discovered overruns in the C–5A program. In January of 1966 he pointed out to his superiors that projected Lockheed overhead increases, if not offset by underruns elsewhere, would result in contract overruns. In late 1966 he reported overruns of one hundred percent and more in key activities in the Lockheed C–5A program. He was also presenting analyses and recommending corrective actions on the Minuteman program. There were as yet no signs that his work was not valued by the Pentagon. In fact, in 1967 Fitzgerald was nominated, though not selected, by the Air Force for two awards. He was one of five employees nominated for the Department of Defense Distinguished Civilian Service Award and one of twenty employees nominated for the Air Force Association's Citation of Honor.

In December of 1967, Fitzgerald wrote a letter to General J. W. O'Neill, commander of the Space and Missile Systems Organization. It was a long ten-page letter about the costs of the Minuteman program and its bluntness was to mortally offend some of the top men on the Air Force team. In criticizing the handling of the Minuteman program, Fitzgerald was in effect criticizing the entire top military establishment for failure to encourage economy in contracts with large corporations.

"In a commercial business situation," Fitzgerald wrote, "similar pressures [to justify more money] are usually countered by a combination of top management restraint and the built-in awareness that excessive costs mean disaster to the business and those dependent on it for livelihood. There are no comparable countervailing pressures in our situation. Indeed, the opposite is true; more costs and, hence, more funds mean increased personal security as long as the increases are tolerated. . . .

"If this situation could be reversed, that is, if managers could be convinced that success in their careers depended at least in part on their ability to achieve difficult cost goals without sacrifice of quality, schedule, or program content, most would view cost reduction and control practices as aids rather than annoyances."

He further pointed out that "in formulating a broad management improvement plan for Minuteman I believe you should consider the problem posed by the mass migration of Air Force officers into the management ranks of contractors with whom they have dealt."

The remark that really struck home, however, was the one noted by Secretary Seamans when he brought the letter before the Proxmire committee. It was Fitzgerald's observation that "I think the Minuteman program has suffered and is suffering from its own credibility gap. Some time back, lying was a way of life in the program. Financial figures were plucked from thin air, and deceptive technical information was presented as a matter of course. I believe this practice has done immeasurable harm to the program. A more serious and lasting effect is the example set for young officers and the damage done to the image of the Air Force.

"The solution to this problem is ultrasimple: Tell the truth, no matter how painful."

The Secretary introduced this paragraph as evidence that Fitzgerald had "hurt his relationship with people in the Air Force by the manner in which he carried out his job."[4]

Seamans responded: "I have yet to meet any responsible person in the military or in the civilian side of the Air Force that I can accuse of lying."[5]

By February, 1968, Fitzgerald's performance ratings had declined to "Satisfactory." In the meantime, he continued to build up a file of correspondence with the Office of the Secretary of Defense concerning procurement policies. On August 27, 1968, he wrote a lengthy letter on acquisition cost control to Colonel Henry M. Fletcher, Jr., director of procurement policy in the Office of the Secretary of Defense. In this letter Fitzgerald complained that economy recommendations from him and other cost analysts were being blocked and that analysts were subject to verbal abuse and other pressures when they persisted in making their recommendations.

"In addition to the Minuteman program," he wrote, "similar situations have arisen on several of our major programs, notably the F–111, including the Mk–1 avionics portion, and the C–5A. Vast cost growth has taken place, and analyses have identified avoidable correctable causes. Proposed corrective actions have been blocked by government management people."

Fitzgerald charged that "opponents of cost control proposals try to ignore the analyses or ridicule the analysts without coming to grips with the facts. . . .

"When consideration of the facts is forced, and the existence of avoidable waste is proven, the opponents make speeches alluding to our commitments to competitive free enterprise, fixed price contracts, and disengagement. They then attack the proponents of improvement measures in earnest. The analysts who prepared the cost figures on which improvement proposals are based receive special attention in these attacks and few survive. Government analysts are transferred, isolated, or motivated to seek other employment. Outside contractor analysts invariably are forced into other lines of work."

By the time Fitzgerald was invited to testify before the Joint Economic Subcommittee in the fall of 1968, the Air Force was well aware of his dissenting views on procurement practices. Exposing these practices to the public was not, he says, a "planned choice": his energies were directed within the organization, where "I still believe that the job can best be done."[6] He did not, however, consider withholding the unclassified information which was available to him and which the committee was seeking.

Up until then, Fitzgerald had been tolerated as a gadfly within the Air Force. But as a witness before a congressional committee, he apparently presented a different sort of threat to his superiors. In the weeks before the hearing, he encountered a number of pressures to prevent or perhaps weaken his testimony.

Before Fitzgerald told anyone about the invitation to testify, Robert C. Moot, the controller of the Department of Defense, called to ask him about the invitation. "I never learned for sure how Mr. Moot came to know about my invitation," he recalled. "I was told later, however, that all mail, even personal mail, with a congressional return address is routinely diverted, opened and read before it is delivered to the addressee."[7]

Fitzgerald relates that "Mr. Moot told me that the Assistant Secretary of Defense for Installations and Logistics was disturbed by the prospect of my testimony. He asked if I would turn the matter over to him, in effect assigning the invitation. I told Mr. Moot that my immediate superior, Mr. Nielsen, was out of town, and I could take no action without consulting him. Later, after it had been decided by the Secretary of Defense and the Air Force, over my objections I might add, that I would appear only as a backup witness, and that I would not prepare a statement, Mr. Nielsen and I met with Mr. Moot to discuss the matter.

"In summary, it appeared that the decision regarding my appearance was predicated on two assumptions. First, that I intended to present testimony which would 'leave blood on the floor.' Second, that Mr. Clifford, then Secretary of Defense, would not agree with my statement. Now there had been no discussion as to what I might say in my statement, so this seemed very strange indeed to me, the assumptions having been made without any discussion of my intent."[8]

Fitzgerald believed there were two reasons for the consternation over his testimony. There was the belief, which he learned later, that Senator Proxmire had seen the file of correspondence between Fitzgerald and the Office of the Secretary of Defense regarding procurement policy. Fitzgerald's contentions that inefficiency in procurement was so widespread as almost to constitute "national policy" might, the Air Force feared, raise annoying inquiries. The more specific fear was generated by the fact that the Joint Economic Committee staff had been looking into the C–5A. As Fitzgerald notes, "There appeared to be a desire at some quarters in the Pentagon to withhold the results of the Air Force analysis which pointed to the huge cost increases on the C–5A."[9] This was, he believes, the principal fear and the one that in fact materialized.

"When I was asked by Senator Proxmire to confirm
his estimate of C–5A cost increases, I committed
truth."[10]

From then on, Fitzgerald was treated as a pariah in
the Air Force. He was immediately taken off major
acquisition programs, and placed in unofficial "isolation," where he busied himself with cost problems of
bowling alleys in Thailand. He was no longer invited
to attend routine management meetings of which he
had been a regular member. One of his two assistants
was reassigned, and the remaining assistant was ordered
not to report to him but to go directly to the military
management deputies. The attitude of his colleagues
underwent a marked change. "My quarantine from the
major programs continued, accompanied by a degree
of social ostracism," he told the committee. "Persistent
rumors cropped up that I was to be fired."[11]

These rumors were given substance only twelve days
after his testimony when Fitzgerald received notice that
his career status had been revoked. He had been granted
career status, as opposed to his original classification
as consultant on a temporary basis, a month prior to
the hearings. The first step toward his dismissal involved
stripping him of any claims to his job. This tenure
claim was removed with the explanation that his career
status designation had been a "computer error."

Meanwhile, unknown to Fitzgerald, his superiors were
carefully scrutinizing the possible ways for getting rid
of him. The possibilities were outlined in a memorandum written on January 6, 1969, to Harold Brown,
Secretary of the Air Force, by Brown's administrative
assistant, John Lang. This memorandum was shown to
Fitzgerald at the time by his superior, perhaps in the
hope of encouraging him to resign. But he refused
to give him a copy. Later both Fitzgerald and Senator
Proxmire received copies of the memo from anonymous
sources. Entitled "Background Information Relating to
the Fitzgerald Case", the memo discussed three ways
in which Fitzgerald might be removed from his job.
The first was a simple "adverse action." Fitzgerald
would be given notice that he was fired. He would, how-

ever, have full rights of appeal under normal administrative proceedings and would retain his job until that process was exhausted. The second method, "reduction in force," involved abolishing the job that Fitzgerald held. Because of his status as a special consultant rather than a member of the civil service, he would have no claim on another position. The memo pointed out that since Fitzgerald "is the only employee in his competitive level grouping and since he did not progress to this position from other lower grade positions, the net result is that he is in competition only with himself. He could neither 'bump' nor displace anyone."

Finally the memorandum noted: "There is a third possibility which could result in Mr. Fitzgerald's departure. This action is not recommended since it is rather underhanded and would probably not be approved by the Civil Service Commission, even though it is legally and procedurally possible. The Air Force could request conversion of this position to the career service, utilizing competitive procedures, and consider all the eligibles from the Executive Inventory and an outside search. Using this competitive procedure, Mr. Fitzgerald might or might not be selected. If not, displacement action would follow."[12]

None of these methods would have to be used, of course, if Fitzgerald left "voluntarily," and on several occasions the wisdom of this course was impressed on him.

On January 8, Fitzgerald was told by his superior, Mr. Thomas H. Nielsen, that as a result of his testimony and the ensuing publicity, "You have lost your usefulness. You work for me and you are not useful to me." Nielsen called him back later to explain that he was not fired and there was no intention to fire him. But a few days later, in a formal performance review, he was told by the same man, Mr. Nielsen, that he had no future in the Air Force. On February 6, he received a copy of a note which stated that Nielsen had requested Fitzgerald's counterparts in the Office of the Secretary of Defense to stop working with him on management systems control problems and to work instead with the military staff in Air Force headquarters. On March 4, he talked with Secretary Seamans who told him that the staff didn't "like" him.

It wasn't until November 4, 1969, that Fitzgerald received official notice that his old team preferred to play without him. They had chosen method number two of the Lang memorandum—"reduction in force"— and abolished his job. Perhaps the Air Force enjoyed the irony of dismissing the outspoken advocate of economy by claiming "economy" reasons. The separation notice explained that the elimination of the position was "necessitated by a reorganization under the current Air Force retrenchment program." It noted that "there is no appropriate available position in which you can be placed at your present grade level or lower" and advised him that "if you believe that this proposed action violates your rights under Air Force reduction-in-force regulations, you may submit a written request for review under the appeal and grievance procedures. . . ." On the same day, the Pentagon issued a press release announcing that the "present Assistant Secretary, Mr. Spencer J. Schedler, has been working on reorganizing plans for several months and with the Secretary's approval has implemented the new organization of his office in conjunction with the current reduction actions in the Air Force."

The Air Force was adamant that the action was not a "dismissal" or "firing" at all. During the hearings when the old team was briefly reunited at the witness table, Chairman Proxmire asked Secretary Seamans with whom he consulted when he fired Fitzgerald. The Secretary corrected the Chairman: "I did not decide to fire Mr. Fitzgerald. I prefer to use the term, the correct term, 'to abolish his job.'" There was a moment's silence. Then someone in the audience guffawed. The staff began to laugh, the press laughed, even the members of the committee laughed. Senator Proxmire commented later, "In my almost thirteen years in the Senate, I remember no occasion in which a witness was so obviously embarrassed by his own statement."[13]

Unfortunately, losing a job is not a laughing matter for the one who loses it; nor is it always the worst that happens. More damaging in some respects is what

Fitzgerald calls the "personal denigration" that may be used to bring about a departure or justify a dismissal. "This aspect of my experiences of the last year is most distasteful for me to talk about," he says. "At the same time I think it is important to bring it out, since I have observed . . . that personal attacks and discrediting innuendo are frequently directed against economy advocates in the defense acquisitions business. I am certainly not unique in this regard."[14]

The most serious were accusations that Fitzgerald leaked confidential documents to members of Congress. In the days following Fitzgerald's dismissal, Spencer J. Schedler, Assistant Secretary for Financial Management, frequented the offices of a number of congressmen to explain why Fitzgerald was departing the Pentagon. The gist of his explanation was that Fitzgerald was not a "team player" and that he had violated security regulations.[15] In hearings before the Armed Services Committee on May 7, 1969, Secretary Seamans made the statement: "It is very interesting that in testimony in front of a number of committees, documents kept appearing, some of which are confidential, that were obtained from Mr. Fitzgerald."[16]

When Fitzgerald tried to talk with the Secretary about the charge, he was denied an audience. He was also denied his request to see copies of the confidential documents he was alleged to have leaked. Even for such a damaging charge he found there were no remedies provided within the civil service. Without the backing of Senator Proxmire and Congressman William Moorhead, the charges, though provably false, might have stood unchallenged. However, when Proxmire and Moorhead pressed Secretary Seamans during the hearings, he retracted the charge, or claimed that his statement had been misinterpreted: "I will say categorically now that Mr. Fitzgerald has not to my knowledge violated national security, and if this has been interpreted in this way, I would say that I am very sorry that this has been the case."[17]

Fitzgerald also discovered that during attempts to get rid of him the Air Force had run a special investigation, now filed away in the Pentagon. He had no way of gaining access to this file nor, it appeared, did a congressional committee. When the Proxmire committee asked for the file, Secretary Seamans denied there had been an investigation. Under pressure he finally agreed to hand over a "sanitized" version of the Fitzgerald file, purged of the names of all informants, who were referred to as T–1, T–2 and so on. From this purged version and from his associate who had been questioned during the investigation, Fitzgerald learned that the Air Force had first tried to establish "moral lapses" but had given that up. Then they tried to establish a conflict of interest by seeking information to show that Fitzgerald had retained an interest in his old management consulting firm while working for the Air Force. They did find clear evidence to exonerate him of this charge, but this information was omitted from the file when it was shown to Senator Proxmire and Congressman Moorhead. All that remained were the charges of anonymous "T's," chief among them the evidence that Fitzgerald was a "penny pincher" because he drove an "old Rambler."

There is an ironic footnote to the "special investigation" episode. These secret files are excluded from the provisions of the Freedom of Information Act which provides that information in "investigatory files" is exempt. However, in its efforts to deny that there had been an investigation, the Air Force theoretically lost its claim to an exemption under the act. Its recourse, however, was effective: it simply refused to produce the file.

CONCLUSION

As he points out, Fitzgerald came through his whistle blowing experience with more help than most people can expect. Immediately after his dismissal, he became a consultant to the Joint Economic Committee, a job which still consumes about half of his time. The publicity that surrounded the episode put him in demand as a speaker; in the following year he made some forty-four speeches around the country. But his career has unquestionably been affected. He is trying to build up an industrial management consulting firm like the one he left when he went to work for the Air Force. He is getting some small clients, but the big companies, where his special cost accounting skills would be most useful, aren't coming to him. Although his former firm handled major companies and supported twelve employees, Fitzgerald is now working alone. "It is not unrewarding," he says, "but as a practical matter, until the attitude of business changes, I won't be getting the kind of work I had before."

At the same time, he is challenging his dismissal by the Air Force and trying to establish precedents that might help future critics of government employers. One potential remedy is the federal statute that forbids anyone to intimidate or impede a witness in a federal departmental or congressional inquiry. Senator Proxmire attempted to enforce this statute by calling on the United States Justice Department to investigate the legality of Fitzgerald's dismissal. No investigation has ever been undertaken. "It is true," Fitzgerald points out, "that civil servants and military personnel appear well protected by statutes providing tough penalties for retaliation against government witnesses before congressional committees. But who's going to enforce them? Would John Mitchell put Melvin Laird in jail? Congress itself would help, but those members who have the power to protect witnesses have not been willing to do so when money for big military contractors is threatened."[18]

The second possible remedy is the Civil Service Commission, where Fitzgerald has filed a grievance asking for reinstatement and back pay. He is contending that he was fired for personal reasons, not for the stated reason of a "reduction in force." He filed his appeal immediately after he was dismissed on January 6, 1970. His first hearing before the commission was not held until May 4, 1971. "We have to exhaust all administrative remedies before we can file charges in court," Fitzgerald commented as the proceedings dragged on. "Instead, those 'remedies' are exhausting us."

At the May 4 hearing, the commission refused Fitzgerald's request for open hearings and conducted six days of closed sessions in May and June. Fitzgerald decided to challenge the commission's closed-hearings policy and went to the American Civil Liberties Union for help. Two ACLU attorneys, William L. Sollee and John Bodner, Jr., both of Washington, D.C., filed suit for him in federal district court contesting the commission ruling.

The first court decision came on June 25, 1971, when Judge William Bryant ruled that no further Civil Service Commission hearings could be held in closed session. On August 20, 1971, the Justice Department served notice that it would appeal the district court order, but by October, Justice lawyers had still not filed an actual brief. Charging stalling tactics, Fitzgerald's attorneys went back to district court in October and argued that the Civil Service Commission was ignoring Judge Bryant's order for open hearings. Bryant noted in the hearing that he had assumed his earlier order would assure open sessions. But he agreed to hear government arguments for holding off open sessions. Those arguments were made on October 22 with the government seeking a further postponement until the case was heard by the United States Court of Appeals. Bryant ruled that Fitzgerald would suffer from further delay of the open hearings because witnesses might be lost and memories dulled. However, he agreed to postpone implementing his order until both sides filed formal motions.[19]

In an order received by Fitzgerald's lawyers on November 22, the United States Court of Appeals set aside Judge Bryant's open hearing order until the appeals court could hear the case.[20] No date was set for those hearings.

This means that when the case is finally heard before the Civil Service Commission, key witnesses may be out of reach. The commission does not have the subpoena power to bring back witnesses once they leave the government.

Soon after his dismissal, Fitzgerald sought support from the professional society he has belonged to since he helped form the student chapter at his college, the American Institute of Industrial Engineers. When he asked the institute to investigate the professional and ethical questions involved in his dismissal, the American Institute of Industrial Engineers suddenly decided it was not a "professional" society; it was a "technical" organization. Thus it absolved itself of dealing with ethical questions. Fitzgerald was not altogether surprised. He believes that the ability of professional groups to deal with such questions is undermined by their practice of allowing "sustaining" or "corporate" members. Large military contractors are contributing members of his own society, for example.

Until the remedies for the public whistle blower are strengthened, conscientious employees may want to consider alternative avenues of reform, Fitzgerald suggests. "I still believe some good work can be done internal to the bureaucracies, especially if you are analytical and keep good notes. If enough well-intentioned, tough, and skillful people take stands inside the Pentagon, the deterioration of stewardship can be slowed, at least temporarily.

"Then, of course, you can always become a 'secret patriot.' Senator Proxmire, Congressman Moorhead, I, and other military economy advocates frequently receive unclassified horror stories from outraged military men and Pentagon civilians who do not wish to be identified. This is a safe and prudent way to surface information the public should have anyway. I believe our secret patriots are making indirect but worthwhile contributions to the education of the taxpaying public. This, in turn, will have a wholesome cumulative effect."[21]

Fitzgerald has not regretted his own decision to speak out, though he is not particularly optimistic about his effect on the military establishment. "I would like to be able to say that even though the experience was costly to me my old organization had learned their lesson, taken the pledge, and had instituted reforms to improve their stewardship. Unhappily, this is not the case. The Air Force, and the whole Pentagon for that matter, are more wasteful, secretive and deceptive than before. . . .

"One of the points of my testimony which really infuriated the Pentagon's leaders was the well-supported charge that contracts with large firms are typically modified to accommodate the financial needs and technical abilities of the favored giants, and that the Pentagon takes a dive, or throws the game, in negotiations with big contractors who might be hurt if their con-

tracts were enforced. Now, mostly because of the Lockheed debacle, this practice is out in the open. But to
my knowledge, no Administration official is taking a
strict constructionist view of contract law and enforcement in this case."[22]

Fitzgerald is now writing a book, tentatively titled
The High Priests of Waste, in which he hopes to go
further in telling the public about the underlying problems of defense procurement policies. The fight is not
over, so far as he is concerned. There is, he believes,
"still an opportunity to capture benefits from the disclosures I and many others have made."[23]

6

Dr. John W. Gofman and Dr. Arthur R. Tamplin

Where the future of the human species is at stake, be very sure your voice is loud enough and incisive enough to be heard and heard well.   —*John W. Gofman*

Few members of the public had heard the names of John W. Gofman or Arthur R. Tamplin before the fall of 1969. They were two of hundreds of scientists laboring in laboratories and universities across the country, scientists whose names are rarely identified with the technology that their labors help produce. But twice that fall, in October and again in November, the names of Gofman and Tamplin made their way into the press, along with their startling estimates that sixteen thousand more people would contract cancer or leukemia every year if the United States population were exposed to the dose of radiation from nuclear power plants presently allowed by the Atomic Energy Commission. The two scientists expressed serious concern. They said they were sure the Atomic Energy Commission shared their concern and asked the AEC to increase the margin of safety by lowering the permissible radiation dose.

One wire service and a West Coast newspaper picked up their story. Drs. Gofman and Tamplin were, after all, AEC men themselves. Both had worked at the AEC-funded Lawrence Radiation Laboratory at Livermore, California, since 1963. Dr. Gofman was an associate director of the laboratory in charge of the Bio-Medical Research Division. He was an eminent scientist whose research on heart disease in the nineteen-fifties led to major advances in the field and was widely recognized by his peers. Dr. Tamplin was a group leader in the division, heading a project to develop an information system for assessing the effects of low-dose radiation. Their information, or so it seemed to those in the press who were interested, came from a respectable source and was, at least, worth reporting.

Even more importantly, after nearly two decades of research, the country was beginning to move ahead with the actual construction of nuclear power plants. No longer visionary shadows on the horizon, operating nuclear reactors were already—or would shortly be—near neighbors of millions of Americans. It was practically certain that the utilities, on the advice of the federal government, were planning to depend heavily on atomic energy. Already, drawing boards indicated one hundred nuclear power stations in the immediate future and five hundred before the year 2000. It was also becoming clear that the reactors would be located, not in isolated places as once thought, but next door to large population centers.[1]

The public was dimly, somewhat uncomfortably aware of questions of safety, centering around the possibility of accidents and the leakage of radiation into the environment. At the time of the Gofman-Tamplin statement, the public knew much more about the clean, cheap, safe electrical power it could expect from the "friendly atom" and about peaceful "nuclear explosives" for recovery of resources such as gas, oil, and metals. The Atomic Energy Commission had diligently kept the citizens informed about the benefits of atomic energy. Talk about safety, on the other hand, was generally clothed in scientific jargon the man on the street found difficult to understand. So far as the laymen could tell, the scientists seemed to be saying there was no way of answering all of the questions short of putting up the reactors.

Questions of safety were deferred to three organizations that promulgated standards to protect workers and the public from the hazards of radiation: the National Council on Radiation Protection, the International Commission on Radiological Protection, and the Federal Radiation Council. The first two groups were private organizations established in the late twenties, and for the next two or three decades were undisputed authorities for the setting of radiation standards. In 1959, aroused by public fears over fallout from nuclear weapons, the federal government established the Federal Radiation Council as a public authority to set more "official" guidelines. The standards established by these three groups were remarkably similar, as were their membership.[2] Few people raised questions about the standards they authorized, though within professional circles some scientists were alluding to doubts. In early 1969, for example, Dr. Brian Mac-Mahon, a prominent Harvard epidemiologist, was writing in a medical journal: "It must be admitted that we still do not have most of the data that would be required for an informed judgment on the maximum limits of exposure advisable for individuals or populations."[3] This might have troubled the average citizen had he heard the statement, which he did not. It might have made him somewhat doubtful about putting the atom to work for him.

A few people were being more specific. In December, 1968, Professor Barry Commoner was talking most specifically about thyroid cancer. He told a meeting of the American Association for the Advancement of Science that radioactive iodine 131 released from nuclear power plants settled in the thyroid gland of animals and human beings. His studies indicated that human beings were subjected to serious risk. "A biologist cannot be satisfied with the statement that the radioactive pollutants released by a given nuclear power plant meet design specifications and government standards," he said. "He must ask, what radiation is released; how does it move through the web of life; what risks to the integrity of life does it involve; and what are their ultimate costs?"

Commoner pointed to the acknowledgment of the Federal Radiation Council that there is a human cost associated with the acceptance of its guidelines for radiation emissions: that "any radiation exposure involves some risk." "If we develop the industry without a full appreciation of what it really costs us," he warned, "we may find—at some future time when we become aware of the full price—that we are unwilling to pay the bill. If that should happen, the development of nuclear power and the nation's reliance on it will come to be regarded as a tragic and costly mistake."[4]

Dr. Linus Pauling had also warned as early as 1958 that radiation damage to human beings from development of nuclear power and other peaceful uses of atomic energy might be costly. But except for a rare voice like this, few cautionary words were reaching the ear of the public, and even fewer warnings of demonstrable dangers.

It was therefore strange to hear talk about risks, specific risks based on specific data, coming from AEC scientists like Gofman and Tamplin, and the public's attention was aroused. The interested citizen could not help but take notice of figures like sixteen thousand extra cancers and cases of leukemia a year. He could not help but follow the reasoning that safety standards that allowed the risk were perhaps no safety standards at all. He was compelled to wonder whether the Atomic Energy Commission and the eminent scientists cared as much for his safety as for their technology. The data supporting the arguments were, perhaps, beyond his ken; but he became interested to know why those data were wrong, if indeed they were wrong. He had, for perhaps the first time, a figure and a focus: sixteen thousand cancers and the AEC standards. For perhaps the first time, a clear route of action was proposed: tighten the standards. These are some of the points it is important to remember when reviewing the case of Drs. Gofman and Tamplin who, among many critics of the Atomic Eneregy Commission, have raised the biggest storm and in some ways made the strongest comment on what it takes to be an effective whistle blower.

The argument was formally launched on October 29, 1969, in a completely correct setting, a nuclear science symposium of the Institute of Electrical and Electronic Engineers. Speaking by invitation, Drs. Gofman and Tamplin presented a paper that outlined their estimates of sixteen thousand extra cancers and cases of leukemia. A review of the data led them, they said, "to have grave concern over a burgeoning program for the use of nuclear power for electricity and for other purposes, with an *allowable* dose to the population-at-large of 0.17 Rads [units of radiation] of total body exposure to ionizing radiation per year. A valid scientific justification for this 'allowable' dose has never been presented, other than the general indication that the risk to the population so exposed is *believed* to be small compared with the benefits to be derived from the orderly development of atomic energy for peaceful purposes."[5]

One month later, they presented the same estimates to Senator Edmund Muskie's Subcommittee on Air and Water Pollution. On both occasions, they emphasized that they were not opposing peaceful uses of the atom and that they sought to work with the Atomic Energy Commission to devise adequate protective measures to encourage that development. They told the Muskie subcommittee, "We should like to emphasize here and now, lest the words be twisted, that the population has *not* received anywhere near 0.17 Rads per year from atomic energy activities thus far. Nevertheless, the industry is only now getting going and the 0.17 Rads per year *is* on the Federal Statute books as *allowable*."

Citing experts who said the dosage is not now and is not expected to be as high as 0.17 Rads per year, the two scientists urged, "Let us immediately codify this into law so that no one can possibly be confused by a high allowable figure and concomitant statement that we will stay well below that figure. Industry urgently needs a real standard that will hold up over time, since a *later* revision downward can lead to excruciatingly costly retrofits to a developed industrial application. It is far better to lower the guidelines now and do our engineering design accordingly. We believe engineering talent can direct its effort to essentially absolute containment of radioactivity at every step in any useful atomic energy development. If we are fortunate enough later to find that some unknown effect operates to protect against the hazards we have demonstrated here, it will be easy enough to raise the guidelines for radiation exposure *then*. In this way we can avoid irreversible injury to our environment and to a whole generation of humans *while* we find out the true facts."[6]

The two scientists had not come suddenly to their position. At Lawrence Radiation Laboratory they were charged with assessing radiation effects. For a number of years they had been concerned about the lack of hard data to assess those effects while the country moved full steam ahead to make them a reality. In 1964, Dr. Gofman told a Plowshare symposium that "data requisite to provide a groundwork for a reasonable set of radiation standards for man are inadequate." At that time, there was little human data on the effects of low-dose radiation, although animal experiments already indicated that the risk might well be higher than generally assumed. Between 1964 and 1969 more human data became available, provided by the survivors of Hiroshima and Nagasaki, by Britishers treated for a form of spinal arthritis by x-rays, by children in the United States who were irradiated in infancy in the neck as treatment to reduce the thymus and who later developed cancer or leukemia, by tubercular patients radiated by fluoroscopy in the course of treatment, by infants irradiated *in utero* incidental to diagnostic x-ray studies in the mother. Direct human data became available down to extremely low total doses from the work of Stewart and Kneale, who found a doubling of the future incidence of cancer plus leukemia for one-third of a Rad delivered during the first thirteen weeks of pregnancy.[7] Gofman and Tamplin extrapolated from this data in order to estimate the effects of the radiation emissions allowed by the federal radiation standards.

Dr. Gofman was to say later, "Certainly I must admit I shared in the ecologically stupid view that standards for human radiation exposure required *human* data. I am appalled by my earlier failure to understand sound public health principles."[8] Even without the human data, he should have realized this, he says. All that was *known* implied risk; safety lay only in the *unknown*— in the hope that there was a threshold below which radiation did not harm the human body, the hope that exposure to radiation over a long period of time produced less serious results than exposure to the same amount of radiation all at once. The question was whether to count on the possibilities rather than the risks. It was an experiment so large they concluded it was unacceptable. Beyond it, they glimpsed the possibility of inadvertent genocide.

In addition, they now had data that showed approximately what the risk would be if the population were exposed to the allowable dose. Having found that, what were they to do with it?

Dr. Tamplin began to include some of that data in a handbook he was developing for the Atomic Energy Commission. AEC spokesmen were later to repudiate the handbook, but before the issue was public it brought no response from the organization. In fact, their principal adversary in the AEC admitted later he had not even read the handbook before Gofman and Tamplin became controversial.[9] If he had, the Atomic Energy Commission might have been prepared for what was to come.

The event that launched the public debate was precipitated, ironically, by the AEC. In the spring of 1969, the AEC asked Dr. Tamplin to prepare a refutation of Dr. Ernest Sternglass, who had written that fallout radiation had caused four hundred thousand infant and fetal deaths in the United States. A member of the faculty of the medical school of the University of Pittsburgh, Dr. Sternglass published these estimates in the *Bulletin of Atomic Scientists* and later in *Esquire*, where the public had a fair shot at it. The AEC was enraged. They strongly and with some justification believed that Dr. Sternglass was wrong, and they picked Tamplin to clear up the matter. Accordingly, Dr. Tamplin wrote a paper for *Environment* refuting Dr. Sternglass but adding his own estimates that fallout might have caused four thousand infant deaths. This was not quite what the Atomic Energy Commission had in mind. In August, 1969, Dr. Tamplin received a telephone call from Dr. John Totter, head of the AEC Division of Biology and Medicine. Dr. Totter wanted Dr. Tamplin to publish his paper *without* his own estimates of deaths. It was a stormy conversation, followed up by a letter from Dr. Totter that repeated, in presumably more delicate language, what he had requested by telephone. (The letter was later widely circulated by the AEC.) He was careful to point out that "our interest should in no way imply that we are attempting to dictate to you what you can and cannot publish." He went on to say, "We are concerned that when numbers are arrived at, particularly any estimation of mortality risk, the seriousness of the subject makes it vital that the greatest care be used in determining these numbers and in assuring that the test truly reflects the uncertainties inherent in their determination. I think in this we all share a mutual concern for accuracy and wise interpretation of the available facts." He still wanted a refutation of Dr. Sternglass for a "fuller understanding of radiation effects," but wanted it separated from any other estimates of infant deaths. He emphasized that a refutation was "particularly worthwhile since Dr. Sternglass has chosen to conduct his debate in the public media and popular magazines."[10]

Dr. Tamplin refused. He and Dr. Gofman, who was present during the conversation, felt that their estimates of infant deaths were accurate and that it would be misleading *not* to include them in the article. Otherwise, they believed, the impression would be that fallout was not believed to have caused infant deaths or at least that there were no other estimates of such deaths. Their response to the conversation with Dr. Totter, the "infamous telephone call" as they call it, was one of immense indignation. It was the beginning of a confrontation that was to consume more of their time and energy than they could have imagined at that moment. And it was, in many ways, a paradigm of the larger debate to follow. Dr. Totter did not refute Tamplin's estimates; neither did the Atomic Energy Commission succeed in refuting the estimates Gofman and Tamplin presented later. Dr. Roger Batzel, who succeeded Gofman in 1969 as head of the biomedical division at Lawrence Radiation Laboratory, said in an interview tape-recorded for the *Atlantic*: "As far as the scientific information is concerned, we have no, at least, I have no fundamental differences about their scientific conclusions." What Gofman and Tamplin were fighting was a political, not a scientific battle, a profound reluctance on the part of most of the AEC to release any risk statistics, or talk publicly about any risks, however well founded, involved in development of atomic energy.

The following fall they made public their estimates of the cancer and leukemia cases that would be caused if the population were exposed to the allowable dose of radiation under AEC standards. They expected their data to be examined and, if possible, refuted. Demonstrating that sixteen thousand extra deaths *would* occur is different from demonstrating that 2 billion extra dollars *have been* spent. Ernest Fitzgerald could point to facts and figures that were tangible, the nuts and bolts, as it were, of a very real aircraft. Gofman and Tamplin had no bodies to present. They had the data that proved to them what *would* happen and said that it ought to be averted. The Atomic Energy Commission immediately challenged them, not by arguing that the estimates were wrong but arguing that the standard-setting organizations believed the risk was "acceptable" and, further, that the population had not been and would not be exposed to the allowable dose.[11] The issue was taken up by the Joint Committee on Atomic Energy in hearings that ran to three volumes. Drs. Gofman and Tamplin submitted further reports; so did the AEC. Far from retreating from their position, in January, 1970, Gofman and Tamplin said their review of the data now led them to estimate thirty-two thousand extra cancers and cases of leukemia a year and between fifteen thousand and 1.5 million additional deaths from genetically determined diseases. They continued to call for lowering the allowable dose from 0.17 Rads per year to 0.017 Rads per year.

By now the one wire service and lone West Coast newspaper that had reported their first speech were being joined by the major television networks, the major newspapers, radio networks, and magazines. Editors were assigning reporters to long-term analyses of the question of radiation safety, and most of them were quoting Gofman and Tamplin. They were turning up on podiums across the country. A good number were professional meetings like those of the Institute of Electrical and Electronic Engineers, the American Association for the Advancement of Science, the Center for the Study of Democratic Institutions, and the Amer-

ican Cancer Society. They went before Congress with
twenty-one reports for the Joint Committee on Atomic
Energy. They spoke to environmentalists at the Congressional Teach-In in April, 1970, and at the University of Minnesota, and in Oregon. They spoke at
the New York City Council hearings on reactor siting
and before the Santa Cruz board of supervisors. In
attempting to trace their activity, the Atomic Energy
Commission staff found twenty press interviews between
October, 1969, and July, 1970. There were probably
more. In November, 1970, they published a book called
"Population Control" Through Nuclear Pollution (Chicago: Nelson-Hall). The AEC staff also reported that
Lawrence Radiation Laboratory set up a special printing arrangement for the Gofman-Tamplin reports,
reproducing twenty-seven thousand copies of their
twenty-one reports at laboratory expense.

But if the directors of the laboratory were generous in
printing their reports, they were doing other things at
the behest of the AEC officials in Washington that
seemed designed to quietly ease Gofman and Tamplin
out of the AEC. Having launched the public debate in
the committee rooms in Washington and in the press,
Gofman and Tamplin were soon fighting to keep their
jobs on the West Coast. In December, 1969, a month
after the Muskie Subcommittee hearings, Dr. Tamplin
was informed that seven of the scientists in his group
of eleven were being "reassigned." A few months later,
two of the remaining three scientists were also reassigned
to "higher priority work on radioecology."[12] It then
became the laboratory's judgment that, having only one
assistant, Dr. Tamplin no longer required a full-time
secretary. He was left as a leader of a "group" of one.

The "reassignments" were subsequently explained by
AEC officials as a reallocation of resources reflected in
a general budget reduction in the Bio-Medical Research Division. Gofman and Tamplin estimate that, of
Lawrence Radiation Laboratory's budget reduction of
three hundred thousand dollars in 1970, approximately
sixty percent of the total cut was taken from Dr. Tamplin's program. They also claim that the reductions and
reassignments so restricted his work that for all in-
tents and purposes he had no program left.

The laboratory's directors than told Dr. Tamplin they would no longer pay his travel expenses when he was invited to speak on his work. They also proceeded to dock his pay when he was away from the laboratory on speaking engagements, even at such notable forums as a meeting of the American Cancer Society in March, 1970. (This meeting took place on a weekend. Dr. Roger Batzel, head of the bio-medical division, was so zealous that he docked Tamplin's pay for Saturday and Sunday. He later refunded the weekend pay.) The subsequent explanation for these measures was that there is a budgetary difference between a trip to deliver a "scientific" paper and a trip to deliver a "technical" paper, the first being worthy of remuneration and the second, not. Dr. Tamplin's speeches were considered "technical" papers.

The most direct attempt at censorship came when the laboratory directors deleted certain portions—the "opinion" portions—of a paper Dr. Tamplin prepared for delivery before the American Association for the Advancement of Science in December, 1969.

Dr. Gofman's work on the effects of low-dose radiation on chromosomes also received a budget cut, from $320,000 to $270,000 for 1970. At the same time, Dr. Totter, head of the AEC Division of Biology and Medicine, was telling newsmen that Dr. Gofman's work was "worthless." He told a *Chicago Sun-Times* reporter that his staff had been urging him since 1966 to "cut out" Gofman and Tamplin. He did not mention that in 1966 Gofman's chromosome work had hardly begun, almost no laboratory funds had been spent on it, and an assessment could hardly have been made. He told the same reporter that Tamplin's information system was "unreliable."[13]

Gofman and Tamplin protested vigorously both their functional restrictions and what they considered personal attacks on their integrity as professionals by AEC staff members. Only a few weeks after their appearance before the Muskie subcommittee, Dr. Gofman wrote AEC Chairman Glenn T. Seaborg—an old scientific colleague—the first of a series of "Dear Glenn" letters, appealing to the AEC Chairman to stop the "harassment by your staff of our efforts to determine and present the truth concerning the hazards of ionizing radiation for man." In January he contacted AEC Commissioner Theos Thompson to ask for "constructive cooperation" and requested that AEC staff refrain from "name-calling, character assassination," and attacks on his and Dr. Tamplin's "scientific integrity and ability."

In June, 1970, after Tamplin received the second of his staff reductions and after Dr. Totter had disparaged them openly to the press, Gofman and Tamplin decided they would not be "cut out" quietly. Like many other professionals, they had little job security and no channels for challenging any cutback in their projects. They were not civil service employees, but employees of the Univeristy of California, which runs the Lawrence Radiation Laboratory on an independent contract with the AEC. They began to contact people outside the AEC: Senator Edmund Muskie, Senator Mike Gravel, Congressman Chet Holifield, Ralph Nader, and members of the press. On July 6, 1970, Ralph Nader wrote Senator Muskie asking him to look into the Gofman-Tamplin case. Nader said the Atomic Energy Commission was trying to "render them voiceless." At the same time, Thomas O'Toole was reporting to readers of the *Washington Post* that Drs. Gofman and Tamplin feared they were being squeezed out. On July 7, Congressman Holifield, chairman of the Joint Committee on Atomic Energy, issued a press release asking the AEC to prepare "a complete and detailed account of this matter." The same day, the AEC issued a press release denying any persecution. On July 21, the AEC delivered to Congressman Holifield and Senator Muskie its "Staff Report on the Gofman-Tamplin Allegations of Censorship and Reprisal by the AEC and the Lawrence Radiation Laboratory." (The report exonerated the AEC and LRL from "motivations" to silence or get rid of Gofman and Tamplin. Every adverse action was carefully explained as a budgetary consideration or laboratory policy.) On July 29, Drs. Gofman and Tamplin wrote Congressman Holifield and AEC Chairman Seaborg that the report was "a shallow, glib, obviously false effort by AEC staff to whitewash one of the greatest scandals in American science." They asked for public hearings. Predictably, Congressman Holifield, a long-time antagonist of atomic energy safety advocates, has not granted this request.

On August 5, Senator Muskie asked the American Association for the Advancement of Science to conduct an independent investigation. Dr. Seaborg promptly wrote Dr. Gofman that the AEC would do nothing until the AAAS review was completed; until then, the budget cuts would stand. On October 17–18, 1970, the AAAS board met and decided to consider the case at its next meeting in December. In December, the AAAS decided to establish a committee to look into cases of alleged scientific repression. By March, 1971, the members of the committee had not yet been announced and Gofman and Tamplin had received no word about an inquiry.

On March 18, Senator Gravel wrote Dr. Athelstan Spilhaus of the AAAS:

> Three months have passed since the AAAS Board of Directors asked its new Committee on Scientific Freedom and Responsibility to look into the Gofman-Tamplin case. Seven months have passed since Senator Muskie first asked the AAAS for its participation. Nine months have passed since Dr. Gofman was threatened with dismissal from the Lawrence Radiation Lab. More than a year has passed since the Lab made its first moves with regard to Dr. Tamplin, who has been without his research team for nine months. . . .
>
> The purpose of this letter is to ascertain what the AAAS is now doing about the Gofman-Tamplin case, why it is not public, and why the action is taking so long. Delay carries a message of its own. Perhaps Congress should look into the problem.

Dr. William Bevan, executive officer of the AAAS, replied on March 23. He said that the board was still seeking "distinguished citizens" to serve as members of the committee.

"It is the Board's view that the Committee, to be fully effective, must be composed of outstanding persons recognized by both the scientific community and the public at large to be of unimpeachable integrity and impartiality. The persons sought by the Board are without exception persons with a great many commitments already, and recruitment does not proceed as rapidly as all of us would like. However, the process has almost been completed. The charge to the Committee is to prepare general policy in this matter of both alleged abridgments of scientific freedom and failure of scientific responsibility and to recommend procedures for the review of such charges. Several cases await the review of the Committee."

Dr. Bevan added, "It is important, perhaps, to point out that the AAAS has not received from either Dr. Gofman or Dr. Tamplin a request to examine the circumstances of their case."

An AAAS staff member told one of the authors of this book that the association did not plan to investigate the case unless Gofman and Tamplin requested it. The new committee would work only on establishing procedures for handling problems of scientific freedom. By midsummer, 1971, the committee had been appointed but did not plan to meet until the fall.[14] By May, 1972, the committee was still considering procedures to recommend to the AAAS and its affiliated societies to handle such cases.

At this writing, Gofman and Tamplin are still at the lab, but barely. Tamplin is working virtually alone except for the assistance of one scientist, Dr. Donald Geesaman, who agrees with his estimates of cancer and leukemia risk. Dr. Gofman's chromosome project funds finally have been cut out. In the fall of 1969, Dr. Totter, already on record as believing Gofman's work to be "worthless" and that the AEC should stop supporting it, ordered a review of the work. Gofman protested to Dr. Seaborg, saying he did not object to a review but to its being conducted by a man already opposed to his work. The review proceeded. A five-man review committee was appointed, composed of three scientists who were sympathetic to Dr. Gofman and two who were not. The committee performed a mathematical miracle and produced seven opinions: three in favor of continuing his cancer-chromosome work and four opposed. The two "extra" opinions presumably were supplied by the Atomic Energy Commission when it reported the findings of the review committee. Dr. Gofman plans to leave Lawrence in January, 1973, after completing several reports on his work. Meanwhile he is searching for independent fundings.

What has proceeded from the Gofman-Tamplin whistle blowing, surely one of the loudest, more persistent examples of blowing the whistle today? Certainly more people are thinking about nuclear safety than ever before. Proponents of present safety standards have not been able to appease their critics, largely because Gofman and Tamplin simply won't be quiet. In the third of three articles on issues raised by Gofman and Tamplin, *Science* magazine (February, 1971) noted that the "sharp national debate over nuclear safety seems likely to continue despite the National Council on Radiation Protection's efforts to lay the matter to rest." The writer credited "the exchange between Gofman and the NCRP" with serving "to focus attention on the important question of how radiation protection standards are set."[15]

Since Gofman and Tamplin first questioned the standards and the method of setting them, the Atomic Energy Commission has been divested of its sole authority for standard setting. Under a law passed by Congress, the Federal Radiation Council has been abolished and its functions transferred to the Environmental Protection Agency. EPA now sets "generally applicable" standards for radiation exposure of human beings, to be implemented by the AEC. In January, 1970, two months after their initial testimony, the then Secretary of Health, Education, and Welfare Robert Finch ordered a complete review of all radiation standards, the first in a decade. (That review took nearly a year to get off the ground.)

Finally in June, 1971, the AEC proposed stricter radiation standards for nuclear power plants, which spokesmen said would reduce the permissible dose of radiation for the public one hundred times.[16] Under this proposal, radiation dosage would be limited to about one percent of the present permissible dose. The rule-making procedures to implement these standards were getting under way by January, 1972.

More scientists are beginning to speak out against the existing standards and to offer estimates of damage even more serious than those presented by Gofman and Tamplin. NCRP spokesmen still claim that "ninety-five percent of the experts" are in disagreement with the Gofman-Tamplin risk estimates.[17] This may be explained by the fact that most of the experts are members of the National Council on Radiation Protection or the International Commission on Radiological Protection, the groups that are responsible for setting standards. It is still the scientists outside the nuclear organization itself who are most vocal as its critics. Dr. Joshua Lederberg of Stanford University, a Nobel Prize-winning geneticist who calls government "the most dangerous genetic engineer," estimates a ten-percent increase in all genetically related diseases under present standards (compared to a five- to ten-percent increase estimated by Gofman and Tamplin). Lederberg says that average exposure to the "allowable" dose of radiation can ultimately result in an added burden of medical and health care costs due to genetically determined diseases of $10 billion annually.[18]

Dr. Linus Pauling, also a Nobel scientist, estimates ninety-six thousand extra cancers a year under existing standards. He calls for lowering the allowable dose "immediately."[19]

In hearings before the Senate Subcommittee on Air and Water Pollution, August 4, 1970, an AEC health physicist, Dr. Karl Z. Morgan, noted his agreement with the Gofman-Tamplin argument, although he did not talk about specific risk estimates.

"I believe present evidence points to the fact that most, if not all, types and forms of chronic radiation-induced damage relate more or less to the accumulated dose, and there is no justification for one to assume the existence of a threshold below which these forms of damage would not result. This, I believe, has been the principal force of the argument presented by Gofman and Tamplin. To this, I agree and lend my strongest support. In this statement, I might say I am supporting also the expressed positions of ICRP (International Commission on Radiological Protection) and NCRP (National Council on Radiation Protection), as well as the Federal Radiation Council. I hope this is or will be made the expressed opinion of the Atomic Energy Commission."

In fact, members of the standard-setting groups have acknowledged that their standards do include risks. Egan O'Connor, assistant to Senator Mike Gravel and specialist in nuclear energy problems, points out that a committee of the National Academy of Sciences endorsed the presently permissible dose while admitting that the price might be a quarter of a million "defective children" if the parents of the present generation were exposed to it.[20]

Question: Even if the population isn't receiving the permissible dose, why are standards permissible that admit the consequences? AEC Commissioner Theos J. Thompson, in an article entitled "Response to Gofman and Tamplin: The AEC Position," wrote: "For the record, the AEC fully concurs with the standards-setting philosophy that all radiation is potentially dangerous and that radiation should always be kept as low as *practicable*" (emphasis added). Question: who is to decide what is "practicable" and what are the implications for public safety versus technological progress?[21]

For the first time these assumptions are being questioned loudly, publicly, and on a broad scale. What are the risks? What is an "acceptable" risk? What are the benefits? Is any risk "acceptable" when it means a technologically avoidable increase in death, disease, and mutation? Who decides?

A growing number of people are also asking whether new institutions are required to offset the promotional bias of government and industry in the development of new technology. Gofman and Tamplin are among those calling for a system of "adversary assessment" of technology that will represent the public interest.

"What is needed is a group of competent scientists who would criticize any new application of science or expansion of technology. . . . It must seem that we are suggesting an end to technological progress. Quite the contrary, we are only suggesting that technology should no longer be an end unto itself, but it should be the means by which society meets its ends."[22]

There are those who believe that Gofman and Tamplin have also had a negative impact on the nuclear safety debate. This is true among those who agree with their risk estimates and give them much of the credit for recent changes in safety standards. These observers say that Gofman and Tamplin's zeal, their impassioned rhetoric and their personal attacks on members of the AEC establishment have clouded the issues and alienated scientists who agree with their basic propositions. Even further, some proponents of better nuclear safeguards fear that the two scientists have discouraged other incipient whistle blowers in the AEC.

Gofman has complained that his critics "only attack my style, my emotion, my sanity, my loyalty, my public forums, my motives. Everything except the issue."[23] Some would reply that Gofman particularly has invited these attacks and contributed to the highly charged nature of the debate. As a whistle blower, Gofman is a brash, impatient, outspoken, passionate man. It is easy to overlook the kernel of his argument and react only to his style. He tends to sweep away objections, even when they come from people who agree with him on the basic issues, and to launch broadsides against the entire nuclear establishment that puts sympathetic colleagues on the defensive.

Gofman and Tamplin have raised almost as many questions about the role of the whistle blower as about the safety of nuclear energy. Other scientists may have been reluctant to criticize AEC policies for fear of being labeled with such terms as "irresponsible," "alarmist," "extremist," and other epithets that have clung to Gofman and Tamplin.[24] Gofman and Tamplin have tended to stamp the image of the whistle blower with their own fervor and an emotionalism highly suspect in the scientific community.

H. J. Dunster, of the United Kingdom Atomic Energy Association, raised this objection to the Gofman-Tamplin book, "Population Control" Through Nuclear Pollution:

"The danger of this book is that it may discourage us from trying to increase the involvement of science in society. This increase can and must be achieved. Fortunately, there is no need to copy the methods used in this book. Some scientists and others may share the authors' doubts about the Plowshare programme or about the feasibility of nuclear warfare, without having to adopt their debating methods or their literary style."25

By fighting so vociferously, Gofman and Tamplin may have lost some of their credibility in the scientific community and frightened some who might have followed a less impassioned lead. On the other hand, would they have been successful? Or would another approach have led to oblivion for the whistle blowers—and for the issues they raised?

Gofman and Tamplin were in an extremely vulnerable position: as professionals they had little job protection of any kind. Like a great number of scientists, they were dependent on grant contracts that carried no guarantees and could be dropped at any time.

Further, when they decided to speak they knew they had no significant support within their scientific constituency and certainly none of any size in the AEC bureaucracy. Had they quietly presented their criticism to the AEC and their peers, they would probably have found themselves quietly eased out of their jobs.

Thus there was a functional objective in their impassioned plea to the lay public. Their simple cataclysmic examples and value-laden language cut through scientific and bureaucratic jargon and became a mechanism to reach the mass media and gain political and popular support. Through the media, they reached legislators, environmentalists, and the public. When they could not be discharged from their jobs without publicity, discharge became less likely.

In addition, as their challenge became stronger, the response from their opponents grew proportionately. The more data they presented and the more often they spoke publicly against the AEC safety standards, the harder their opponents tried to silence or discredit them. The only choice was to submit, be quiet and take the consequences, or renew their challenge in ever stronger terms, which in turn brought forth stronger attacks. In light of this challenge-response phenomenon and their lack of any but public support, Gofman and Tamplin's success may be due to the very course they took.

There is no question but that Gofman and Tamplin's championship of the cause of nuclear safety has helped

to improve safeguards for the public. They are instruc-
tive whistle blowers, both with regard to the vulnerability of the professional who speaks out and the
requirements for being heard. Others might have acted
differently in the same role. But Gofman and Tamplin
followed their own view of the public critic: "Where
the future of the human species is at stake, be very sure
your voice is loud enough and incisive enough to be
heard and heard well."[26]

7

Edward Gregory

*I'd catch the brass when they came through the plant
and tell them about it.*   *—Edward Gregory*

In 1969, General Motors announced what was up to
that time the largest automobile recall in history. Involved were 2.4 million Chevrolets recalled to repair
faulty exhaust systems that allowed carbon monoxide
to enter the passenger compartments. Behind the unprecedented recall, which is said to have cost over
$100 million, was a safety inspector who had been
warning General Motors for three years that the defect
existed. When the company persisted in ignoring his
reports, the inspector informed outside critics of the
auto industry. His information played a major role
in the eventual call-back of Chevrolets from the 1965
to the 1969 models.

The interesting part of the story is that Edward
Gregory is still inspecting automobiles for General
Motors and still blowing the whistle when he has to.
The latter is inevitable, one concludes after meeting
Gregory. He is probably as incapable of keeping silent
about a rear quarter panel he knows is inadequately
welded as he would be if another man called him a liar.
To Gregory, the two are equally personal affronts.
What is remarkable is that he has pitted his kind of
old-fashioned code of behavior against a corporate
ethic that says an individual's sense of duty must yield
if it conflicts with company demands, and he has
survived. He has also achieved some success with his
suggestions for safety and quality improvements,
though not nearly as much as he would like. He has

done it by following routine channels established by the company itself and by holding management strictly to its own rules. When these channels fail and the company ignores its own procedures for improvement, he goes elsewhere for help.

Gregory is the first to say that life as a whistle blower is not always pleasant. "As a result of the 'stink' I caused, I have been ridiculed and downgraded by company officials who look upon me as a thorn in their side, not only because of [the exhaust problem] but because I am constantly on the outlook for safety defects and poor quality on the line. At one time, they threatened to fire me, stating that I was costing the company too much money with my suggestions."[1]

But Gregory has not lost his job and in some ways is more effective than before. There are several reasons, not the least of which is Gregory's readiness to fight to the hilt any harassment by supervisors. Also, he has an unblemished record of being right when he brings up a safety issue. Even more important has been the backing of his union and the support of an outside public interest organization. Because he is able to count on some measure of job security, Ed Gregory is not a one-time but a full-time whistle blower. As he puts it, "Safety to the driving-riding public is foremost in my mind so I have continued my 'minority campaign' to give the American motorist what he should be getting without us 'thorns.' "[2]

It was 1953 when Gregory went to work as a quality inspector in the huge General Motors complex in St. Louis. He moved to St. Louis from Hannibal, Missouri, where he had lived since he was ten. Except for service in Italy and Africa during World War II, which earned him three combat wounds, a Bronze Star, and Purple Heart citations, his life had centered around Hannibal and nearby Ellsberry, Missouri, where he was born. In Hannibal he worked as a railroad brakeman, shuttle car driver for a limestone mine, and employee of United States Steel's Atlas Portland Cement Company. He was thirty-five when he moved with his wife and two daughters to St. Louis.

In the Fisher Body plant where Gregory went to work,

the bodies of Chevrolets are made, painted, and trimmed, complete with doors, seats, windshield wipers, and seat belts. In the final process, the bodies are lowered over the engines and sent to another plant, where extras are added. Quality inspectors are stationed at certain points along the assembly lines to check the parts as they are installed on the cars. It is not an easy job, and sometimes the pressure of meeting a production deadline is severe. The work must be done quickly and often under the eyes of a harried foreman, who carries the responsibility of meeting the production quota.

Gregory advanced in the ranks of inspectors until by 1966 he held what he considers the "best," or most crucial, inspection position. This position is "buy-out" (sometimes referred to as "the hold"), where the final product is inspected before it is moved out of the plant.

General Motors employees are encouraged to make suggestions to the company that will improve production. Ostensibly, these suggestions cover a broad range. As outlined on the special form printed for employee suggestions, they include "labor savings, material savings, safety improvement, housekeeping improvement, quality improvement, and reduced scrap or repairs." But the emphasis in the "Rules of the General Motors Suggestion Plan" is clearly on savings to the company, and most employees understand the "suggestion plan" to mean ideas that will cut company costs. For example, an employee may be awarded several thousand dollars for making a suggestion that will delete two or three jobs.

Suggestions are reviewed by a suggestion committee composed of management representatives of major departments. The suggestion form says that every idea submitted will be "systematically investigated for merit" with the final decision on adoption left to the committee.

The incentive to make money-saving suggestions is most explicit in the awards section of the rules. Awards are based on the savings that result when "the benefits are measurable." Where there are no measurable savings resulting from an adopted suggestion, the amount of the award is left up to the committee. The maximum of any award is ten thousand dollars.

There is no award specified for suggestions that cost the company money. (Any mention of "expensive" suggestions is avoided on the form.) Nonetheless, safety and quality improvement are specifically included. Conceivably, suggestions in these areas could mean adding employees or materials, thus increasing the company's production costs. Technically, at least, employees are invited to make suggestions along these lines and the company obligates itself to investigate the suggestions. Gregory was to put General Motors and its suggestion plan to its own test when he submitted a suggestion that would have immediately added eight employees to each shift at Fisher Body.

Gregory's first major safety suggestion was a by-product of his avocation as a rock collector. One day in 1966 when he and a friend returned from a rock hunting expedition in the friend's 1965 Chevrolet, Gregory noticed that the trunk of the car was filled with quarry dust. Another man might have failed to notice the dust or simply let it go, but this was Gregory's field. He knew that dust should not have gotten into the trunk if the car was properly sealed. Further, he knew that if dust was entering the trunk, deadly carbon monoxide could be seeping in as well, and from there entering the passenger compartment. He investigated and found that the quarter panels on the rear of the car were not properly sealed, and he traced the problem to poor welding. He immediately reported the problem to his superiors at the Fisher Body plant and, following the company's rules, submitted a suggestion: the defect should be corrected on all models currently in production, and older models should be recalled for repair when it was determined which models had the welding problem. This was not, obviously, a money-saving suggestion. But it seemed clear to Gregory that the problem was a real one and was potentially very serious.

When he reported the defective quarter panels to his superiors at Fisher Body he got nowhere. He demonstrated the defect on automobiles at the plant. They said it wasn't a problem because no complaints of leaking carbon monoxide had been reported in the field. He found cars in the field with the defect. Still came the answer: no complaints from dealers or customers.

Gregory refused to drop the matter. "I'd catch the brass when they came through the plant and tell them about it," he says. Such behavior became embarrassing to his supervisors. Over his vehement protests he was moved off "buy-out" to a part of the plant where "I couldn't make waves with an outboard motor." He was assigned to the "ink" section, making side mark-ups, far from where he could act as a daily watchdog over the suspect quarter panels.

This move did not succeed in silencing Gregory, however. He immediately filed a grievance with the union over his transfer and filed a second "suggestion" on how to correct the hazardous Chevrolet quarter panels. The second complaint was also turned down by the suggestion committee and a supervisor gave Gregory to understand that he had better let the matter go if he knew what was good for him. He did not. He was still finding the problem on cars whose exhaust systems had been damaged. He kept telling his superiors that if they acted now they could actually save money because, he was confident, the defect would have to be corrected sooner or later. He still speaks with incredulity over his company's obtuseness in refusing to seek out and correct a potentially expensive, not to mention hazardous, problem.

The union, Local 25 of the United Auto Workers, was backing Gregory in his grievance suit over his job transfer. The union position was that under the contract Gregory was entitled to his old job on "buy-out." Union officials said they agreed with him on the safety issue, too, but they claimed that the union had no control over the product that went out of the plant. They said the contract gave the union no authority to demand that an inspector not be forced to "buy" defective vehicles. Gregory set to work—and is still working —to strengthen the union position on the safety issue.

Finding the company intractable and the union apparently powerless to help him, Gregory began to consider other ways to move the company. The routine channels had obviously failed. The "suggestion plan" was a dead end so far as this case was concerned. He himself had been shifted to a position in the plant where he could not easily point out the defect on current models. All internal routes seemed tightly blocked. Several months after he first discovered the problem, Gregory read that a Senate committee was holding hearings on proposed safety standards for automobiles. Testifying at that moment in Washington were his own boss, James Roche, chairman of the board of General Motors, and a leading critic of the auto industry, Ralph Nader. Convinced that he needed help to get the defect corrected, Gregory was perfectly prepared to look for it where help seemed likely. The question of loyalty to his company never occurred to him. He had used the prescribed channels and gotten nowhere. People were in danger. He decided to contact Nader. He went to the phone and called the Senate committee room where the hearings were in progress. "I told the woman who answered who I was and what I wanted. I told her to get Nader." The woman was unable to provide Nader instantly, as Gregory would have liked, but she got the message through and a few hours later Nader called back. After talking with him, Nader began to check out the complaint.

Several weeks later Gregory got another call from Nader asking permission to use the information in a speech he was to make in New York. Gregory agreed. A couple of days after that, he was working overtime on the night shift. He and some of the foremen were "standing around talking about fishing and waiting for one of the lines to finish. I knew them all real well. One of the foremen and I used to fly together. Then somebody comes up and they all draw away from me into a huddle. They look over at me and they're suddenly cold toward me. I tell the foreman I've got to go call my wife. He says OK so I go call her and she says it's all over the radio and TV. The next day the white shirts from Detroit are down. None of them says a word to me. But it is obvious what's going on."[3]

More time passed. It was now well into 1967, which meant that the poor sealing on the quarter panels would not be corrected on the 1968 model Chevrolets. In spite of the fact that the whistle had been blown on General Motors and the problem made public by Nader, the company still showed no signs of action. Gregory was still filing complaints whenever he found another of the defective parts. On the advice of the union he had his third "suggestion" notarized. He recalls that this caused a flurry of concern among members of the suggestion committee. According to the instructions on the suggestion form, the committee was obliged to investigate any suggestion made by an employee. Gregory believes that the committee never investigated his complaints about the quarter panels and therefore failed to live up to its part of the bargain implied on the suggestion form. What angered him was that whether or not he was right on the issue, which he did not doubt, the company was failing to follow standards it had set for itself and its employees. No one contradicted his discoveries; they simply ignored them. These were factors that Gregory felt justified his decision to make the matter public.

For two years, Gregory kept up his badgering until events occurred that the company could not ignore. On July 11, 1968, a truck driver heading east on U.S. Route 40 about seventy-five miles from Salt Lake City noticed a 1968 Chevrolet Impala parked on the side of the road. Later that day, making his return run on the same road, he saw that the car was still there. He reported it to authorities in Salt Lake City, and a policeman rode out to investigate. He found the bodies of three people and two dogs inside the car. The dead were Charles L. Hunt, a Navy chief petty officer from Alameda, California, his wife, and a niece, Susan Koehler. The Hunts had been returning to California from a visit with relatives in Grand City, Missouri, and were taking Susan with them. Medical examinations showed they had died from asphyxiation by carbon monoxide. Chevrolet engineers traced the leak to a damaged exhaust system.

Within three days tragedy struck again. On July 14, a 1966 Chevrolet ran into another car when it stopped for a red light on a street in Baton Rouge, Louisiana. It was a minor accident, but two occupants of the Chevrolet were found unconscious and one woman was dead. It was found that Mrs. John Dunaway died from carbon monoxide poisoning, which had overcome, though not fatally, her husband and mother-in-law. The leak was traced to a tail pipe that had rusted through.

The "field reports" whose absence the company had long touted were at last coming in. Chevrolet engineers subsequently found twenty-eight other cases in which exhaust emissions were claimed to be entering the cars. Several of the passengers were temporarily overcome or reported such complaints as headaches and eye irritations.[4]

The recall announcement came on February 26, 1969, three years after Gregory first alerted the company to the problem—three years and at least four known deaths. General Motors said it was recalling 2.4 million Chevrolets made between 1965 and 1969 to fix the faulty sealing on the quarter panels that allowed seepage of carbon monoxide into the cars under certain conditions. At the same time, the company recalled 2.5 million 1968 and 1969 vehicles suspected of having a carburetor part that could break and jam the throttle in an open position. It was a massive, unprecedented recall that according to Gregory's estimates cost General Motors $100 million, with another $10 million in postage to notify automobile owners. Even so, only approximately 2.5 million vehicles of the 4.9 million autos involved in the recall campaign were eventually corrected. As is true with most recalls, many cars never made their way to dealers for correction, often because owners could not be located or failed to heed the recall.

In announcing the recall, General Motors spokesmen emphasized that only thirty cases had been reported in which exhaust fumes entered the cars and that certain conditions, including a wornout exhaust pipe, must exist before it could happen. "The whole affair," said GM's statement, "is like calling in the haystack to find the needle."[5] But others, such as Dr. William Haddon, Jr., former director of the National Highway Safety Bureau, differed. "If there are thirty cases where carbon monoxide is suspected, the actual number probably is considerably higher," Haddon said in a statement urging police officers to be more thorough in investigating cases where cars run off the road.[6] Too often, he said, these cases are routinely written off as "reckless driving" or "heart attack" and the possibility of a defect in the automobile is never considered. Carbon monoxide, it should be remembered, is odorless, colorless, and tasteless, thus making it difficult for motorists to detect.

Gregory had previously been a nuisance to the company; now he was an embarrassment and potential threat. In the face of his earlier warnings, General Motors clearly stood to be accused of negligence. Had it not been for his warnings many months earlier, and the fact that he had made them public through Nader, the recall would not have been so damaging to the company's image nor so potentially costly in terms of possible damage suits.

The company refused to admit negligence in a series of careful denials. Company spokesmen brought out the old allegation that Gregory's original proposal was rejected because there were no field reports of the problem. Then they insisted that the problem was not what Gregory reported anyway: it was not due to the way the metal panels were sealed, they said, but to plugs dropping out of the inside panels. When Nader made public Gregory's transfer to an innocuous inspection job, the company denied vigorously that it had tried to silence or intimidate him.

There was no way, however, for General Motors to avoid admitting that its method of fixing the recalled Chevrolets involved a sealing process similar to that originally proposed by Gregory. The company chose a novel course out of the predicament. Without admitting it should have heeded his earlier warnings, General Motors awarded Gregory ten thousand dollars, the maximum under its suggestion plan.

Gregory's career as a whistle blowing automobile inspector was by no means ended by success. In some respects, it was only begun. He has become an unofficial ombudsman at the Fisher Body plant for employees who find safety problems but are afraid to report them. His publicity during the recall affair has brought him calls and letters from unhappy Chevrolet owners throughout the country. Friends and neighbors in St. Louis frequently consult him about the service they get from local dealers. All the complaints he faithfully passes on to the company. If nothing is done about them, he funnels the information to public-interest groups concerned with auto safety. At last count, Gregory had submitted fifteen suggestions for improvement to Fisher Body's suggestion committee; one safety suggestion and two quality suggestions have been adopted.

An example of his reports is a suggestion submitted on June 22, 1970:

"I suggest that you use pop rivets on lower quarter panels extension. . . . When they repair it with a torch it burns out seal and also paint off the finished job. You shouldn't use heat on this quarter panel any place. I have got you stopped using brass in stress points. You should hang up a spot weld gun at Chevrolet and the two main holes at Fisher Body. One at the west end hole and at Chevrolet door at Fisher Body side. This is unsafe practice."[7]

Information from dealers and Chevrolet owners led to Gregory's reports that taillights on the 1969 Chevrolets were corroding and the springs rusting out. He reported faulty turn signals. Gregory spends hours of his spare time working over the cars of people who come to him with problems. Frequently these cases stimulate a report to the company, such as the following:

"I have reports that the 1969 and 1970 General Motors ball joints have to be replaced at around 30,000 miles. Poor design or quality in the joints should be checked. Also I have a tie rod off a 1965 Chevrolet Impala with 60,000 miles on it where the right wheel joint is out and the $50 tire was ruined. No grease fittings in the tie rod were found and we couldn't buy a General Motors tie rod with grease fittings but we did find a Moog that had fittings and he [the car owner] bought it. I would not own a car if it did not have grease fittings. They could go out at any time."[8]

He is also concerned about the safety of employees working for General Motors and has submitted six suggestions concerning a fire hazard in the body shop:

"At bay M–16 there is an overhead motor speed reducer. Paper and rags accumulate on the motor base which is a fire hazard. The last fire which resulted from this condition was Monday night, January 18, 1971. This is not only a fire hazard but a safety hazard to employees because in the fire Monday I suffered smoke inhalation and had to be sent to the nurse and then home for the balance of the shift. The nurse said that this was a personal sickness and my doctor stated that it was a direct result of the fire. The safety engineer, Jimmy Venson, was contacted and he stated that he had been overruled on taking steps to correct this situation."[9]

A suggestion filed simultaneously noted:

"On Wednesday, January 20, 1971, a second serious fire took place at M–16 bay when a trash bin caught on fire setting the sprinkler system off. The fire was ignited by sparks from the spot welder. The same situation prevailed Saturday night. The whole shop is in a dirty condition and is only cleaned up when 'company' arrives. It should be kept clean at all times for the safety of plant personnel."[10]

Gregory is tolerant, though somewhat disgusted, with his fellow employees' reluctance to report hazards. "They're scared," he says. "They tell me, you go ahead and send this [suggestion] in. They'll listen to you and you got Nader. But don't sign my name to it."

But if Gregory is an example, the role of the in-plant whistle blower could become less precarious. The worst he suffered—something he resented and fought vigorously—was his transfer off "buy-out" during the quarter panel controversy. No reduction in salary was involved and the work on the new job was no more difficult. "Buy-out" is simply where the most important safety inspections are made and that is where Gregory wants and feels he deserves to be. The grievance he filed in 1968 was in its third stage of arbitration, before a third-party referee, when Gregory was finally re-assigned to his old inspection post, beginning with the 1972 model year.

Only once has he been directly threatened with dismissal. In November, 1969, Gregory testified at a trial in Marshall, Texas, involving the defective quarter panel on a 1968 Chevrolet Impala. He was away from work for two days. When he returned, he was refused his pay for the absence and further found that his line foreman was preparing to fire him. "He said he already had the papers drawn up," Gregory recalls. "I blew up." He immediately called his committeeman (the

union representative who deals with members' grievances), and the firing attempt, which was apparently
never endorsed by higher company officials, got no
further. But the committeeman and the union refused
to fight for Gregory's lost pay, even though his absence
from work had been in obedience to a court order.
Gregory was irate. He marched to the telephone and
called UAW president Leonard Woodcock in Detroit.
The next day Gregory got his back pay.

Gregory is also critical of some General Motors
dealers, many of whom, he says, could not care less
about the customer after he buys a car. A man who
read about Gregory in the newspaper came to see him
when the engine on his 1970 Chevrolet blew up with
only twenty-eight thousand miles on the car. He had
left the car with a dealer, and when Gregory got there
"they had taken the engine completely apart. Then
they told the customer that the trouble was just carbon
on the engine. They told him they didn't put on any
new parts. And they charged him $324." Gregory was
incensed. He wrote four letters to the dealer and the
local General Motors zone office demanding restitution.
The dealer and zone officials agreed to meet with the
customer, who insisted on bringing Gregory along. The
company refused to meet with Gregory, and an official
told him, he says, "Stay out of this. You're an employee
and you're not to get involved."

From Gregory's point of view, he should be very
much involved and he is acting in the company's interests when he is. "They lost four sales on that deal," he
says, referring to the treatment of the customer whose
engine blew. Shortly after, the man bought new cars for
three members of his family and traded in his old
Chevrolet. None of the cars he purchased were made
by General Motors. (Gregory himself owns two Chevrolets.) What Gregory resents and believes is detrimental to the company is "a lack of responsibility of
the dealer and the zone office to the customer. The little
dealers are best. I've worked with them and I know.
They've got to give the customer service to make a
living. The volume dealers don't care."[11]

There have been other kinds of pressures to keep
Gregory from playing his chosen role. In May of 1970,

he says he was offered a supervisor's job. He didn't take it because he believed it was an effort to remove him from the line, where he can more easily detect defects. Sometime later, a company official, whom Gregory declined to name, asked whether he could talk to him. "I said, sure, you can talk to me. Anybody can talk to me about anything. Then he said that if I played my cards right I could get anything I wanted out of the company, including a lot more money. I said, 'yeah? That's good to know,' and let it drop."

Somehow, the feeling that the world is too big, the corporation too large, and the individual powerless never caught hold of Ed Gregory. An item in the newspaper that offends his sense of justice can set him off on a new campaign. Recently he read that seven people had died in Iowa from carbon monoxide poisoning. Gregory did some work and concluded that a stricter automobile inspection system could have prevented the problem. He is now trying to get his union to help him campaign for a national inspection law that would prevent such fatalities.

The ten thousand dollars he got from General Motors helped to finance his most recent campaign. Gregory used twenty-seven hundred dollars of his award money to buy an eighteen-foot Monarch Bell with which he patrols the polluted areas of the Mississippi River, fifteen miles from his home. Gregory is an avid fisherman, and originally the boat was meant to serve that purpose. But the fishing gear has not been unpacked for a year now. Gregory is too busy with his camera.

With an Instamatic and a Polaroid 350, Gregory has photographed the Mississippi from St. Louis to Hannibal, photographed it where old refrigerators and washing machines tumble into the river from the make-shift dump of an appliance company, where hopper cars have been cleaned of old bone meal and cement that now clog the river and its banks, where a glass company has disposed of its wornout molds and oily rags, where sludge has accumulated at the perimeters of a steel company, and where piles of brown foam ride the river's waves. Gregory takes care with his photography, and the color pictures are usually clear enough for the newspapers in Hannibal and St. Louis to print. Gregory also sends copies to the local office of the United States Army Corps of Engineers.

In four cases, Gregory has followed the photographs with formal charges against the polluters under an 1899 law that forbids discharging into waterways without a permit. Three of his complaints filed with the Corps of Engineers, involving a railroad company, a steel company, and a glass company, resulted in large-scale cleanups and stopped further dumping.

Gregory spent sixty-five hours in his boat last year and never dropped a line into the water. He regrets the temporary loss of his fishing, but not enough to interrupt his pollution campaign, which started after a fish kill a few years ago. Gregory went out to the river that day, smelled the rotting fish, and scooped up a handful of dirty suds on the surface. He remembered that "when I was a kid I used to go fishing with an old man. When I was thirsty he'd tell me to lean over the boat and take a drink. Now you couldn't pay me a thousand dollars to take a drink out of that river." He decided to do what he could, to blow the whistle on the people who had done that to the river.

Compared to some whistle blowers, Gregory is fortunate. His union has provided him a measure of job security, and Nader's organization gave him the means of getting his information to the public. He has had his share of unpleasantness as a result of whistle blowing, but he has not had to forfeit his family's income or his career for a single act. He has been able to continue as a "thorn" to prod his company toward being responsible for public safety, and he has preserved his integrity as an inspector. Many fellow employees who were shocked when he made the Chevrolet exhaust problem public now admire the way he has risked the company's wrath. Gregory's advice to other automobile inspectors is "Do not buy [defective] MVSS (Motor Vehicle Safety Standard) automobiles regardless of who orders you to do it."[12] He is thinking of the times when a harried supervisor rushing to meet a deadline tells an inspector to "buy," or approve, a part that ought to be corrected. He is thinking of inspectors who "buy" a defective automobile for fear of costing the company money.

As for blowing the whistle, Gregory says, "A guy shouldn't do it unless he has evaluated the problems and sees what will happen. He shouldn't blow the whistle until he has used all the routes within the company. Then if they don't move, blow it."[13]

8

Dr. Jacqueline Verrett

Given the same circumstances, having adequate data in hand, if the occasion arose I would not hesitate to discuss them openly. —Jacqueline Verrett

For fifteen years scientific writing contained doubts about use of the artificial sweetener cyclamate. Yet it was not until a scientist in the Food and Drug Administration told the public through a television interview about her research on cyclamates that the first government ban on the chemical was announced October 18, 1969.

It did not occur to Dr. Jacqueline Verrett to refuse when a reporter asked her for an interview. "I saw no reason not to discuss the matter with the media," she recalls. She had been reporting her research to FDA officials for a year and a half. Other findings that cyclamates might be harmful to human beings had been circulated in the scientific community and had gotten into the press. So she hardly considered her interview as whistle blowing. But in fact it turned out to be. The public attention she aroused succeeded in moving FDA officials to act where internal reports and scientific journals had not.

Dr. Verrett received censure rather than credit from her superiors in the Department of Health, Education and Welfare. But she is still in her FDA laboratory injecting food additives into chicken eggs. She has even received a promotion in the meantime. And she says readily she would do the same thing again. She is not the only whistle blower to have survived the displeasure of superiors—in fact, to have outlasted them. But

Jacqueline Verrett remains one of the most visible and refreshing examples of candor in the federal government today, firmly convinced of the scientist's responsibility to communicate with the public.

Dr. Verrett went to work for the Food and Drug Administration in 1958 after completing her doctoral work in biochemistry at Fordham University. She was assigned to the division of pharmacology and toxicology and worked on a program surveying foods for radioactive fallout, work related to her doctoral research. When the radiation surveillance program was dissolved not long after her arrival, she was transferred to a small program just being initiated by FDA using the chicken embryo to investigate the toxic effects of materials involved in the food-processing industry. The program was new but the method of testing was not. Dr. Verrett explains that "since the time of Aristotle, the developing avian embryo has been thoroughly investigated, and modern-day nutritionists and toxicologists have used it to study the effects of countless materials."[1] FDA was beginning an attempt to study all the materials under its jurisdiction that Americans were consuming along with their food, and decided to apply the chick embryo technique to the investigation.

In the course of her work, Dr. Verrett began to find disturbing effects in the chick embryos injected with cyclamate. Soon she became convinced that her research showed a firm relationship between the chemical and deformities that developed in the embryos. On March 7, 1968, she reported these findings to a high-level FDA science seminar. It was at a time when concern about the safety of artificial sweeteners was growing, even within FDA, and the seminar had been convened for the express purpose of drawing together research efforts on these chemicals. In her 1968 year-end report, Dr. Verrett again reported her research findings to her FDA supervisors, but received no reaction. The FDA did not acknowledge her work and continued to give its official blessing to cyclamates. In April, 1969, a superior of Dr. Verrett's, concerned about the agency's failure to consider her results seriously, carried two deformed chicken embryos to the office of FDA Commissioner Herbert Ley. Dr. Ley

remained unmoved by the sight of such deformities as
wings growing out of the wrong part of the body, a leg
rotated in the socket, and extreme curvature of the
spine.[2] Again in her 1969 midyear report, Dr. Verrett
informed her superiors of the evidence against cyclamates. Still the sweetener remained, undisturbed, on the
FDA Generally Regarded As Safe (GRAS) list. Cyclamate manufacturers continued to assert that "the
American housewife need have no hesitancy about
using artificial sweeteners in the preparation of foods
and beverages."[3]

Warnings about cyclamates were not confined to Dr.
Verrett's neglected reports to the Food and Drug Administration. On November 15, 1968, *Medical World
News* reported that another FDA scientist, Dr. Marvin
Legator, cell biology research chief, had found that
rats injected with cyclamate showed dangerous genetic
effects. Dr. Legator was also trying to get the FDA to
consider his findings. In one memo to Commissioner
Ley he urged, "The use of cyclamates should be immediately curtailed, pending the outcome of additional
studies."[4]

Thus, Dr. Verrett hardly considered her research a
secret when a member of the press approached her
about it. Hers and other studies had been discussed in
scientific groups outside the FDA, although they had
not been published. They had also received mention in
the press, including a newspaper column on cyclamate
research by Jean Carper which reported both Dr. Verrett's and Dr. Legator's findings. It was this column
that led NBC's Paul Friedman to ask Dr. Verrett for
an interview.

Another reason that Dr. Verrett was not particularly
surprised or concerned about the interview was that
working in the FDA laboratory was hardly like working
behind closed doors. Indeed, FDA liked to encourage
publicity—at least certain kinds of publicity. She recalls that "during these years our laboratory operations
have been used in FDA films and other consumer-
oriented material to illustrate some of the new research
methods that FDA uses in their efforts to assure the
safety of commodities under their control. Additionally,
research reports of our studies presented at national

scientific meetings have on several occasions been singled out by, and reported in, the lay press. Our laboratory is a tour stop for visitors, and the major networks as well as other groups have filmed our operations. And of course visits by scientists from this country and many foreign countries have been numerous. For several years, the FDA had been using our laboratory as a showcase, and publicity about our activities was certainly not unusual, whether initiated by FDA or the press."[5]

For these reasons, the request for an interview by NBC-TV in late September, 1969, "did not strike me as unusual. Nor did I expect, although I probably should have, the furor it would cause in HEW."

But furor there was. When Dr. Verrett routinely notified her superiors of the prospective television interview, within minutes her office was full of a dozen people who tried to persuade her that "presentation of these studies in the news media might lead to 'undue public concern.' . . . While I could not control the nature of the interview or what would be revealed, I indicated that I felt that these findings could be presented in a manner which would not cause public panic."

There was also a recent event that made her superiors' "obvious reluctance to have this material discussed on television" even more incomprehensible and was, she says, "the overriding factor in my decision to proceed with the interview." The previous summer, Dr. Verrett had produced a preliminary study of another suspect additive, monosodium glutamate (MSG). It was a "totally inconclusive preliminary experiment" using only 180 eggs. Although the test did not find any harmful results, she emphasized to her superiors that it was in no way conclusive and in fact "gave no information whatsoever on the safety of MSG." Nonetheless, Commissioner Ley immediately presented Dr. Verrett's study to a congressional committee and hailed it as an "exquisite, sensitive, new toxicological approach." His implications were that MSG was thoroughly safe so far as FDA was concerned. At the same time, Commissioner Ley refused to utter a word about Dr. Verrett's cyclamate data, which used about thirteen

thousand eggs and established a definite causal relationship between the chemical and embryo deformities.
"It was clear to me," she says, "that as long as the
method [chick embryo research] could be paraded before the public as one of FDA's new techniques without
indicating any particular chemical, publicity was not
only acceptable but sought after. But when it raised
serious questions about the safety of a chemical, as in
the cyclamate study, then discussion should be restricted
to my scientific peers who could evaluate it but still
keep it closed to public view."[7]

The alarm in Dr. Verrett's office before the interview
spread to the commissioner's office after it was aired
on October 1, 1969. Commissioner Ley insisted that it
was the first he had heard of her research, despite her
four internal reports over the prior eighteen months.
He then asked the National Academy of Sciences/Na-
tional Research Council to review Dr. Verrett's work
as well as the research of Dr. Legator, which had been
mentioned in the NBC film. As for Dr. Verrett, "in the
following two weeks I was put under 'house arrest,' all
communication with the press was barred, and I was
told to confine my activities to the preparation of the
cyclamate data for presentation to the Academy."[8] She
was not even allowed to answer her office telephone.

Coincidentally, the same week the academy was
meeting to consider the FDA studies, the manufacturer
of cyclamate, Abbott Laboratories, reported that it had
found bladder cancer in rats that were fed cyclamate.
Shortly afterwards, on October 18, the then Secretary
of Health, Education, and Welfare, Robert Finch,
apologetically announced a ban on cyclamates; he chose
to ignore the FDA studies and referred only to the
manufacturer's findings of rat cancer. At the press conference Secretary Finch made his reluctance clear: "I
have acted under the provisions of law because . . . I
am required to do so." It was, he said, the rat cancer
findings, also unpublished, that "forced" the agency to
remove cyclamates from the GRAS list.[9] The results
of Dr. Verrett's and Dr. Legator's research "were
deemed by the Academy as not relevant to the human
consumption of cyclamate," she recalls.

But FDA officials went further than denying that her

research had in any way affected their decision. At the press conference announcing the ban, they criticized "the subject doctor" for speaking out of turn, for making unwarranted claims, being overzealous and "unethical." Asked whether he was happy with FDA handling of the issue, Secretary Finch said, "By and large, yes. I was unhappy and expressed my unhappiness about the subject doctor in the Food and Drug Administration who chose in the case of the eggs to go directly to the media without having consulted with their superior and with the office. That is not a procedure I approve and certainly they did not act in a very ethical way."[10] Surgeon General Jesse Steinfeld added his word of censure: "These experiments must be communicated, but the problem is that people to whom they should be communicated are other scientists working in the field who do have the ability to interpret them and relate them to other ongoing research. I think it unfortunate to publish them in general media along with interpretations which at this moment certainly are far from justified."[11]

Secretary Finch's charges were patently false, since Dr. Verrett had not sought the television interview and had cleared it with her superiors, to whom she had been reporting her data for eighteen months.

Dr. Verrett also firmly rejects Dr. Steinfeld's charge that she should have first published the material in a scientific journal, where it could be evaluated by her scientific peers. "This is usually a very lengthy and frustrating process," she says. "It usually takes several months to clear a scientific paper within FDA, and there is further a one or two year lag before it appears in print. Had I followed that route, my findings would probably not be in print as yet, and would remain unknown to this day.

"Further, from past experience, our publications have not yet elicited any constructive criticism or actual repetition of the work which in any sense negates or refutes the findings of prior investigations. The point of relevance of chick embryo data to humans is a valid one; however, we have serious limitations in our ability to relate animal data directly to humans no matter what the test species. All of this was, in any case, beside

the point because the same observations of the effects
of cyclamate on chick embryos had been made and
published by research workers in Italy a year prior to
my television appearance. This goes to show that the
prerequisite of publication in scientific journals is no
assurance of gaining the attention of other qualified
scientists, government officials, or the public. In fact,
publication in scientific journals is in many cases a
most decent form of burial."[12]

Dr. Verrett has survived the storm she precipitated.
In the wake of the cyclamate publicity, the Food and
Drug Administration underwent a complete reorganization. But the chick embryo research has neither
been curtailed nor expanded. "Strangest of all," Dr.
Verrett says, "seven months later I received the first
promotion I had had in seven years."

There may be several reasons for her survival, among
them the pressure on the Food and Drug Administration to step up its testing of additives and Dr. Verrett's
undiminished reputation for excellence in working with
the chick embryo method. There is also little pressure
the agency could apply short of firing, because her
laboratory work does not depend on the cooperation
of a great many associates and is too important at this
point to curtail through the familiar method of cutting
off funds.

Dr. Verrett says she does not regret the episode in
any way and would not hesitate to do it again if the
occasion arose. If anything, the cyclamate affair simply
confirmed her view of the responsibility of scientists
and of public servants, a view that led her to become
and remain one of the most successful whistle blowers
in the federal bureaucracy.

"It has been my observation over the years that data
that are negative, and frequently of inferior quality,
are readily accepted by FDA officials in support of the
safety of chemicals. However, data indicating an adverse effect in any animal system must be subjected to
endless repetition, confirmation, and critical review,
often while the questionable chemical remains in the
marketplace. This apparent double standard is certainly not in the consumer interest, and merely serves
to support existing FDA policy and maintain the eco-

nomic interests of the proponents of its use. Hence, given the same circumstances, having adequate data in hand, if the occasion arose I would not hesitate to discuss them openly, even though they might be in conflict with current FDA policy that had been developed in the absence of this new information."[13]

Whistle blowing involves responsibilities and rules to which Dr. Verrett gives articulate testimony. "In similar situations," she says, "there should be no reason for reticence in discussing scientific information openly. I feel that scientists are obliged to present their information in a manner that is readily understandable to the public, but being cautious to keep it in proper perspective so that it is not unnecessarily alarming. I also feel that it is the duty of the press not to sensationalize such information, distorting its meaning and significance. There was no exaggeration in the reporting of the cyclamate data by the press.

"Finally, I feel that officials are remiss if they downgrade the significance of findings, however difficult they may be to interpret, and then issue placating but meaningless statements to reassure the public, as was done by HEW officials in the case of cyclamate. They frequently stated that the rat cancer data were not applicable to humans, and further ridiculed the federal law requiring the cyclamate removal, when in fact this law is the only real protection we have."[14]

Dr. Verrett's experience illustrates that whistle blowing may involve the *translation* of information to the public in an understandable fashion and making it generally accessible. She disclosed nothing new in her television interview, unless making esoteric reports buried in even more esoteric journals understandable constitutes disclosure. In candidly answering the questions put to her, she fulfilled a fundamental obligation of a professional in our society: the duty to communicate the meaning of one's work to the public.

9

William Stieglitz

The standards were, in my opinion, a hoax on the American public, creating an illusion of improved safety which did not, in fact, exist. I could not be a party to this.
                                              —William Stieglitz

William Stieglitz received his copy of the first federal safety standards for automobiles along with the rest of the public on February 1, 1967. This was unusual because Stieglitz himself had been in charge of drawing up the standards as consultant to the Undersecretary of Commerce for Transportation. But ten days before the standards were issued he was abruptly assigned to other duties. When he saw them again in final form they were vastly different from those he had proposed.

Stieglitz took the regulations to his Washington hotel room and began to study them. It was approximately 5 P.M. At midnight he wrote out his resignation. That resignation, which Stieglitz personally handed to his superior the next morning, did more than any other single act to focus public attention on the deficiencies of the federal auto safety standards. As word of his departure carried to the press, newsmen rushed for an explanation. Stieglitz told them that he could not "in good conscience continue to serve."[1]

The next day press reports on the new standards featured Stieglitz's resignation prominently along with his comments on the failure of his former agency to follow sound safety policy. The *New York Times* commented in its typically restrained language that "Mr. Stieglitz's resignation adds another dimension to the furor that has grown since the twenty safety standards were issued. Heretofore, the criticism of the regulations came from outside the agency."[2] To the press and the public, the act of resigning was a powerful criticism in its own right. There were other critics, but Stieglitz's credentials as a long-time safety expert and above all as the man formerly in charge of the standards gave weight and substance to the criticism.

Stieglitz had not anticipated the publicity that attended his exit from the National Highway Safety Bureau. He had prepared no public statement and credits the press with being the real whistle blowers. "My only actions were to resign from a position that I found totally untenable on the basis of my professional convictions, and in reply to questions asked me by members of the press, to state the reasons for my resignation. The whistle blowing was done by the press in their coverage of my resignation and the reasons therefore, and by my professional peers who supported my actions."[3]

But if Stieglitz had not planned it, the effect was the same. Nor was his experience so different from others who have acted in accord with their standards of professional integrity and, in so doing, have exposed the failure of their organizations to achieve those standards. Stieglitz had no new information to divulge, but he exposed something equally serious: the refusal of the National Traffic Safety Agency to heed the advice and urging of one of its own chief experts. He also made public an example of professional responsibility that was to challenge and encourage other engineers. Finally, he became the focus, however inadvertently, of the criticism of the first auto safety standards.

If Stieglitz was surprised at the attention his resignation commanded, it may have been in part because it was a natural—he says "inevitable"—thing for him to do. For over thirty years he had worked in aviation safety and more recently had developed an expertise in automotive safety. Thirty years earlier he had promoted the idea that design errors lie behind many driver errors that lead to crashes. Throughout his career in private industry, where he has spent most of his life, and in the private consulting business he built later, he was concerned with designing vehicles that were "crashworthy," that protected, as far as possible, the occupants in crashes.

In February, 1971, Charles O. Miller, director of the Bureau of Aviation Safety of the National Transportation Safety Board, writing in the MIT *Technology Review*, pointed to Stieglitz as a pioneer safety advocate, one of the earliest to point out the design challenge to professional engineers. "In 1948," Miller wrote, "William Stieglitz, who is still quite active in automotive as well as aviation safety, gave the landmark paper in what today has become known as system-safety engineering. 'Safety,' he said 'must be designed and built into airplanes just as are performance, stability, and structural integrity. . . . A safety group must be just as important a part of a manufacturer's organization as stress, aerodynamics, weights, and so forth.' "[4]

Born in 1911 in Chicago, Illinois, Stieglitz studied electrical engineering for two years at Swarthmore College and graduated from MIT in 1932 with a bachelor of science degree in aeronautical engineering. He went to work in the aircraft industry as a specialist in aerodynamics and flight testing and was soon deeply involved in safety problems. While chief of the Fleet Wings division of Kaiser Aircraft, he lectured on aviation safety at Princeton in 1941–42. In 1944 he went with Republic Aviation, where he spent the next twenty years as a design engineer.

In 1946 Stieglitz organized a design safety group at Republic, the first such group to be formed as an integral part of the industry. In 1950, on loan from Republic, he worked with the Air Force on accident prevention and flight safety research. From 1950 to 1955 he was a member of the subcommittee on aircraft fire prevention for the National Advisory Commission for Aeronautics, the predecessor of NASA. During 1952–55 he was also a member of the NACA committee on aircraft operation problems.

Meanwhile, he was broadening his field to include automotive safety engineering, applying to automobiles the same ideas on "crashworthiness" he applied to aircraft design. In 1959 he testified before the House Subcommittee on Interstate and Foreign Commerce, chaired by Representative Kenneth Roberts, which was then holding the first congressional hearings to consider automobile safety. He submitted a paper on crashworthiness written in 1950. The paper was addressed to aircraft but, as he was to show, applied equally to automobiles. For example, he cited aircraft crashes in which "many of these fatalities could have been prevented by stronger safety belts and seats."[5] He said the same design factors pertained to the automobile—to dashboard design, access of controls to the driver, and shiny chrome and high gloss paint that can blind the driver.

"Quite frankly, from personal observation of automobiles," he told the subcommittee, "it is my conviction that the interiors of these cars are designed, not from the standpoint of effective human utilization, but . . . from the standpoint of appearance and style. I think unquestionably there are a large number of needless accidents resulting from improper consideration of the human being in design."[6]

By the time Dr. William Haddon, head of the new federal traffic safety agency, persuaded him to become his chief engineering consultant, Stieglitz had built a reputation as one of the foremost safety experts in the country.

In the fall of 1964, Stieglitz resigned as manager of Republic's design safety and reliability division to set up a private consulting practice on aviation and automotive safety in Huntington, New York. Two years later, he was contacted by Dr. William Haddon, who had been appointed to head the new National Traffic Safety Agency. Dr. Haddon came to New York and asked Stieglitz to accept a consulting position and take charge of drafting the standards. Stieglitz was not enthusiastic. In a subsequent meeting with Haddon and Alan Boyd, then Undersecretary of Commerce for Transportation, he suggested several people he considered better qualified for the post. Haddon and Boyd objected to all of them. They wanted Stieglitz.

Stieglitz's reluctance was partly based on the fact that the job involved certain personal sacrifices. "It meant abandoning the consulting practice which I had spent two years building up, and a way of life that I enjoy."[7] But there were more serious misgivings.

"In the discussion prior to my accepting the position, I called attention to my earlier testimony before committees of both the Senate and the House of Representatives on the then pending traffic safety bills. One of the measures being considered involved merely extending to all vehicles the standards of the General Services Administration for automobiles purchased by the federal government. I had opposed this vigorously in my testimony, stating that in my judgment these standards were inadequate. I therefore told Dr. Haddon and Undersecretary Boyd that I could not and would not be a party to issuing these same standards as the initial federal motor vehicle safety standards. I was assured that whether or not this were done would be my responsibility."[8]

Stieglitz had indeed made his position absolutely clear during hearings before the Senate Commerce Committee and the House Committee on Interstate and Foreign Commerce in March and April of 1966. He criticized the General Services Administration standards as "woefully and totally inadequate to provide the level of safety that they are intended to provide." He then attacked the bill that would apply these standards to 1968 cars driven by the public, standards "which, on the industry's recommendation, are written around what they had in the 1965 cars." If that were done, he said, "we have improved nothing. We have applied a label, we have spread some whitewash, we have said, now it is safe. But we have not changed a thing. We cannot get safety this way, gentlemen. We cannot protect people by just giving a blessing to what already exists, and which we know hurts people or kills people. There is no reason we cannot write these standards."[9]

Haddon and Boyd still wanted Stieglitz, wanted him to write the standards. Finally, having been assured, to some extent at least, that the standards would be his responsibility, Stieglitz agreed. "I felt obliged to accept. Had I refused the position and then found the standards to be inadequate in my engineering judgment, I could only blame myself for not having tried."[10]

Stieglitz directed the first two phases of the initial safety standard–setting process, the preparation of the advance notice requesting suggestions for standards, and of the proposed standards published in the Notice of Proposed Rule Making. But already a fundamental difference was developing between Stieglitz and his superiors at the agency. The industry's strong argument was that the proposed safety features, as Stieglitz and his staff drafted them, could not be developed for the 1968 models. They wanted standards to reflect what they had already planned. Henry Ford threatened that the proposed standards would close down the industry, and House minority leader Gerald Ford demanded an explanation. Stieglitz was willing to acknowledge that the industry needed time to institute some of the new features. But he argued that the standards themselves should require building at least some crashworthiness performance into vehicles in which forty-eight thousand people were dying yearly and millions were being injured.

During the last phase of preparing the final standards, Stieglitz found the ground slipping from under him. Others in the agency were leaning toward industry's argument of what was "practical." They were demanding what he considered serious weakening of the standards. He objected strenuously. Finally, ten days before the final standards were issued, he was assigned to other duties and not consulted again.

When he read the standards in his hotel room on the night of February 1, he found that of the initial twenty-three standards, three—relating to tires, wheel rims, and headrests—were dropped on the grounds that more technical data were needed. Of the twenty standards issued, all were reworded, most were softened, and six were substantially compromised and scheduled for future rulemaking. The date for most to go into effect was moved forward four months.[11]

"They offered no advance in safety but were basically a rubber stamp of what would have been done in most 1968 automobiles without standards," he says. "From this point of view, they were, in my opinion, a hoax on the American public, creating an illusion of improved safety which did not, in fact, exist. I could not be a party to this. Under the circumstances I had no alternative to resigning. It was not an agonizing decision."[12]

When their differences became public, Haddon explained that Stieglitz's recommendations were "preposterously impossible."[13] In hearings before the Senate Commerce Committee in March, 1967, Stieglitz explained his position and stressed the problem of lead-time. "In my opinion, what should have been done on many of these standards was not to weaken the standards but to change the effective date to provide a legitimate lead-time requirement of industry. . . . I am perfectly willing to say that some of the proposed standards could not possibly have been met for 1968 automobiles. I didn't think they could be when I proposed them. But I felt that things had to start moving forward, and this lead-time block had to be broken."[14]

Rather than abandon the provisions which had value but truly could not be incorporated in the short time available between issuance of the standards and the new car production beginning in July, 1967, Stieglitz argued that two-part standards should be issued, with the first step applicable to 1968 vehicles and the second step applicable to 1969 vehicles. In this manner, the agency would not be merely endorsing existing industry practice from year to year but rather would be assuring orderly priority for safety advances. As had already been documented in the 1966 hearings leading up to the passage of the safety legislation, without mandatory requirements there is little priority or urgency in the auto companies to build safety features into motor vehicles.

Stieglitz documented his skepticism about industry arguments for lead-time. He cited as an example the Chrysler request for twenty-five to seventy-nine weeks to change their brake hoses to a type using a different reinforcing braid in order to comply with the proposed standard. Chrysler said it would require one engineer and one mechanic two weeks to work out the front wheel brake hose installation (even this Stieglitz stated was excessive). Further, to accommodate the various Chrysler models there would have to be eleven different installations, or a total of twenty-two weeks (two weeks for each of the eleven installations). Stieglitz chided Chrysler for implying that in all its corporate divisions there was only one engineer and one mechanic capable of routing a brake hose.

Stieglitz also criticized the agency for unnecessarily bowing to industry pressure. He cited as an example the proposed motor vehicle safety standard 101, "Control Location and Identification." As proposed, the controls listed had to be within the operational reach of a fifth-percentile adult female driver restrained by an upper torso restraint with enough slack to permit "a five-inch movement of her chest." The standard as finally issued required controls to be within the reach of "a person," with a "reasonable degree of slack" in the upper torso restraint.

As Stieglitz pointed out, the final standard contained numerous loopholes. The seat position was not defined, thus allowing compliance with the seat in the most forward position (even if the subject could not drive the car in such a position). The manufacturer could interpret "reasonable degree of slack" very broadly, even if the amount of slack made the restraint virtually ineffective. But most important, the "person" in the standard could be a six-foot, five-inch male with extra long arms. The standard was clearly meaningless.

The agency, according to Stieglitz, deleted the reference to fifth-percentile female because it claimed it did not have sufficient data on arm reach. Stieglitz cited a study providing data on the measurements of Air Force female pilots and flight nurses obtained in 1946. The agency rejected this information as nonrepresentative of the public. Stieglitz also cited a 1961 Society of Automotive Engineers publication, "Human Body Size and Passenger Vehicle Design," by Ross McFarland and Howard Stoudt of the Harvard School of Public Health. The authors said their data were approximations of the general driving population interpolated from several studies (including the 1946 Air Force information) and that: "Although the adjusted and weighted values in Table 1 are tentative, we believe they do, for most practical human engineering purposes, approximate sufficiently closely the true body measurements of this group to enable them to be used with confidence."

The agency refused to base its standard on these careful approximations. This difference in the arm reach of fifth-percentile Air Force flight nurses and the estimate by McFarland and Stoudt is two-tenths of an inch. The arm reach of a tall man—who would qualify as a "person" in the agency's standard—is many times greater than these values. Stieglitz concluded: "Thus in order to avoid a possible discrepancy of a fraction of an inch, the standard permits controls to be nine or ten inches beyond that of even a tall woman. I do not believe that the standard as written can be claimed to contribute appreciably to safety."

Stieglitz assesses the influence of his action on the agency as "negligible." "Many standards that I have objected to in February of 1967 are still basically in effect and have yet to be revised to a point where they are meaningful." But he does see one major change. "In one respect I do find the bureau acting in consonance with what I then argued for; that is, establishing standards on a basis of safety requirements and setting an effective date that allows adequate lead-time rather than weakening the standards to endorse what would be immediately achievable. I cannot say that this was the result of my influence, although it does represent a position I had taken before my resignation."[15]

The response from many fellow engineers has given Stieglitz tremendous personal satisfaction, however, and he credits his peers with helping him blow the whistle. He cites in particular the support of Frederic Salinger, an engineer in Seattle, Washington, and the Washington Society of Professional Engineers which, in response to a motion by Mr. Salinger, passed and forwarded to Senator Magnuson a resolution supporting Stieglitz's position and urging Senate committee hearings into the circumstances. "Judging from letters and comments I have received," he says, "it may be that my actions gave encouragement to other engineers who also feel strongly about their professional responsibility."[16]

Stieglitz has worked actively to encourage safety

committees in industrial plants, like the one he started at Republic Aviation in 1946. He has also encouraged physicians with special knowledge in treating crash victims to support safety measures. In an editorial written for the *Medical Tribune* on June 23, 1965, Stieglitz urged physicians to support the then pending bills to create a federal auto safety agency and set federal standards. "It is essential that the legislation be supported by all those interested in automobile safety," he wrote, "but especially by those with professional knowledge in crash injury and accident prevention."[17]

His experience has not been without some hardship. "From a personal standpoint it unquestionably was expensive economically," he says. "I had not only to start over, but was faced with the attitude of some clients expressed as 'You walked out on us once. Can we be sure you won't do it again?' Against this, of course, were new clients who had heard of me through the publicity attending my resignation, and who had approved of my stand. Nevertheless, it took considerable time to rebuild the practice to the level it had reached prior to my going to Washington."[18]

When asked whether he would take the same action again, Stieglitz responded that "there is no question in my mind that under similar circumstances I would do the same thing, and I sincerely believe that in the same situation I would do it in the same way. I wish to stress the words 'the same situation.' No two cases are ever the same, and I think that the manner in which one performs an action of this type must depend on the particular circumstances."[19]

To others who find themselves in similar situations, Stieglitz says, "There is no question that there are probably economic penalties which in some situations may be prohibitive. One's responsibilty for supporting a family may be so great that blowing the whistle publicly is impossible. Further, there is the pressure exerted by retirement plans, for one's investment in such a plan could make resignation almost impossible. This would be particularly true for older men.

"None of these factors, however, should inhibit a man from privately calling the situation about which he is concerned to the attention of someone who can act, and will protect his source of information. The cost of violating one's sense of professional integrity must be weighted against possible economic loss, in determining one's course of action. Peace of mind is intangible, but very important."[20]

10

Fumio Matsuda

I believed that the best policy for the company was to inform users about defects in their automobiles and to repair the defects.
                                            —Fumio Matsuda

In 1957, Fumio Matsuda got the job in the Japanese auto industry he had been looking for since he finished industrial college nearly a decade before. He went to work for Nissan Motor Corporation as a service engineer. Eleven years later he quit to become one of Japan's most vocal critics of the industry's safety performance.

With his fledgling Japan Automobile Users Union, Matsuda has raised a ground-roots protest movement rarely seen in that country, much less in the giant automobile industry. Six court cases are now pending in the Japanese judicial system involving automobile defects on which Matsuda blew the whistle. Japanese citizens are able to buy for a small cost a magazine in which Matsuda meticulously details for them how much yen they are paying for poor servicing and shoddy parts and points out hazardous features of cars the Users Union has tested. Some of the defects are those he discovered while he worked for Nissan and tried to get the company to correct. He is far more effective, he has found, now that he is working on the outside. But the information he gathered during his years inside the industry gives him unique documentation and he was able to set up a network of industry employees and dealers to feed him additional facts.

In January of 1971, Ralph Nader met Matsuda during a speaking tour in Japan. Through interviews with

Matsuda, his staff, newsmen, consumer advocates, and others, Nader's associates were able to bring back the story of the Japan Automobile Users Union and of a unique whistle blower. Matsuda's experience closely parallels that of whistle blowers like Ed Gregory, the General Motors quality inspector. In Japan, he represents the most persistent technical criticism yet to challenge the auto industry in that country.

Fumio Matsuda was born in 1924 in the small town of Katsuyama, in Fukui Prefecture in northeast Japan, bordering the Japan Sea. His family had lived in Katsuyama for four hundred years and had been leading citizens of the town. Three generations before Matsuda, the family gave the town a mountain which they owned and assured Katsuyama of a large forest area unusual in most villages in Japan.[1] Matsuda was often told this story when he was a child and says that the example of social concern made a great impression on him.

The family's prosperity dwindled, and by the time Matsuda was born the family was no longer prosperous. Matsuda's father owned a small market that sold rice and kitchenware. Although Matsuda was the eldest son, his father released him from the traditional obligation of carrying on the family business (the second son is now running the market) and at age nineteen he entered an industrial college, Kogyo Senmore Gukao, in the town of Nikone. He studied engineering, his interests being mainly in design, although his career plans were vague. He graduated after three years, spent one year as an assistant at the school, and another studying economics. In 1948 he began to look for work. In Japan's postwar collapse he could not find a job in industry and finally became an examiner in the engineering office of the Self-Defense Department in Tokyo. During the first year he worked primarily on purchasing specifications for the internal combustion engine, and so began a lifelong preoccupation with the automobile. His aim was to become a design engineer in the automobile industry, an aim he was to fulfill in a highly unorthodox manner twenty years later.

During the time he worked as a civil service employee, Matsuda briefly moonlighted as an inspector of automobiles and trucks at the American maintenance depot. "I wanted to see it, [the depot] so I applied for a night job," he says. The double duty was wearing, so he soon quit the job at the depot. Finally, dissatisfied with his civil service job and unable to break into the infant auto industry, he joined the Japanese Self-Defense Force in 1949 as an inspector of vehicles. He was promoted to lieutenant, then to captain. Switching to the Air Force, he became an instructor at a technical school teaching service and maintenance of vehicles.

In 1957 he achieved his goal of entering private industry by getting a job as a service engineer with Nissan Motors. His first choice was design, but because he had no experience in the field he was assigned to the service department—a personnel decision that was to prove costly for the Japanese automobile giant. His duties included writing a technical manual for dealers and users, receiving complaints from dealers and users, and servicing automobile parts.

His concern with safety grew gradually. His first major discovery was that many consumer complaints could be traced to faulty design or to inferior material in parts. Subsidiary companies manufactured parts for Nissan and they were inspected by "lot tests." Matsuda realized that there was a difference in the quality of the items that composed the lots. Other defects occurred in the process of assembling the parts.

His list of discoveries grew longer. A transmission gear lacked the proper strength. A rear axle shaft broke because of a defect in design. A bad dust cover for the ball joint of the steering linkage tie rod allowed dust to get inside and wore out the ball joint quickly. "I began to find defects in all of the parts," he says, "in suspension, brakes, steering, everything."

At least twice a month in meetings with designers, Matsuda talked about these defects. He pointed out, for example, that inadequate coating on a brake tube allowed the tube to become rusted and cause crashes. These were the kind of defects, he says, that would only be found by service engineers, the people who heard the consumers' complaints.

The difference between Matsuda and his superiors

soon hinged on the extent to which the company was willing to inform customers of defects. He found that the policy was never to let them know—except in special cases when the user himself spotted the defects and the manufacturer allowed the service department to repair them. In cases where there were complaints of defects and a crash occurred, the policy was to "recall" the defective vehicles by secretly requiring repair when the consumers brought their cars for the regular two-year inspection required in Japan. This was accomplished by collusion with the Japanese government. One of several flaws Matsuda saw in this system was that not all cars made their way to the inspections. The rest continued with the unacknowledged defects.

The picture Matsuda began to see unfolding was one in which the automobile user was generally ignorant of serious defects and, even when he was aware of them, was unable to call the manufacturer to account and receive free repair or compensation for injuries in auto crashes. "After the car had crashed, no one could see the original defect and even if the owner knew about the defect, he was unable to prove it without assistance."

The next realization was that the service engineer was the best—or even the only—person equipped to aid the auto consumer. But he found little support among his fellow service engineers. "Their attitude was not to do anything that would jeopardize the company," he says.

As a service engineer, Matsuda did not belong to any automotive engineering societies. The employee union was "so close to the company" that he found no support from its ranks.

The pressure to act became intense as Matsuda saw drivers being held responsible for crashes that he believed stemmed from defects. Drivers were judged guilty of negligence that he knew was not theirs. His colleagues repeated the phrase "do nothing that will hurt the company." But Matsuda was evolving the theory that the best he could do for the company was to urge practices and policies that would win the trust of auto consumers. "I believed that the best policy for the company was to inform users about defects and repair the defects," he says.

Five years after he began working for Nissan, Matsuda suggested that the company publish a list of a thousand defects which he had documented. At that time, secret repairing of serious defects was costing Nissan some 1–2 billion yen a month. Publication of the defects could cost the company two or three times as much money. The company rejected his suggestion.

Next Matsuda suggested that the company recall all cars of a model that had been involved in an accident when a defect was recognized. His immediate boss rejected the suggestion; Matsuda went to his superiors, which infuriated his own supervisor. Again and again he went over his own superior to higher officials in the company until the relationship between him and his supervisor became strained. The supervisor began making damaging reports about Matsuda to the main office, falsely charging him with accepting bribes from dealers and leaking information to the press.

At the same time Matsuda was involved in a fight with the employee labor union, which he had charged with corruption. Specifically, he charged union leaders with spending union money on personal entertainment. He was also frustrated because the union failed to support his reform efforts.

Finally, discouraged by his attempts to help the automobile consumer within the company and by his rapidly deteriorating relationship with his superiors, he resigned in August, 1968.

He was now free to do what he wanted to do: to give automobile owners all the information they needed about defects. He developed a plan for an organization through which he could become an effective critic of the industry. But he knew that he faced tremendous difficulties. For over a year he did nothing but study auto design, earning a living by writing articles for magazines and newspapers and doing consulting work. Most of his acquaintances, even those who supported his ideas, believed then that his project would fail and he would never "beat the manufacturers." His family was skeptical and his wife complained as he began to spend more and more time in the one-room office he rented in Tokyo. Some publishers refused to print

his articles, but reporters began coming to him for
assistance and gradually he began getting his ideas into
the public media.

During this time, he formed an important alliance
with Masataka Itoh, a top reporter for the prestigious
newspaper *Asahi Shimbum* in Tokyo. In June, 1969,
Itoh broke a story that caused a furor in Japan. He
reported that Japanese auto makers were recalling
defective automobiles in the United States under the
United States safety law requirements, but were not
recalling the same autos sold in Japan, which had no
recall law. After substantial newspaper publicity and
public hearings in the Diet, a voluntary recall system
was instituted for Japanese owners by the companies.
Itoh followed this story with other reports on the Japanese auto industry, often using tips from Matsuda
whose reliability he came to respect. Itoh in turn helped
Matsuda with plans for his auto users union and became
an invaluable source of support.

Matsuda was looking for people to back his new
organization with financial support as well. The man
who provided a large part of it was Haruo Abe, a
Tokyo lawyer. In November, 1969, Abe asked Matsuda's help on a suit involving a Honda N–360, a case
that became front-page news in the Japanese press.
Abe was representing the family of a victim, who believed it was the car, not the driver, that caused the
crash. But the lawyer needed the testimony of an expert. At first Matsuda turned down Abe's request on
the ground that the job was too big for him to handle
alone. But the family of the victim called him and he
yielded, primarily because he realized they had nowhere
else to turn. For forty days he investigated the mini-
car, refusing pay, and came up with evidence that the
early model Honda N–360 had a serious stability defect that caused it to go out of control when the car is
fully loaded (with the maximum of four passengers)
and the car is decelerating. Through some of his contacts, he says he found that Honda durability tests
themselves indicated a problem. He brought these tests
to the attention of police investigators, and the family
of the victim sought to press criminal charges of homi-
cide against the president of Honda. As a consequence,

the Ministry of Transport ran a series of tests on the vehicle, some new information was published in the press, and a police investigation was undertaken. Apparently, however, the prosecutor has declined to bring charges against the company or the president.

Another consequence of the Honda case was backing from Abe for Matsuda's automobile users union. Largely through Abe's influence, sixteen "founders" contributed 20 million yen (fifty-five thousand dollars) to found the Japan Automobile Users Union, officially organized on April 20, 1970. The names of the founders have been kept secret for fear of retribution by the powerful automobile industry, but Matsuda says they include several high-ranking members of the judicial system.[2] By the spring of 1971, ten thousand members were paying a monthly membership fee of 300 yen, or ten dollars a year, for which they received the monthly JAUU magazine. The magazine is also sold on the newsstands. Matsuda had assembled a staff of twenty. Three assistants and a secretary were working with him in the small office; the others, mostly volunteers, worked in research institutes during the day and came into the office at night. At that time, the union was able to act on about sixty percent of the complaints it received. The office was getting eighty to one hundred visits a week from auto owners, two to three hundred letters and around two hundred phone calls.

An essential part of the union's effectiveness has been Matsuda's network of contacts inside the auto industry, with salesmen and dealers, customers and service engineers. This network is carefully guarded, and Matsuda contacts them secretly. Professors in five universities work for him regularly without pay, he says, doing research and tests and writing articles for the magazine and feeding him information.

From his informants Matsuda has obtained lists of defects still kept by auto companies and given to dealers who make secret repairs, that is, repairs the customers pay for when they have their cars inspected without knowing that the defects existed when they bought the cars. Matsuda has charged that most auto defects are still handled secretly in Japan. He has also directed lawyers and police investigators to sources of information within the companies of which they were previously unaware, for example, manufacturer drawings and durability tests and receipts at servicing plants for repair fees.

Whenever Matsuda has made a new discovery he has approached the auto manufacturer first. If the manufacturer is unresponsive, the union has taken its case to the press. The result has been, says Matsuda, that every manufacturer except one has begun to respond to his requests for repair and redesign. His biggest weapon is their fear of publicity. Finally, the union looks for legal aid to help victims sue manufacturers. There are now six major pending law suits brought by public prosecutors which were instigated largely by the Users Union on behalf of crash victims. The union is cooperating in ten other auto liability cases.

Matsuda is working for the auto user from another angle: the expense of auto parts. In his magazine he informs consumers of the original price of the parts—which he obtains from informants—and then tells them what profit goes to the manufacturer and dealer. Recently, the union began to sell a new type of engine oil and antifreeze to its members at one-third to one-half the market price. A cooperating university researcher developed the products. The union keeps three percent to cover handling expenses but makes no profit.

Matsuda's organization has been harassed a good deal, which is one reason for his care in keeping secret the names of his informants. The office has been broken into once but no records were taken because Matsuda was sleeping there that night. When the organization was beginning, members of his staff received telephone calls from anonymous callers who accused one or another staff member of being a spy for one or more manufacturers. Staff members' families and neighbors received phone calls telling them that the union was subversive and would fail. He has managed to work out most of these staff problems.

In the fall of 1971, pressures against the Users Union took a new and more formidable turn. On November 2, Matsuda and Abe were arrested by the district prosecutor in Tokyo on charges brought by Honda. Honda claimed that their efforts to reach cash settlements with the company in behalf of the victims of Honda N–360 crashes constituted extortion. The prosecutor, in behalf of the company, charged that the amounts they sought ($5 million for two hundred victims and their families) were too high; that Matsuda and Abe "threatened" Honda with publicity and court action; and that they refused to release the names of all the victims they represented. Matsuda and Abe were jailed for twenty-five days before they were released on bail set at approximately fifteen thousand dollars each. Denying the charges, they plan a vigorous legal defense and offense. The prospect, at this writing, according to observers in Japan, is for lengthy court proceedings that could stretch over a ten-year period and could seriously impair, if not destroy, the work of the union.

Thus, at this time, the future of the Japan Automobile Users Union and of Fumio Matsuda is highly uncertain. So too, are the implications of the case for the consumer movement in Japan. When we talked with him, Matsuda said he saw himself as "a test case for other whistle blowers in Japan." He hoped that his experience, successes by his organization, and a mounting constituency for auto safety and consumer rights would encourage other Japanese citizens to follow his example. How effective he was may be measured by the response of the Honda Company in its recent efforts to suppress him and his organization. On trial now with Matsuda is the right of citizens to use those tools available to corporations—negotiation, court action, and exposure of abuses—to strengthen consumer safety and corporate responsibility.

11

A. Dale Console

I reached a point where I could no longer live with myself.
                                        —Dale Console

In 1960, Dr. A. Dale Console, a former medical director at E. R. Squibb and Sons, gave the public and Congress their first detailed view of the way drug companies increase sales through exploitation of physicians and manipulation of improper prescription of drugs. In testimony before the Kefauver hearings on drug price competition, he described the "inroads the [drug] industry has made into the entire structure of medicine and medical care."[1]

"Unfortunately drugs are not always prescribed wisely," he told the committee, "and while the physician and patient among others must share the responsibility for this with the pharmaceutical industry, it is the industry that carefully nurtures and encourages the practice. . . .

"The pharmaceutical industry is unique in that it can make exploitation appear a noble purpose. It is the organized, carefully planned, and skillful execution of this exploitation which constitutes one of the costs of drugs, which must be measured not only in dollars but in terms of the inroads the industry has made into the entire structure of medicine and medical care. With the enormous resources at its command, it has usurped the place of the medical educator and has successfully substituted propaganda for education."[2]

Dr. Console went on to indict the industry—not Squibb alone—for promotional techniques that included:

1) a "barrage of irrelevant facts [the physician] has neither the time, the inclination, nor frequently the expert knowledge to examine critically,"[3]

2) the hard-sell tactics of detail men who follow the maxim "If you can't convince them, confuse them,"[4] and

3) the testimonials that "are used not only to give apparent substance to the advertising and promotion of relatively worthless products, but also to extend the indications of effective drugs beyond the range of their real utility."[5]

He was equally severe in his criticism of physicians and their organizations for the "unhealthy" and "in many ways corrupt" relationship with the drug companies they allowed and sometimes welcomed, frequently associated with the large grants and gifts the industry makes available to physicians.

It was a dramatic indictment, the more so because it came from the "inside," from someone who had been close to the drug industry as few critics had been before. For six and a half years, Dr. Console had worked as a drug company doctor, having resigned four years before the Kefauver hearings. Both then and in 1969, when he testified before Senator Gaylord Nelson's Monopoly Subcommittee of the Select Committee on Small Business, he gave the public a rare and vivid portrait of the individual who is forced to sacrifice his scruples to the will of the organization. His testimony was both a severe criticism of the industry and a comment on the manipulation of corporate employees to serve corporate aims.

As an example, Dr. Console described the company doctor's function of "reviewing" and "approving" advertising copy:

"Drug companies boast that *all* advertising copy is reviewed or approved by the medical staff. Most [ads] require 'approval' since review is pointless if the doctor has no voice in determining what is and what is not acceptable. This poses problems for the doctor. In the first place, *all* advertising copy makes a mountain of paper, some of which is difficult to digest. Overall, the task is dull and boring. In addition, the doctor who does not approve the majority of copy that reaches his desk is not likely to keep his job. Yet over and over again he is faced with advertising that is obviously misleading and which he cannot approve in good conscience. The dilemma is best resolved by a bizarre process of reasoning. . . .

"The doctor who reviews advertising copy must learn to ask himself not whether the advertisement is misleading, but rather whether it can pass. . . . Under [certain] conditions the advertisement can be defended against any attempt to prove it false or misleading. The doctor who wishes to keep his job in the drug industry will find it mandatory to use this kind of reasoning. In desperate situations what can pass can be stretched to almost infinite limits. The determining factors are the mental and verbal facility of the doctor or lawyer who must defend it."[6]

The list of what a drug company doctor must learn if he is to advance in the industry became so long, so personally and professionally obnoxious, that Console finally had enough.

He had found that the drug company doctor "must learn the many ways to deceive the Food and Drug Administration and, failing in this, to seduce, manipulate, or threaten the physician assigned to the New Drug Application into approving it even if it is incomplete.

"He must learn that anything that helps to sell a drug is valid even if it is supported by the crudest testimonial, while anything that decreases sales must be suppressed, distorted, and rejected because it is not absolutely conclusive proof.

"He must learn to word a warning statement so it will appear to be an inducement to use the drug rather than a warning of the dangers inherent in its use.

"He must learn, when a drug has been found too dangerous for use in this country, he can approve its use in other countries where the laws are less stringent and people have less protection. He must learn, when a drug has been found useless on one side of the Rio Grande, it can be sold as a panacea on the other side and that he is expected to approve the claims made for it.

"He will find himself squeezed between businessmen

who will sell anything and justify it on the basis that doctors ask for it and doctors who demand products they have been taught to want through the advertising and promotion schemes contrived by businessmen. If he can absorb all this, and more, and still maintain any sensibilities he will learn the true meaning of loneliness and alienation.

"During my tenure as medical director I learned the meaning of loneliness and alienation. I reached a point where I could no longer live with myself. I had compromised to the point where my back was against a wall and I had to choose between resigning myself to total capitulation or resigning as medical director. I chose the latter course."[7]

Dr. Console resigned from his position at Squibb in June, 1957. The next two years he spent on a psychiatric fellowship paid for by Squibb. When his relationship with the company was completely severed in 1959, and he began practicing psychiatry in Princeton, New Jersey, Console considered writing a book about the industry. His intention was not to pillory his former employer. On the contrary, he has defended Squibb as one of the "more ethical" pharmaceutical firms, and he destroyed the records in his private file when he resigned, records which might have been used as proof of specific abuses concerning specific drugs had Dr. Console chosen that route. He decided instead to offer "a distillate of my experience and the opinions I have formed as a result of that experience."[8]

But he was concerned about the possibility of a libel suit if he wrote the book. He was confident such a suit would not be successful, but it would mean heavy financial costs for him. Then the invitation to testify before the Kefauver committee offered him the platform he sought. It was an opportunity for whistle blowing that was certain to attract public attention and assured him immunity from "legal" harassment by the industry.

The fifty pages of testimony he subsequently produced for several congressional committees provided a strong witness for the need to strengthen government control over the testing and marketing of drugs. His evidence undermined notions that the industry was

successfully policing itself or that physicians were providing a viable check to abuses. As a physician himself, Console was a unique critic of his own profession's willingness to turn over "postgraduate medical
education" to the drug industry.[9] He reminded them
that "we are still human in spite of being physicians.
As humans, we are vulnerable to all forms of flattery,
cajolery, and blandishments, subtle or otherwise." He
then demonstrated how "the drug industry has learned
to manipulate this vulnerability with techniques whose
sophistication approaches perfection."[10]

Reflecting later on what motivated him to become a
whistle blower, Console said, "While I am convinced
that I am motivated by a deep sense of moral indignation, I am equally motivated by a deep personal feeling of resentment. The roots of that resentment run
deep, and my contribution was an incredible degree
of idealism and unrealistic expectations that set me up
as a patsy for disillusionment and disappointment.

"I grew up with the concept that medicine is a noble
profession. I spent some fourteen years, or one-quarter
of my present life span, cloistered in an ivory tower.
For four years I was a medical student. Eight years
were spent in postdoctoral (or residency) training, and
the remaining years I was a member of the faculty of
the medical college. Throughout these years I was
exposed to all the very best that medicine has to offer.

"I had been exposed to, and was appalled by, shabby
practices I had observed when I served as a substitute
intern in small hospitals during medical school vaca-
tions. These were brief stints and after each of them
I returned to the cloistered life in the ivory tower.
Naively I came to believe that the totality of my personal experience was a true and accurate representation
of the reality of medical practice."[11]

What he discovered when he entered the drug industry was far different. He concluded that "in today's
practice of medicine one of the simplest professional
tasks a physician is required to perform is the writing
of a prescription. Since it is simple and uncomplicated,
many physicians would like to reduce the practice of
medicine to the practice of writing prescriptions. . . .
Since a drug company's profit is dependent on the num-

ber of prescriptions written for its products, its advertising and promotion practices carefully nurture the concept that the prescription pad is omnipotent. The end result is what I once labeled a *folie à deux*. The physician and the drug company each serves his own purposes. Both of them dance but the patient pays the piper."[12]

Console also observed the transition of Squibb, indeed of the entire drug industry, from a "family corporation" to the "modern corporation," huge, largely anonymous, concerned with profits and an ever-increasing market rather than with consumer interests. "When I joined it, twenty years ago, Squibb was still a family corporation, management was still guided by the philosophy and the policies of the company's founder, and the medical director was a physician's physician. In time, ownership of the company changed hands, management changed, and most important the entire drug industry changed. Having written some fifty pages of testimony on the nature, meaning, and consequences of those changes, I now find myself in the position of trying to say it all in one sentence. I heard the sentence frequently spoken by a vice-president who offered it as fatherly advice and as an unsubtle threat: 'It's easy to find a lawyer who will tell you that you can't do something; the trick is to find one who will show you how you can do it, even if he costs more.' To me this single sentence always has been, and still is, the epitome of shabbiness and all of its ramifications."[13]

To counter the new corporation's focusing of enormous resources on narrow interests, Console is convinced that people within the organization must speak out. "We could make no greater mistake than to be lulled into a sense of false security by believing that some disembodied force called the government will act like a beneficent big brother and make certain that the special interests will not predominate. If the general welfare is to be protected, it will be protected by the actions of people, not the government, and the actions of people are one of the primary concerns of this Whistle Blowers Conference."[14]

His view of whistle blowing (a term Console himself prefers not to use) is that it should ideally be a lifetime affair, carried on in the private as well as the public sphere. In addition to his public statements, he has criticized the medical profession through private correspondence for serving the interests of the drug industry and has tried to institute change through internal channels. Recently, for example, he wrote the editor of a state medical journal criticizing the journal's practice of blatantly endorsing the products of drug companies that bought advertisements. This journal scattered through its pages boxed notices urging its readers to "Patronize Our Advertisers. They Merit Your Support." Even worse, he found one issue to contain the notice: "Not everyone can advertise in this JOURNAL. When you see an advertisement here you know that the company or the service has been stamped 'approved.' As you read our advertising pages, you get a compact little course on what's new. And if you tell the company that you saw his notice in these pages you remind him that this is a happy medium for his services or his company. These pages deserve your consideration."

Console protested that "stamped as 'approved' " suggested the society or journal had actually tested the products. It was at least an unjustified endorsement of products based solely on the willingness of companies to purchase advertising space in the publication, he said. The medical society reviewed the practice, and it has since been discontinued.

Console has also made a study of the difference between claims made for drugs marketed in Italy, where restrictions on advertising and labeling are few, and claims for the same drugs in the United States. The comparison shows, he says, that "any notion of the morality of the drug industry is a hollow mockery." Drug companies blatantly omit warnings to physicians and consumers in markets where regulations do not require them, even though their products must carry such warnings by law elsewhere. His study was prepared for a congressional inquiry into drug company practices abroad.

Though he analyzed his own motivation to speak out, Console refused to do the same for the hundreds who fail to do so. "We are faced with the knotty problem of why a small handful of people do act while the vast majority remain passive even though its vital interests are at stake. A partial answer to this question is found in the simple fact that only a small handful of the people are ever exposed to a naked view of the operations, techniques, and methods used by the special interest groups. This is, at best, a partial answer since it is also obvious that only a small percentage of those who do gain access to this restricted information elect to 'speak out' while the majority elects to 'go along with it.' "[15]

One reason may be that there is not always a way out of the organization, such as Console found when he entered psychiatry as a private practitioner. For the drug company doctor who remains in the industry, there is little protection. What recourse does he have against losing his job if he refuses to "approve" a worthless drug or a misleading advertisement? The answer is, none. Console makes the point that policing of the industry cannot be done entirely through government regulation. Professional watchdogs within the organization, acting on a daily basis, have a far greater opportunity to assure that the public is not harmed and physicians are not gulled by unsafe drugs. But until the medical profession provides protection for the conscientious drug company doctor, he may, like Console, find his "back against a wall" with the untenable choice of "resigning himself to total capitulation" or resigning as medical director.

12

Christopher Pyle and Ralph Stein

What is important is that the story be told, that those who can effect change learn the truth, and that the telling of the story be legitimated.   —Ralph Stein

Few whistle blowers have given more thought to how to speak out effectively than Christopher Pyle and Ralph Stein, who disclosed in early 1970 the Army's deep involvement in the surveillance of civilians. Their disclosure led to widespread public indignation, two court challenges of the practice, over fifty congressional inquiries, a congressional hearing, and finally an announcement by Defense Secretary Melvin Laird of limited curbs. But it took far more than a simple announcement to get that far, and Pyle and Stein are still working for a meaningful resolution to the constitutional questions they have raised.

Both former Army intelligence officers, Pyle and Stein left military service convinced that the data collected on the personal lives of thousands of citizens had no bearing on the military's legitimate responsibility for national security. They were acutely disturbed by the huge computerized data bank being assembled at Fort Holabird, Maryland, and its implications for the exercise of guaranteed freedoms.

At the same time, they knew that the military establishment had formidable resources to fend off criticism and to weather a storm unscathed—and unchanged. There was probably no other organization so fortified against outside criticism. A single disclosure might shock the public momentarily and move a few congressmen to demand explanations. But would it lead to fundamental reform or even to a close scrutiny of the surveillance practice by the institutions with the power to correct it, the Congress and the courts? Pyle and Stein thought not. Success, they were convinced, depended first on presenting an irrefutable case of carefully documented facts that suggested the magnitude of the problem. They needed to bolster their own first-hand knowledge with that of other former and present intelligence officers. It depended, too, on their ability to touch the levers of political power in the right way and at the right time. Finally, it depended on mobilizing people within the military establishment to enforce such curbs as might be imposed by blowing the whistle if they were ignored.

It was a bold experiment, as much a test of the political system as of the Army's right to probe the private lives of law-abiding citizens. They were also determined that it should be an example of responsible dissent. Pyle and Stein were not, and did not want to appear as, antimilitary or opposed to military intelligence. At one point, in fact, Stein was so attracted by intelligence work that he applied for a job in the Army's civilian career program. Pyle insists, "We are friendly critics in the best sense of the term."

For two years, as a captain in Army Intelligence, Pyle taught at the intelligence school at Fort Holabird, central Army Intelligence headquarters. His course, an elective, was on constitutional law, and it was usually crowded. The fare served up in the mandatory courses tended to be too dry for many of the young officers, and they liked Pyle as well as his course. One day one of his students asked Pyle whether he knew about the intelligence files kept in a building not far away from the classroom where he was teaching. Pyle did not. The student told him about the surveillance program, about the data bank, and about the infiltration of Army intelligence agents into groups the Army wanted to watch. Pyle was astounded. Through his students, he began to put together the whole picture of the CONUS (Continental US) intelligence program. Former students, now agents in the field, gave him more information as he considered making the program known to the public.

The picture as he began to see it was that after the 1967 summer urban riots the Army greatly increased its coverage of civilian activities and enormously, without any real direction, expanded the guidelines as to collecton of information. Stein later described the result: "In several central locations and in many local offices the Army maintained . . . files on individuals and organizations engaged in left wing, right wing, racial, and antiwar activities. While the names of many of the individuals would perhaps be well known, the great majority of those whose lives and activities are recorded in Army files can truly be described as anonymous Americans who did no more than exercise the rights guaranteed them under the First Amendment."[1]

Army special agents infiltrated antiwar groups, lived with black Americans in Resurrection City, penetrated college groups, monitored campus activity, photographed and videotaped dissenters and "compiled dossiers and published reports too numerous to be itemized in a brief statement."[2]

The Army itself was later to tell a congressional committee that it had dossiers on 25 million American "personalities," including persons loosely described as "considered to constitute a threat to security and defense" as well as such public figures as Senator Adlai Stevenson. The data bank contained files on 760,000 organizations and incidents and processed 12,000 requests for information a day.[3]

Pyle had enough of this information soon after he left the Army to write an article outlining the program and giving a number of startling particulars. This article, published in the *Washington Monthly* of January, 1970, was the first the public—and many civilians in the Pentagon—knew about the Army's domestic spying activities. The article pointed out that CONUS intelligence far exceeded—in large part had nothing to do with—the Army's needs in preparing for plots.

Stein commented later that "most of the information

collected in no way improves upon or positively adds to the Army's ability to perform its assigned civil disturbance function. All of this activity has been accomplished without statutory authority and in contravention of our long tradition of keeping the military apart from civilian affairs." Further, their investigations showed, it was accomplished without the knowledge of the civilian authorities who traditionally direct the military and were placed in the uncomfortable position of "learning about the Army's intrusive presence in civilian affairs from newspapermen and former intelligence agents."[4]

As Pyle had expected, the Army high command lowered a blanket of secrecy over its intelligence activities after his article appeared. The Pentagon's Office of Public Information refused comment, and agents were forbidden to discuss the program with newsmen. Army General Counsel Robert E. Jordan III suspended all replies to congressional inquiries, and the Army did not even acknowledge their receipt.

Criticism was so great, however, that by the end of the month the Army issued the first in a "series of partial admissions." As Pyle reported in a second article in the *Washington Monthly* (August, 1970), the Army confirmed the existence of a nationwide intelligence apparatus but included the false assurances that it collected political intelligence only "in connection with Army civil disturbance responsibilities" and did not include "individual biographies or personality data."[5] The Army acknowledged that it published an identification list of "persons who have been active in past civil disturbances activity" but failed to mention that the list also included detailed descriptions of people and organizations never involved in civil disturbances.[6]

The denials failed to settle the storm, and congressmen continued to demand full explanations. The leader of the critics, Senator Sam Ervin, chairman of the Senate Subcommittee on Constitutional Rights, said in a Senate speech on February 2, 1970, that "the Army has no business operating data banks for the surveillance of private citizens; nor do they have any business in domestic politics."[7]

Meanwhile, the civilian hierarchy in the Pentagon was also trying to find out what was going on in the CONUS program and launched its own investigation. In mid-February, Pyle reported, General Counsel Jordan went to Fort Holabird and "watched as the computer bank on dissidents disgorged a lengthy printout on Mrs. Martin Luther King."[8]

On February 25, Jordan sent an identical letter to more than thirty congressmen which included the brief confession: "There have been some activities which have been undertaken in the civil disturbance field which, on review, have been determined to be beyond the Army's mission requirements."[9] He assured them that the data bank and the published identification list had been ordered destroyed.

Jordan's promise placated some congressional critics, though not all, and it definitely did not satisfy Pyle, who by now was working with another former agent also concerned about the CONUS intelligence program. Ralph Stein became concerned about the "over-broad scope of military intelligence activity" while working as an analyst at the Counterintelligence Analysis Branch, specializing in left-wing activities. "Along with several other analysts," he says, "I attempted to present briefings and write reports which forced the listener or reader to focus on the Army's legitimate concerns with regard to civil disturbances, rather than on political matters and on the personal lives, thoughts, and associations of American citizens. Frequent discussions with my associates, both on and off duty, convinced me that public disclosure would be necessary to curb the rapidly expanding activities of military intelligence."[10]

When he left the Army, Stein was planning to write an article himself when Pyle's piece appeared in the *Washington Monthly*. He contacted Pyle, and the two decided to work together to keep the issue before the public and Congress.

They were immediately concerned with the fact that the Army's bland assurances were actually no assurances at all. Their investigations of the total intelligence apparatus proved them right. The promise to destroy the computerized data bank at Fort Holabird and the identification list failed to mention over 375 copies of a two-volume, loose-leaf "encyclopedia on dissent," containing descriptions of hundreds of organizations and individuals; a computer-indexed microfilm archive of intelligence reports and documents; a computerized data bank at the Continental Army Command head-quarters in Fort Monroe, Virginia; noncomputerized regional data banks at each stateside Army command and at many military installations; and noncomputer-ized files at most of the Intelligence Command's three hundred stateside intelligence group offices.[11]

These facts were also brought to public attention, and criticism began again. Senator Ervin was clearly dissatisfied with the Army's assurances. Now Pyle and Stein began an intensive information-gathering effort, contacting military personnel, students, businessmen, and professionals across the country. They also de-cided to make their information "available where it would do the most good, specifically to Senator Ervin's Subcommittee on Constitutional Rights and to the American Civil Liberties Union."

Both men were in school in New York City, where Pyle was a doctoral candidate in political science at Columbia University and Stein was enrolled at the New School for Social Research. The decision to undertake the kind of whistle blowing that was re-quired was not easy. As Stein recalls, there was a moral decision in the first place and, second, practical and personal considerations:

"The decision to reveal information gathered by intelligence methods and sometimes subject to security classification was not an easy one for moral and legal reasons. The decision to actively investigate the Army and travel about the nation soliciting the help of others was even more troublesome. A question of divided loyalties pressed urgently on my conscience. It was necessary for me not only to reflect on my subjective feelings, but to study at great length the issue involved from a legal and historical perspective. I arrived at the, for me, inescapable conclusion that the Army's do-mestic intelligence activities were proscribed by the First Amendment and by the weight of almost 195 years of American tradition and history and that to

reveal the activities of the Army's Intelligence Branch
was the only moral course.

"I would like to say that I have encountered no
personal problems in carrying out my convictions,
but, as I early discovered, dissent causes many to be
fearful of consequences. My wife, while always helpful and strongly supportive, was nonetheless appre-
hensive and probably she still is today to some extent.
Friends and relatives called to warn about the danger
of being rejected for future employment, sometimes
citing examples of which they claimed to have personal
knowledge. Far more distressing, however, were the
warnings of those who cautioned against speaking out
because of indefinable, inhibiting dangers which these
people felt precluded one from taking a controversial
position with regard to the government.

"This demonstrated inhibition, this chilling effect
on First Amendment rights, caused to no small degree
by the latitude and indiscretion of both military and
government surveillance, convinced me, as no other
factor did, of the urgency of airing this issue and
securing remedies, both legislative and judicial."[12]

Their coast-to-coast investigation of the Army uncovered numbers of former intelligence agents and
military personnel who were willing to help, either by
speaking out publicly or by giving their information
anonymously.

The report that most alarmed the politicians, including the President, was former agent John M.
O'Brien's letter to Senator Ervin in December, 1970,
reporting that the Army had spied on and collected
information about Senator Adlai Stevenson during
1969 and 1970, when he was Illinois state treasurer.
O'Brien's letter, which outlined Army spying on some
eight hundred civilians and activist organizations, laid
the groundwork for hearings that Ervin's subcommittee
held in February, 1971.[13]

At those hearings, other former agents stepped forward. Laurence F. Lane told the committee of an incident in which 119 demonstrators outside a gate at
Fort Carson, Colorado, included no less than 53
undercover agents from all services. Intelligence gathered by agents, whether reliable or not, Lane said,

was forwarded to Fort Holabird, where it went into the computers and then out again to other commands as substantiated facts.[14]

Oliver A. Pierce, another former Fort Carson agent, told of being ordered to infiltrate a young-adult project sponsored by the Pike's Peak Council of Churches that operated a recreation center for emotionally disturbed young people. He was ordered to see if its leader was influencing local GIs. After six months, Pierce said, he reported no influence but was kept on the job. He also reported that the Army sent an informant to the 1968 SDS (Students for a Democratic Society) National Convention in Boulder and sent five agents to monitor an antiwar vigil in the chapel of Colorado State College.[15]

Shortly after the hearings were concluded, Secretary Laird issued a directive limiting the military's surveillance activities and placing authority for such activities in the hands of designated civilians. Members of the subcommittee, however, still saw a need for controlling legislation. Pyle is now helping the subcommittee staff draft the legislation.

Pyle and Stein have also assisted the American Civil Liberties Union in litigation aimed at bringing about a judicial review of the constitutional questions raised by military surveillance of civilians. Stein testified in a Chicago case, *ACLU* v. *Westmoreland*, which is now on appeal. The ACLU has also filed a suit in the District of Columbia. But the difficulty of getting key documents as court evidence, before they disappear in the labyrinth of the military establishment, is an impediment in the suits. The District of Columbia District Court refused an ACLU motion to confiscate certain documents; the delay in appeals procedures will make it difficult for the ACLU to keep its evidence up to date.

Having started the machinery for reform, Pyle, Stein, and their associates have found that even the smallest success requires painstaking research and digging for facts. Above all, it requires the help of others who know the situation on the inside. "There is a pressing need," Stein says, "for more military intelligence personnel, both active duty and former, to step forward and publicly relate their experiences where surveillance and record keeping of civilians is involved.

"In some areas of the country and under some personal circumstances this may not be easy, as I have discovered even among my closest friends, and I respect the many people who have aided our investigation after receiving our promise of anonymity. What is important is that the story be told, that those who can effect change learn the truth, and that the telling of the story be legitimated.

"All the promises of the civilian authorities cannot safeguard us if the individuals who must take part in the actual conduct of intelligence operations do not remain alert to the dangers inherent in domestic intelligence and retain a sense of higher loyalty to the nation and the American people. In this age of technology and with all the ills of bureaucratic accretion, we cannot be protected from a full-scale resumption of this surveillance activity in the future if the citizen–special agent and the junior officer and career civilian remain aloof to the problem or are fearful of exposing abuse because of possible consequences."[16]

13

Charles Pettis

You've got to stand up against pressures on that kind of thing to live with yourself. —Charles Pettis

In February, 1966, Charles Pettis went to Peru as resident engineer on a $47 million project to build a road across the Andes. It was a huge undertaking, financed in the main by United States assistance, with $12 million authorized by the Agency for International Development (AID) and $23 million by the Export-Import Bank. Pettis worked for Brown and Root Overseas, Inc., an international engineering firm and subsidiary of the Brown and Root worldwide construction company, which had been hired by the Peruvian government to oversee the project. The contractor was another international construction company, Morrison-Knudsen. As resident engineer, Pettis was charged with making sure the project met contract specifications and protecting the interests of his firm's client, the Peruvian government.

It wasn't long before he began to be seriously disturbed by the engineering design which called for cutting channels up to three hundred feet deep through the mountains, with sheer cliffs on the sides of the road. The Andes are well known for their instability and frequent slides. Yet Pettis found that the design team had taken inadequate geological borings to determine where slides might occur. Other problems began to develop, and Pettis concluded that the road designs needed drastic overhauling. He also estimated that large contract overruns would occur, for which the Peruvian government would have to pay, if he went along with the plans. Despite his misgivings, Morrison-Knudsen, the contractor, proceeded with construction.

Pettis's fears were realized almost immediately when the road project sustained a number of serious slides, in which thirty-one men were killed. The first direct confrontation between Pettis and Morrison-Knudsen came when the contractor demanded that the monthly payroll be amended to include charges for slide removal. Pettis refused. He told the company that the extra charges were not included in the contract and that in his judgment the Peruvian government should not have to pay them.

His own company, Brown and Root, supported him at first, but in February, 1968, their attitude began to change. There was a high-level meeting that month, at which Morrison-Knudsen began to put pressure on Brown and Root. The Morrison-Knudsen representative said his company had bid the job low because of prior associations with Brown and Root. They hoped that their fellow corporation would not do anything to impair their happy working relationship in other parts of the world by being stubborn in Peru. The implications were not lost on Brown and Root. Morrison-Knudsen wanted a break and they got it. Pettis was incensed and told his employers he "wouldn't be a party to such a thing."

Brown and Root nevertheless ordered him to boost the payroll as Morrison-Knudsen demanded. When Pettis continued to refuse, he was replaced by another engineer, B. W. Donelson, who proved exceptionally pliable. Not only did Donelson order extra payments to the contractor, he apparently decided that he would obtain some extra business for himself as well. According to Pettis, he persuaded Morrison-Knudsen to give him a subcontract to feed the workers and by cutting food costs gleaned a substantial profit. His allegations were subsequently confirmed by investigators from the General Accounting Office.

Pettis, meanwhile, was under enormous pressure to bail out Brown and Root by assuring the Peruvian government that everything was proceeding properly on the project. He refused to do so and Peru stopped payment on the road. Frantic, Brown and Root offered Pettis his pick of jobs anywhere in Latin America if he would cooperate. At the same time, other subtle pressures were applied. The American consul in Lima gave him a temporary passport and tried to pass it off as a bureaucratic error. Contractors' children threw eggs at his children and refused to associate with them. More and more isolated, without any support but his own convictions, Pettis stuck to his position. In December, 1968, he was fired.

The next few years were a full dose of what offending a corporate employer can mean. Pettis got job offer after job offer but in every case, after he gave a prospective employer his past job references, the offer was canceled. The obvious explanation was that Brown and Root were giving him an "unreliable" label. He contacted the American Society of Civil Engineers but was unable then to get any action in his behalf.

Pettis and his family moved to Spain, where they made plans to build a school. Meanwhile, he was exploring the possibility of a breach-of-contract suit. When he asked his lawyer to contact Brown and Root, the lawyer wrote Pettis that the company's position "seems to be that your first duty was to the Brown and Root 'team' rather than to the Peruvian government, and that by your action you violated this duty." Pettis vehemently disagreed, as he had all along, maintaining that his professional duty was to the client whose interests he was hired to protect.

In January, 1971, Pettis's lawyer came to Washington to attend the Conference on Professional Responsibility. The next day he talked to an attorney in the Public Interest Research Group about legal remedies available to people like Pettis who are fired for taking an unpopular stand in the course of duty.

A month later, Pettis himself came to the United States. He went to see Martin Lobell, a member of Senator William Proxmire's staff, who was helping Proxmire look into contract policies of international construction companies, particularly those with large contracts in Vietnam, which included Brown and Root and Morrison-Knudsen. Lobell got Pettis an appointment at the General Accounting Office, the agency of Congress charged with keeping an eye on spending by the executive branch, which made a preliminary inquiry into the circumstances of his dismissal. In March, Senator Proxmire made a formal request for a major investigation by the GAO.

On December 25, 1971, Senator Proxmire released the GAO report, which confirmed Pettis's charges of fraud, improper construction, unauthorized payments, and use of inexperienced employees and improper equipment.[1] The GAO also criticized the Agency for International Development and the Export-Import Bank for failing to supervise the project properly. "The U.S. Mission in Peru and AID/Washington were aware of many of the project's problems by early 1967," the GAO said, "but did not take substantive action until the end of 1968."

Among Pettis's charges which the GAO substantiated were:

—"The consultant's [Brown and Root Overseas, Inc.] design for the Tarapoto road was deficient because, among other things, no core borings had been made to determine subsurface conditions."

—"The consultant's regional engineer had ordered the contractor [Morrison-Knudsen, Inc.] to perform work totaling almost $1 million without having authority to do so from the Government of Peru or the U.S. Mission."

—"The consultant's design had not called for proper placement of drainage pipes under the roadway."

—"During the early stages of the project, the contractor did not have employees experienced in road construction."

—"A fellow consultant employee had improperly used contract funds derived from food payments for personal expenses and had charged the Peru contract for material and labor used to construct a private house for himself." (The GAO report included a picture of the house with the caption: "Pictured above during its construction in 1968, the consultant employee's house was the only luxurious residence in Tarapoto."[2])

—"The consultant changed its position [after meeting with the contractor] and authorized payment to the contractor for slide removal," which would have added $2.2 million to the cost of the project, without the approval of Peru or AID.

The GAO did not find documentation for Pettis's assertion that he had been blackballed in the construction industry, but added the following concluding paragraph:

"The question of whether Mr. Pettis has been blackballed cannot be established as any such action would, by definition, be informal and not necessarily documented. We could not find any overt action to blackball Mr. Pettis. The fact remains, however, that he has applied for thirty-one jobs since 1969 and has been unsuccessful in obtaining employment in the engineer-construction field."[3]

Since February, 1970, neither Brown and Root Overseas, Inc., nor Morrison-Knudsen has worked on the project, which has been taken over by Peru. The government of Peru has filed a court suit against the two firms, which includes charges of poor workmanship, fraud, and collusion.

Pettis is still living in Spain and is still unemployed. The GAO report, as well as the support of William H. Wisely, former executive director of the American Society of Civil Engineers, who made his own inquiries and has interceded on Pettis's behalf with prospective employers, may change his heretofore bleak employment prospects. Meanwhile he is suing Brown & Root both for what he considers its breach of his contract and for recovery of funds due the United States. He is also writing a book about his experiences—in which several publishers have expressed a keen interest.

Of his action, Pettis has said, "You've got to stand up against pressures on that kind of thing to live with yourself. You sure won't make much money that way —I mean what the hell did I have to gain out of this? —but you have to do it."[4]

14

The Colt Workers

"Professional responsibility" as the term is used in this book really means "individual" responsibility. Edward Gregory, the Fisher Body Plant inspector who appeared at the Conference on Professional Responsibility, is not a professional in the ordinary sense—he is not a doctor or a lawyer or an engineer. Seven employees of the Colt Firearms Company at West Hartford, Connecticut, who publicly revealed massive fraud and deception in the testing of Colt M–16 rifles bound for Vietnam, are not "professionals" in that sense either. Yet their revelations represent an expression of personal responsibility for the quality and consequences of their work that "professionals" rarely equal, but which is part of what "professionalism" is all about.

On November 1, 1971, the Connecticut Citizens Action Group (CCAG) released a report[1] charging that Colt was engaged in a systematic program of subverting government inspection procedures for the M–16 rifle. The report, which called for a congressional investigation and an investigation by the Justice Department for possible violation of federal criminal law, was based on extensive interviews with Colt employees. Seven employees later submitted affidavits affirming the truth of the charges to Congressman Les Aspin of the House Armed Services Committee and to Connecticut Senator Abraham Ribicoff.

The Colt workers and the CCAG report maintained that Colt management ordered its employees to tamper with endurance tests and interchangeability-of-parts tests—the successful completion of which is necessary before the Army may accept any particular shipment of rifles. Colt also ordered employees to repair weapons that failed an accuracy test by bending the barrel "either by straining the muzzle between the mounting beams or by striking the flash suppressor against the floor."[2] As the CCAG report expressed it, "It is difficult to conjure up a more amazing image than the picture of a worker in a modern factory grasping the world's most sophisticated rifle by the butt and 'whacking' its flash suppressor on the target range floor."

Both the endurance test and the interchangeability-of-parts test are performed on weapons selected at random by government inspectors from six-thousand-rifle shipment lots that have completed all other Colt quality control tests. Four weapons are used in the endurance test, ten in the interchangeability test. In the endurance test, each weapon of the four is fired six thousand times in eight hours, with periodic forced-air cooling and regular disassembly and washing of parts. In the interchangeability test, the ten weapons are disassembled, their parts are thoroughly mixed, randomly grouped, and reassembled into ten (hopefully) acceptable performing weapons. In either case if any weapon is rejected because of malfunctions or failure to function, the whole set of four or ten is rejected and a new set randomly chosen from the same shipment. The second set is then tested in the same manner. If the second set must also be rejected, the entire shipment of six thousand rifles is rejected by the government and must be totally reprocessed.

During the endurance test, the Colt workers reported, "It is standard practice that if the gun should fail to feed and fail to fire, we pull back the charging handle, recharge the gun and continue firing without the government men detecting it. The Colt's weapon technician would keep the government agent occupied during the cover up. If a weakened extractor spring is causing trouble, the Colt's men might give you a new spring without the government man knowing it."[3]

A similar pattern was revealed in the interchangeability tests. Out of view of government inspectors, Colt workers were ordered to inspect the test weapons for parts that might need replacement: "We always

changed the parts whether it was before the breakdown or after reassembly. Orders for switches were
given by the quality control man or the range master."[4]
Frequently, workers were required to come to the plant
before or after the regular work day to put in overtime—again, beyond the view of government inspectors
and contrary to government regulation—in order to
"prepare" the weapons for the interchangeability test:
"I have seen the whole upper receiver—the barrel—
changed during overtime, with the new receiver selected from outside the test group. I have seen the
guns test-fired during overtime, and corrected, to insure
that good results would be had during the government-
witnessed regular test-firing."[5]

Who are the workers who signed the affidavits
charging such astonishing, if not criminal, irregularities? And why did they speak out?

"The lead poisoning. That's what did it for me,"
Wayne Handfield told one of the authors. When the
company first installed a "dry tank" for bullet testing,
Handfield and others became concerned about the possibility of inhaling or otherwise absorbing lead. When
rifles are fired in the dry tank, the bullets pass through
a series of baffles. As a result, the bullets are pulverized
to dust and tiny particles. "We told them two years
back we'd have a problem with the dry tanks. We even
filed a grievance. But they didn't listen. Then after we
had the blood tests that showed the lead in our blood,
they were content to let the situation go on. It seemed
so callous to me. They just didn't give a damn."

William Sklar, a law student at the University of
Connecticut Law School and a volunteer at the Connecticut Citizens Action Group, literally stumbled on
the M–16 situation when he spoke to Handfield and
other Colt workers about their complaints of lead pollution in the West Hartford plant. The company's attitude toward the lead hazard jolted Handfield out of
going along with the company on the M–16 test tampering. "I'm sorry I didn't say something about that sooner.
Weapons go back a long way with me. When I got the
job in the plant, I was real excited. I was going to
work on the 'world's most sophisticated shoulder
weapon'—that's what they call it. Then I saw what was

going on and I got disillusioned. But I got in a rut. You lose perspective, you know, about a job and security. I might have let it go if this lead business hadn't come up."

Handfield is a gun purist: "I've loved guns since I was a boy. To me weapons are things of beauty." He has always read avidly "anything about armies and war" and at age sixteen he exaggerated his age in order to join the National Guard unit in his hometown, Florence, Massachusetts. At seventeen he quit school and joined the Army for the first of his two stints in the military. In 1964 he went to work at Colt's main plant in Hartford as a filer on small-arms pistols. When a job came open in the West Hartford plant, where the M–16s are made, he bid for it and got it. For Handfield, the gun enthusiast, this was the ultimate. But he was soon disillusioned, both with the M–16 and with Colt.

He was the first of the weapons testers to get sick from exposure to lead-filled dust. "I was tired at the end of the day, which isn't like me. I wanted to sleep all the time. Colt had promised to give us blood tests every three months, but they gave us only one test when we first started using the dry tank. So I went and got a blood test. The level of lead in my blood was .07 ppm [parts per million]. Then everybody else got tests too."

When the company still failed to put in a ventilation system or institute other precautionary measures, Handfield, incensed, went to the *Hartford Courant* in June, 1971. It was the *Courant* story that led CCAG representatives to contact Handfield and other Colt workers. For two weeks after the newspaper's story on the lead problem "company VIPs were in and out of the plant." Also, after the story, Handfield was given a three-day suspension for "saying something to a foreman," which he says was a bogus charge.

Later that summer, Handfield filed a complaint with the United States Labor Department under the Federal Occupational Safety and Health Act. Government investigators came in, and by early fall Colt had installed a ventilation system that Handfield says has reduced the dust.

Handfield, who is married and the father of three children, was again suspended, this time indefinitely, when it became generally known at the plant that CCAG was looking into possible test tampering. This time he was again told that he had been suspended for "saying something to a supervisor," but three days later he was back at work, having produced a witness who denied the foreman's charge. The "supervisory personnel are nice to me now," he says. "The people I work with consider me something like a hero. I don't know why."

Vic Martinez, a fifty-four-year-old veteran of twenty-two years service in the Marine Corps, joined Colt in October, 1961, as an archery equipment inspector at the Hartford plant. In 1968 he became a process inspector at the West Hartford plant. In May of that year he went onto the range as a targeter and range inspector for the M–16.

"I began to notice these irregularities right away. The minute I saw what was happening, swapping the parts and all the rest, I wanted to get it stopped. But who would believe one man? No one would stick together then. They were afraid they would lose their jobs." Then blood tests revealed that the people who worked in the range had high levels of lead in their blood. Martinez had the highest level on the first tests, with .08 ppm. He asked to be taken out of the range and was, along with three others.

William Sklar of CCAG contacted Martinez, as he would later other Colt workers, about the lead situation. As he talked, Martinez began to describe what else disturbed him, primarily the dishonesty in the testing procedures. This was the first time he had told anyone outside the plant about the problem. Previously, "every time something would happen I informed the government men. But I guess they were in the same boat we were in. Their superiors would tell them to smooth it over and nothing would happen."

When Sklar asked Martinez if he would make the problem public, "I was a little leery. You must understand, I had my wife to consider, it wasn't just me. So I first questioned her, told her I might lose my job and that the company might blackball me." But his wife supported him, and he decided to do it, particularly since he liked and trusted Sklar. "My reasoning was, being a Marine twenty-two years, that the men in the field were put in a position where it could happen that their gun just wouldn't fire. I was in the service and what was happening to them could have happened to me.

"Don't get me wrong. The M–16 is a beautiful little weapon. You can't beat it. But it's only as good as its parts. If you cover up malfunctions, then there's no sense in having tests. You've got to catch these defects and have the guns in A–1 condition before they go out of the plant and before they are in the hands of the boys in the field. There, your life depends on your gun. How many boys have died because their guns didn't fire or because a part didn't fit? We'll never know. It's too late to uncover these things in the field."

At the time of this writing, neither Martinez nor the other Colt whistle blowers have suffered serious repercussions at the plant, despite persistent rumors that they would soon "get the ax." Since November 2, 1971, Martinez has been back on the range, but "they haven't given me the chance to check on many of these things. The barrel-bending is still going on. They do that where everybody can see it." Martinez acknowledges that the majority of his colleagues are "scared stiff" of losing their jobs, but some are "glad these irregularities have come out."

The final chapter of the Colt episode is yet to be written. The results thus far, in terms of getting action from Congress, the Department of Defense, or the Justice Department have been disappointing at best. Congressman Les Aspin (D., Wis.), a first-termer on the House Armed Services Committee, published the CCAG report and later the affidavits of the Colt workers in the *Congressional Record* and sought hearings on the matter before his committee. Committee Chairman F. Edward Hébert (D., La.) referred the matter to the Defense Department. Connecticut Senator Abraham Ribicoff requested that the Senate Armed Services Committee look into the matter. The Defense Department's response was subsequently released as "Fact Sheet— M–16 Rifle," which Senator Barry Goldwater published

in the *Congressional Record*.[6] The Army Material
Command, the fact sheet reported, would begin an
"expedited" investigation, but it went on to state that
the Army had conducted tests on the rifle since November, 1967, that "clearly refute the allegations" in
the CCAG report. One reads the fact sheet's four
paragraphs in vain to find *any* of the allegations of
the Colt workers refuted. Colt Firearms president Paul
Benke later announced an investigation into the irregularities, but specifically declined to "formally rebut"
the report, though he also asserted that no one at
Colt has ever "knowingly" shipped any defective guns
out of the factory to any customer. Thus, both the
government and the company have denied the charges
before the investigations which each have announced.
The FBI has started an investigation, but early press
reports reflect some concern at precisely what the
FBI is investigating. CCAG spokesmen fear the bureau
might be investigating the workers and CCAG rather
than the substance of the report and the affidavits.[7]

15

Whistle Blowers
Beyond the Headlines

It would be a mistake to assume that whistle blowers always reach the headlines. The opposite is probably closer to the truth. As Ernest Fitzgerald has said, "The only thing that makes me unique at all is that I have not gone away quietly, whereas most of the others have." Most whistle blowers are relatively unheralded, their reports buried in bureaucratic crypts, their fates unknown to the public even when the public benefits by their courage and honesty. They are whistle blowers who have spoken out far from the centers of power and the national press, and thus have not gained public attention. Or they have quietly given their information to those who they believed could take corrective action and have played only a background role in the ensuing debate. In some cases, they have acted anonymously to bring their information before the public.

This chapter touches briefly on a number of whistle blowers, some practically unknown or little known outside their organizations. In some cases, the reader will recognize the issue but not the name of the individual who first brought that issue to public attention. In other instances, he may recall a news story and wonder what has happened to the person who spoke out. Each case offers an alternative for action when the time comes that a man or woman cannot justify the organization's behavior and must choose between his or her view of the public interest and duty to an employer.

1. Carl W. Houston and Stone and Webster

In February, 1970, Carl Houston went to work as a welding supervisor on the construction of a nuclear power plant in Surry, Virginia. An engineer, he was an employee of the Stone and Webster Engineering Company of Boston, Massachusetts, which was overseeing construction of the plant owned by the Virginia Electric Power Company.

The first day on the job Houston noted defects in the welding of steel pipes, some of which would carry cooling water to and from the nuclear reactor. He informed the company the same day. In succeeding days he found more defects and was soon writing Stone and Webster in Boston in an effort to have corrections made.[1]

The danger of poorly welded pipes was critical, Houston pointed out. If cooling water were lost through a break in the pipes, temperatures within the reactor would rise with extreme rapidity. Though a nuclear explosion would be highly unlikely, in such a "big accident," as nuclear power experts have described the eventuality, the entire reactor would melt within a few hours, perhaps rupturing both the containment vessel surrounding it and the containment slab under it. Large quantities of radioactive material at very high temperatures would be released in the neighborhood of the plant through steam explosions. A molten mass of reactor material would sink into the ground to remain hot and radioactive for years, possibly contaminating underground water reservoirs and creating a long-lasting threat to all life in the vicinity of the plant.

The emergency cooling system that would be activated in such a situation has never been tested in any nuclear power plant, and Houston understandably doubted its effectiveness. The Union of Concerned Scientists, a group of nuclear physicists, engineers, and environmental experts including Dr. Henry W. Kendall of MIT, Dr. Ian A. Forbes of the Lowell Institute of Technology, and Dr. James J. MacKenzie of MIT share Houston's concerns about the adequacy of the emergency system.[2] As Dr. Ralph Lapp, a member of the Manhattan Project team, which developed the first American atomic bomb, has pointed out, the untested system would have to work perfectly within the first five to ten seconds after a break in the cooling system in order to prevent disaster.[3] Faced with this uncertainty and doubts about the resolution of other nuclear power safety issues, Senator Mike Gravel (D., Alaska) has introduced a bill which would impose a national moratorium on reactor construction until the fail-safe system to control the "big accident" has been designed and proven and until other safety issues have been resolved.

But Carl Houston's efforts were in vain. The company replied with increasing irritation to his pleas for better welding.

Two months after he signed on the job, Houston resigned after he was told by a Stone and Webster welding inspector that he was to be fired for "lack of experience in welding," a charge Houston found hard to take seriously, since he had been a journeyman welder for twenty-four years and his engineering experience was mostly in welding.

From April to June he wrote letters trying to get some action on the faulty welding. He wrote Governor Linwood Holton of Virginia and Senator Harry Byrd without replies. He wrote the Atomic Energy Commission with the same result. Finally, he wrote Tennessee Senators Albert Gore and Howard Baker, both of whom contacted the AEC. In mid-July, AEC officials visited Houston, who had moved to Johnson City, Tennessee. They promised to investigate eight of his allegations.

In August the AEC began an investigation of the Surry plant, which lasted for two months. They confirmed Houston's reports of defective welding. Late in October in a letter to Stanley Ragone of the Virginia Electric Power Company, John G. Davis, director of Region III of AEC's division of compliance, confirmed defects in welding, testing of welding rods, and the pouring of concrete, none of which met AEC construction standards. On December 28 the then AEC Chairman Glenn T. Seaborg wrote Senator Gore that "the general validity of Mr. Houston's eight allegations was verified."

The AEC then proposed, according to Houston, to bring all welding and other construction methods up to standards but *not* to correct past defects. AEC representatives told Houston that if there were failures in the operation of the plant, the plant emergency safety system would prevent danger. Houston pointed out that the safety devices to control the heat in the reactor if the normal cooling system failed had never been tested in an actual crisis. He had strong doubts that they would prove adequate.

In April, 1971, the AEC ran six tests on the safety devices in a plant in Idaho Falls, Idaho. All failed. As reported by Thomas O'Toole in the *Washington Post,* "the cooling water that bathed the heated elements was allowed to escape, as it would in a 'loss of coolant' accident that might result from a ruptured pipe. Emergency or backup coolant was then pumped into the reactor vessel to keep the nuclear core cool while procedures were begun to shut the core down.

"Test engineers discovered that high steam pressures kept almost all of the emergency cooling water out of the pressure vessel. One description of the test suggested that the pressurized steam blew the emergency coolant out through an outlet before the water even reached the hot core.

"A second problem occurred when the tests showed that the temperatures of some of the fuel elements in reactor cores might go higher than anticipated during a loss of coolant."[4]

Houston had already predicted these possible failures in the emergency cooling system.

Despite his accuracy, the AEC has not responded to Houston's criticism of the welding in the Surry, Virginia, plant with efforts that he deems adequate. Nor does he have much faith that the agency will insure proper construction in the future. Houston contends that the AEC has insufficient manpower to keep a close eye on the building of nuclear power plants. He is also critical of an AEC policy decision to delegate all quality control at the project level to the owner of each project. The AEC fails to understand, he believes, "that the owner's primary objective is frequently to meet the date scheduled for completion of construction" rather than to take all necessary safety precautions.

In the Surry plant, the need for enforced standards is especially critical, he believes. Virginia is one of the states that have not even adopted the minimum codes and standards of the American Society of Mechanical Engineers; welders at the Surry plant are therefore not bound to comply with ASME standards.

For his pains, Houston has been out of work ever since he left Stone and Webster in April, 1970. He is living in Johnson City, where he has attempted with little success to start a private consulting business. His applications for full-time jobs have been constantly rejected. He believes, though he cannot prove, that he has been blackballed in the construction industry since he criticized his former employer.

In October, 1970, Houston brought suit against Stone and Webster claiming slander and breach of contract. The suit was not heard in federal district court in Richmond until a year later, in October, 1971. At that time, the breach of contract charge was dismissed on grounds that Houston had submitted his resignation. Then Stone and Webster asked that the name of its Virginia agent be joined as defendant along with the company, to which the judge agreed. The case was then remanded to state court. The case thus promises to stretch into a lengthy legal battle far beyond Houston's scant financial means. He has already had to sell his house in Johnson City, Tennessee, to pay his attorney's legal fees. He has also used up six thousand dollars of savings and borrowed five thousand from friends, relatives, and a local bank to support his wife and three children.

He is still trying to force the Atomic Energy Commission to take action on past welding defects at the Surry plant. Virginia Lieutenant Governor Henry Howell has intervened in the matter, and the AEC has scheduled a hearing in February at which Houston will testify.

2. Henry M. Durham and Lockheed

In the midst of the controversy over the proposed bail-out of the Lockheed Aircraft Corporation with a $250 million federal loan guarantee, a former Lockheed employee publicly charged the company with inefficient and wasteful management.

Backed with a sheaf of documentation, Henry M. Durham, a former assistant division manager at Lockheed-Georgia, said bluntly that many of Lockheed's troubles were the company's own fault.

According to documents Durham gave to the *Washington Post,* mostly memoranda he had written to his superiors, inefficient supply practices at Lockheed accounted for a substantial part of the $2 billion overrun on the C-5A transport plane.

In the fall of 1969, Durham found that numerous parts issued and presumably installed on sections of the C-5A were missing. By certifying that these sections were complete, Durham contended, Lockheed received payment from the Air Force for work that still had to be done.

In the spring of 1970, Durham reported to his superiors that the company's methods for ordering "very small parts" (VSPs) and disorderly storage that resulted in parts being thrown away had raised the cost of VSPs from $560,000 per aircraft to over $1 million per aircraft.

Other parts, he reported in another memo to his immediate superior, were purchased and then returned to stock because they weren't needed. Such practices, Durham told the *Post,*[5] wasted "thousands and thousands of dollars. It happened on all ships, constantly."

Durham went on to relate other examples of mismanagement that he had observed and documented in memos to his bosses. Most of the problems, he believes, were kept from the top company management by lower-ranking employees anxious not to rock the boat.

Durham's attempts to improve Lockheed's supply program led, he says, to his demotion in the spring of 1970, with a twenty-dollar-a-week pay cut. He protested, even taking his case to the president of Lockheed-Georgia, R. H. Fuhrman. This interview had no results except, as Durham later wrote Lockheed chairman Daniel Haughton, "I was ostracized, criticized, pushed into a corner, and eventually downgraded."

Rather than take a demotion, Durham said he would leave Lockheed. Haughton replied that he would ask for an investigation but ended his letter, "I hope you find a job that you will be happy with." Durham has not heard of any investigation of his case.

In the next few months, Durham was twice asked to return to Lockheed. The second time he agreed, taking a job at eighty dollars a week below his former salary at the Chattanooga, Tennessee, plant, one hundred miles from his home in Marietta, Georgia.

Once in Chattanooga, however, Durham said he continued to find "shabby performance," and he continued to protest. Finally, in May, 1971, he again left the company. Durham says he asked to be laid off. W. P. Frech, director of manufacturing at Lockheed-Georgia, told the *Post* that Durham left when he was told he would have to take a "downgrade" because of employment cuts.

Durham's public disclosures of mismanagement in July, 1971, brought immediate disclaimers from his former bosses who said, in effect, that Durham didn't know what he was talking about. However, Senator William Proxmire asked Durham to testify before his Subcommittee on Economy in Government. He did on September 29, 1971, reiterating and amplifying the story he gave the *Post*.

At the hearings Durham also reported what had happened to him and his family since he made his accusations public. They were ostracized by friends in Marietta, Georgia, and subjected to "an apparent organized telephone attack threatening in almost every instance my life and frequently the lives of my wife and children. We took these cases rather lightly at first, but the offensive language and brutal tones of the voices we listened to quickly made us realize that some of these people, at least, had murder in their minds."

Now Durham is trying to start a business selling Aerosol products in the Atlanta area. His wife has gone to work to support the family.

Morton Mintz, the reporter who wrote the story for

the *Post,* found Durham an "unlikely" whistle blower.
For most of his nineteen years at Lockheed, Mintz reported, Durham worked eleven-hour days and seven-
day weeks. His devotion to his company was such that
"if Lockheed wanted it, I assumed it was good."

Why, then, did he blow the whistle? In a letter to
Fuhrman, he wrote, "I have been very disappointed
with my superiors for lacking the fortitude and courage to go to the top if necessary to get serious problems corrected. . . . I realize now that it is because
certain members of management feel they must conform and not rock the nice, tight little boat they have
constructed. I believe *one cannot afford to jeopardize
the company by conforming to such standards.* One
must operate with directness and integrity in the best
interests of the company, not the individual." (Emphasis added.)

3. George B. Geary and U.S. Steel

George Geary, a sales executive with the United States
Steel Corporation's oil and gas industry supply division
in Houston, Texas, strongly objected to the sale of a
new type of pipe which he believed was inadequately
tested and likely to fail under high pressure. He told
the company that in his judgment use of the pipe could
result in serious physical injury to customers and the
public as well as property damage. He urged his immediate superiors to perform more tests before marketing the product.

Geary was not an engineer, but during his fourteen
years with U.S. Steel, he had had extensive experience
with the technical aspects of tubular steel products manufactured for use by the oil and gas industry.

Despite his reservations, mid-level managers decided
to pursue the sales program for the pipe. Geary reluc-
tantly agreed to participate but carried his objections
to officials in U.S. Steel's main office, who were ultimately responsible for the product. Because of his good
reputation with the company and the potential seriousness of his assertions, these officials ordered an immediate re-evaluation of the new line of pipe. Shortly

thereafter, the product was withdrawn from sale pending major retesting.

Geary was discharged on July 13, 1967. The reason given: insubordination. Apparently, even though he may have saved the company substantial costs had the pipe been prematurely marketed and saved users of the pipe from physical and financial injury, he had ignored the rules of the game and breached the etiquette of hierarchical management.

Unlike whistle blowers who lack the means or the persistence to pursue available legal remedies, Geary has sought and continues to seek relief in a number of legal forums. Through a damage suit, his attorney hopes to develop a new principle of law: that any employee, under appropriate circumstances, can sue and obtain compensation for "wrongful discharge." Heretofore, only members of labor unions have had similar protection when their collective bargaining agreements contain provisions limiting discharges to cases in which the employer can show "just cause."

Geary's application for unemployment compensation also raised a question similar to that of dismissal for "just cause" before the Unemployment Compensation Board of Review of the Pennsylvania Department of Labor and Industry. Under the applicable laws, if an employer can show that the employee was discharged for "willful misconduct," the latter can be denied unemployment compensation even though he would otherwise be entitled to benefits. U.S. Steel chose to seek such a finding in Geary's case. After several hearings and appeals, the Pennsylvania Board of Review held on May 3, 1968:

> No company places a man in the position held by the claimant and pays him the salary received by the claimant simply to have him quietly agree to all proposals. The claimant did not refuse to follow orders, but, in fact, agreed to do as instructed despite his opposition to the program proposed. Although he may have been vigorous in his opposition and offended some superiors by going to a vice president, it is clear that *at all times the claimant was working in the best interest of the company* and that the welfare of the

company was primary in his mind. Under these circumstances, giving due regard to the claimant's position
with the company, his conduct cannot be deemed willful
misconduct. [Emphasis added]

The board was not making a determination on the
separate question of whether or not Geary had been
wrongfully discharged. Nevertheless, its decision indicates that judicial bodies are capable of reasoned judg-
ments about an employee's conduct with respect to his
employer in a whistle blowing situation.

4. Warren Braren and the National Associaion of Broadcasters

As manager of the New York office of the Code
Authority of the National Association of Broadcasters,
Warren Braren was responsible for seeing that television commercials complied with the code standards for
honest and accurate advertising. He particularly urged
the NAB to take steps against cigarette commercials
considered in violation of the standards. His superiors
were reluctant to take decisive action against tobacco
companies, which contributed millions to broadcast
treasuries. These differences between Braren and Code
Authority leaders became increasingly tense during the
late nineteen-sixties as public opposition to the broadcasting of cigarette commercials grew.

In 1969, congressional hearings were held to determine the legislative course to follow expiration of the
first federal cigarette-labeling act. Tobacco interests lob-
bied vigorously against regulation of cigarette advertising, as did broadcast interests. NAB president Vincent
Wasilewski testified before the House Commerce Committee in April, 1969, arguing against regulation on the
grounds that the NAB code enforcement program provided sufficient "self-regulation" in the public interest.
The committee was unaware that Braren, within the
NAB, had been arguing that the Code Authority's regulation was far from adequate.

Not long afterwards, on May 1, 1969, as a result of
their longstanding differences, the NAB president asked
for Braren's resignation.

Shortly after resigning, Braren went to Congressman

Brock Adams (D., Wash.) and disclosed confidential NAB reports which illustrated the failure of "self-regulation" with respect to cigarette advertising. On June 10, Congressman Adams held a news conference and released Braren's information. The House committee had issued its report on the Public Health Cigarette Smoking Act three days earlier, but on hearing of Braren's criticism of NAB regulation, Chairman Harley Staggers hastily called a meeting of the Commerce Committee to hear Braren and NAB representatives discuss his charges.

Braren told committee members that they had been misled into believing that the NAB Code Authority exercised effective regulation over cigarette ads. The Code Authority stuck to its guns and Congressmen from the tobacco states subjected Braren to vicious cross-examination on his motives for speaking out. They attempted to discredit his testimony as the bitterness of a recently fired employee. They also asked why Braren had not come forward while the hearings were still in session and why he had not gone to the chairman when he did speak. Braren admitted that, not versed in the byzantine code of congressional protocol, he had gone to the only committee member with whom he was acquainted. He delayed coming in the first place, he said candidly, while he struggled to decide whether to let the matter go or end the possibility of further employment in his profession by speaking out. "It is not an easy decision, I can assure you, to face the eventual possibility of never being able to work again in your chosen profession," he told the congressmen.

Braren accurately predicted his employment future. The industry has not touched him since. He served for a time as executive director of the National Citizens Committee for Broadcasting, a public interest group, and is now assistant director of Consumers Union.

5. *Kermit Vandivier and B. F. Goodrich*

Kermit Vandivier had worked as a scientific writer for the B. F. Goodrich Company for six years when he was assigned, in early 1968, to write reports on raw data developed from tests of the brakes for the A-7D

aircraft. Goodrich was building the A-7D brakes for
the Air Force under subcontract from the Ling-Temco-
Vought Company. In the course of his work, Vandivier
was ordered to falsify figures so that test results which
had not met contract specifications would appear to
have been successful.

He followed instructions under protest until his conscience would no longer let him remain silent. In addition to the implication of fraud, he feared for the lives
of A-7D pilots who would have no knowledge of the
actual brake test failures. In June, 1968, he went to
the FBI. The local agent promised to begin an investigation but urged him to remain on the job. Five months
later, having heard no further word from the FBI, he
resigned in protest.

Before he quit, Vandivier had already lined up a job
as a reporter with a local newspaper, the *Troy* (Ohio)
Daily News. Later, the paper ran an exposé on the
A-7D scandal.

In August, 1969, Vandivier and another former
Goodrich employee, Searle Lawson, an aeronautical
engineer, testified before the Joint Economic Committee of Congress. It was revealed at the hearings that
the Air Force had been seriously concerned with the
performance of the brake before Vandivier's story became public knowledge, but had been refused access
to the raw test data (which would have demonstrated
the falsifications) on the grounds that such information was "proprietary."

As a result of Vandivier's testimony and a subsequent Air Force investigation, the A-7D brakes were
withdrawn and substitutes developed. The Air Force
took issue with Vandivier's contention that the brakes
constituted a serious threat to the safety of test pilots,
but by its action supported his allegations concerning
falsification of test data. No action was taken against
Goodrich or any of its employees.

6. *Carl Thelin and General Motors*

When Ralph Nader's *Unsafe at Any Speed* was published in 1965, Carl Thelin was working as an engineer
for General Motors. His specialty was design of chassis

suspension systems and steering mechanisms. (One of his design innovations culminated in the experimental vehicle which eventually became the Oldsmobile Toronado.) In addition, he provided engineering liaison for General Motor's legal staff and in that capacity found himself in the middle of the Corvair issue.

Thelin and his associates were charged with developing engineering and technical support for General Motors' defense in damage suits brought by Corvair victims or their families. They conducted accident investigations, produced films to be shown to juries, and held seminars on vehicle dynamics for defense lawyers who would have to question witnesses. Thelin also prepared an index and critique of materials considered important in the Corvair litigation.

In the course of piecing together these materials, Thelin discovered inexplicable gaps in company records. He refused to accept explanations that the missing records never existed. When he persisted, he was finally provided with documents which he later described as "dynamite." He was warned, however, that these papers were never to be shown to anyone who might be called on to testify in behalf of General Motors. Later, Thelin himself was removed from cases when General Motors executives thought he might show the records to potential witnesses.

Several years later, Gary Sellers, a legal consultant to Ralph Nader, discovered in a review of some of the Corvair papers that Carl Thelin's name cropped up repeatedly. Sellers went to see Thelin, who by then had moved to Buffalo, New York, to head the design and test section of the automotive safety department at the Cornell Aeronautical Laboratory. Thelin revealed to Sellers, and on a separate occasion to *Washington Post* reporter Morton Mintz, that General Motors had concealed test reports from its own witnesses to prevent their surfacing in court. According to Thelin, one of the documents proved that with suspension systems like those installed on later models the early Corvairs would have been almost impossible to roll over. It revealed further that top General Motors officials knew this even before the first Corvair was offered for sale.

Thelin said that when Nader's book first came out

he had accepted uncritically the "straight party line" of his company. Later he came to believe that General Motors was obligated at least to produce the suppressed documents. When Sellers, Mintz, and, later, investigators from Senator Ribicoff's Government Operations subcommittee sought his cooperation in finding the truth, he said he had no choice but to help them.[6]

7. George Caramanna and General Motors

George Caramanna was a member of the General Motors team that designed and tested the Corvair. From mid-1957 to 1970 he was senior design and development technician with the research and development section of Chevrolet. In 1970, Caramanna resigned and moved to California for family reasons and began operating his own service station in Spring Valley near San Diego. When new revelations about the Corvair were reported late that year, principally those made by Carl Thelin, Caramanna began to reconsider his earlier decision to remain silent about the defects of the car.

In early May, 1971, he contacted Alexander Auerbach of the *Los Angeles Times* and unfolded a new chapter in the history of the Corvair. Auerbach's story appeared in the *Los Angeles Times* on May 28, 1971.

General Motors had never publicly conceded the unsafe characteristics of the 1960–1963 Corvairs, even though the company instituted several "product improvements" in the 1964 and 1965 models that substantially reduced the car's tendency to roll over unexpectedly. Caramanna's first-hand knowledge conflicted sharply with the official company line.

According to Caramanna, the very first Corvair, a prototype, rolled over in its first trial run. Contrary to claims by General Motors, the rollover was purely accidental and not part of any test program. Production models suffered the same fate, he told Auerbach, adding that "it doesn't have to be at high speed. It can happen at thirty miles per hour or even less in a sharp turn."

More disturbing was his report that the research and development section had been directed to design modifications for racing versions of the Corvair which were not put on the car sold to the public. "You could not turn it over the way we fixed it," he said. He contended that the modifications were simple and inexpensive. They included a stabilizer bar, for which a mounting spot was embossed into the body of the regular Corvair three years before the bar itself became standard equipment. Auerbach noted in his story for the *Los Angeles Times* that General Motors engineer Charles Rubly said in 1960 that the roll stabilizer bar was left off the early Corvair because "we felt the slight amount of gain realized did not warrant the cost." Caramanna maintained that several engineers and technicians on the project, including himself, had told Chevrolet officials point blank that without the stabilizer bar the car was unsafe.

Finally, Caramanna supplied the missing link to the mysterious General Motors test films used by defense counsel in many of the hundreds of suits filed by Corvair crash victims or their families. The film showed a Corvair being put through rigorous test maneuvers without mishap. Caramanna confirmed that the car was a standard Corvair without special adjustments. However, he revealed that he had developed special driving techniques to counter the car's inherent tendency to roll over. The ordinary driver, Caramanna pointed out, would tend to take corrective action that would have precisely the opposite results and substantially accentuate the roll tendency.

8. Ronald Ostrander and Proctor and Gamble

Ronald Ostrander was project engineer on the Procter and Gamble research team which developed Tide laundry detergent in the late nineteen-forties. In December, 1970, he wrote Congressman Henry Reuss (D., Wis.), chairman of the House Conservation and Natural Resources Subcommittee, that "the most important knowledge bearing on. . . . the subject [of phosphate detergents] apparently is known to a limited number of people and I am one of that number."

Ostrander revealed that the optimum amount of detergent for effective washing is substantially less than recommended by most manufacturers. Housewives, he wrote, could achieve better results at substantially less cost while reducing by ninety percent the amount of phosphates entering the water. Most manufacturers call for a minimum of one and one-quarter cups of detergent for top loader washing machines and one-half cup for front loaders, when in fact one-eighth cup would do well for both, he said.

Procter and Gamble, which Ostrander still describes as a "marvelous" company, initially instructed consumers to use much smaller amounts of Tide than other laundry products. But the company discovered, he said, that housewives preferred to see large quantities of suds in the mistaken belief that suds represent cleaning power. Old habits were hard to break and manufacturers apparently decided not to attempt to break a profitable one.

Ostrander left Procter and Gamble in 1949 to take over a family business. Except for a stint with the Army Chemical Corps during World War II, he had been with the company since he graduated from engineering school in 1935. He was not a "disgruntled employee," as Procter and Gamble spokesmen were to charge twenty-one years later in response to his letter to Congressman Reuss. On the contrary, he had planned from the first to leave the company before he became too dependent on its tempting, but late-vesting, pension plan. He remained through the Tide project only because he found it exciting. Both then and later, Ostrander viewed the project as an intriguing industrial version of the supersecret Manhattan Project, which developed the first American atom bomb. When the project was complete, he left satisfied with the company and his own performance.

Now fifty-nine, Ostrander is with the Wisconsin Department of Natural Resources, largely because of a personal commitment to help achieve a better environment. That commitment grew out of his efforts to alert first his friends, then the local media, then the Federal Water Quality Administration, and finally Congress to the truth about optimum use of detergents. His experience suggests that older professionals and technically

skilled citizens have much to offer, that one can em-
bark on a second career in the public interest, and that
it is never too late to blow the whistle.

As a direct result of Ostrander's letter, Congressman
Reuss has called on the Federal Trade Commission to
conduct a major investigation based on Ostrander's
charges. That investigation is now in progress.

9. Frank Serpico and David Durk and the N.Y.P.D.

One of the major facts that came out during the Knapp
Commission investigations of corruption in the New
York City Police Department was the effort by two
members of the force to get something done about
graft within police ranks and the refusal of high-
ranking police officials to listen to them.

Patrolman Frank Serpico and Sergeant David Durk
were the two policemen responsible for the exposure
of misconduct among "New York's Finest" over the
past several years and, ultimately, for the convening
of the Knapp Commission. The effort took five years
of contacting one police official after another, a fruit-
less appeal to City Hall and, finally, an appeal to the
public through the press.

Frank Serpico grew up in the Bedford-Stuyvesant
section of Brooklyn and joined the New York City
Police Department in 1959 after graduating from City
College. As he was to describe it later, he found a
well-developed system of shakedowns and payoffs
within the department involving not only patrolmen
but higher-ups who either actively participated or tolerated the graft.

He also found that the pressure to join the system
was intense, and, as he consistently refused to become
a part of it, Serpico was increasingly isolated from his
fellow policemen.

In 1966, a Bronx gambler offered Serpico and his
partner a bribe, which the partner accepted. Serpico
turned down his share of the payoff, three hundred
dollars, and got in touch with Detective David Durk,
a close friend. An Amherst graduate, Durk had been
working successfully to recruit college graduates for

the New York police. He, too, had become concerned about the demoralizing effects of corruption within police ranks.

Serpico and Durk began contacting officials in the department who had the power and the responsibility to investigate departmental corruption. But nothing happened, and Serpico particularly became mistrustful of his superiors. He feared that they would not back him up in his allegations, and he was under no illusion about the risk he took in making his information known.

As months went by and no action was taken, Durk arranged a meeting with Jay Kriegel, special counsel to Mayor Lindsay on police matters. He and Serpico asked that their identity not be disclosed and that the mayor, whom they offered to meet, not inform their superiors in the police department of the meeting. Reports of that offer vary, but the undisputed fact is that neither he nor Kriegel acted on their information.

The mayor later told the Knapp Commission that "I could not under any circumstances as mayor accept those ground rules. Police Commissioner Leary had been on board for a year and three months at this point. It would have undermined him totally. It would have been a signal to him of no confidence, and if I'd been a police commissioner under those circumstances I expect I'd have handed in my resignation. . . ."

Kriegel told the commission that he did not tell the mayor of Durk and Serpico's belief that the top police command was not acting on their allegations, because of their request for secrecy. Durk, however, said that Kriegel refused to act because it might stir up the police and implied that the city could not afford that with the possibility of summer riots near.

In spite of the official rebuffs, Serpico and Durk kept trying. Durk next went to see the person responsible for policing official misconduct, Commissioner of Investigation Arnold Fraiman. Fraiman barely listened to him and told Durk at one point that Serpico seemed to him a "psycho."

Finally, in October, 1967, a year after Serpico first stated his charges, the police department launched an investigation. Serpico and others believe that it did so only after officials learned that he had talked to Kriegel and Fraiman. That investigation led to indictments against nine patrolmen and one lieutenant. For Serpico it was a bitter victory because not one higher-ranking official was involved, which meant to him that the system of graft could continue relatively uninterrupted.

As a last resort, Serpico and Durk went to the press. The *New York Times* investigated their allegations and in May, 1970, published a long article on police corruption. Here at last they had found a lever that brought some response. Mayor Lindsay heard about the *Times* article one day before it was to be published and appointed a commission to study police misconduct. That body became the Knapp Commission, which during six months of hearings in late 1971 uncovered lengthy evidence of payoffs to police.

New York City Police Commissioner Patrick Murphy has praised Serpico's efforts as "the highest form of loyalty to . . . fellow officers." It is apt praise, particularly in view of Serpico's concern for the kinds of oppression to which patrolmen, in particular, are subject when their superiors encourage a system of corruption or simply close their eyes to it. However, others in the department, those who have most to fear from his allegations, have not been so generous. In February, 1971, Serpico was shot in the head by a narcotics pusher. While he was recovering in a hospital, he received a "get well" card signed "with sincere sympathy . . . that you didn't get your brains blown out, you rat bastard. Happy relapse."

Yet it is not his fellow policemen, it is his superiors against whom Serpico is most bitter. On the witness stand of the Knapp Commission, which called him to testify only after criticism by the newspapers, Serpico urged reform so that "police officers in the future will not experience the same frustration and anxiety that I was subjected to for the past five years at the hands of my superiors because of my attempt to report corruption."

Durk also told the commission why he and Serpico gave five years of their lives to reform their organization:

"We wanted to believe in the rule of law. We wanted

to believe in a system of responsibility. But those in high places everywhere, in the police department, in the D.A.'s office, in city hall, were determined not to enforce the law and they turned their heads when law and justice were being sold on every streetcorner.

"We wanted to serve others, but the department was a home for the drug dealers and thieves. The force that was supposed to be protecting people was selling poison to their children. And there could be no life, no real life for me or anyone else on the force when, every day, we had to face the facts of our own terrible corruption.

"I saw that happening to men all around me, men who could have been good officers, men of decent impulse, men of ideals, but men who were without decent leadership, men who were told in a hundred ways every day go along, forget the law, don't make waves, and shut up.

"So they did shut up. They did go along. They did learn the unwritten code of the department. They went along and they lost something very precious: they weren't cops anymore. They were a long way towards not being men any more."[7]

10. Gordon Rule and the Air Force

A ranking civilian procurement official in the Naval Material Command, Gordon Rule has publicly criticized Navy procurement practices on two separate occasions. Several years ago, he complained to procurement policy makers about the Navy's mishandling of the F–111B fighter contracts, which had resulted in enormous cost overruns. He later revealed the substance of his in-house criticisms in testimony before a subcommittee of the Joint Economic Committee.

For his efforts to protect the public purse, he was passed over for the Legion of Merit, which was awarded to several of his subordinates. The Navy subsequently reversed itself and granted him the Distinguished Service Medal. Rule also got a delayed promotion.

On May 24, 1971, he returned to the same joint committee and revealed that the Navy awarded two contractors $135.5 million in claims without determining whether the government was legally obligated to pay anything. One of the contractors was a subsidiary of the Lockheed Aircraft Corporation, then seeking a $250 million loan guarantee from the federal government. In response to a question from Senator Proxmire, Rule described the proposed guarantee as "most unwise." "If we do this for Lockheed," he said, "we're setting a precedent we'll never live down. . . . If their management is so lousy, let them go broke."

The Navy has taken no action against Rule as yet for his heretical statements.

11. John McGee and the Navy

John McGee, a civilian employee of the Navy, was serving as fuel inspector in Thailand when he became concerned that Navy procedures in handling Armed Forces fuel in Thailand were not providing adequate protection against theft. McGee's attempts to raise these issues with his superiors were frustrated. No one in the Navy, it appeared, was interested. So in March, 1968, he contacted Senator Proxmire's office.

Senator Proxmire instigated an investigation by the General Accounting Office that sustained McGee's allegations of laxity. The GAO found 5.5 million gallons of fuel in Thailand stolen or unaccounted for between January and October, 1967. The report was made public in January, 1969.

The immediate response of the Navy to McGee's allegations was to reprimand him, deny him a pay raise and threaten him with discharge. After Senator Proxmire intervened, however, the reprimand was withdrawn and McGee cleared of any charges.

Having weathered bureaucratic reprisals, McGee has now been promoted from a GS–11 to a GS–12. He is assigned to an interim project office in Pensacola, Florida.[8]

12. Ronald Ridenhour and My Lai

An Army enlisted man left the service to investigate and reveal an incident that led to one of the most sustained examinations of Army procedures in this

century, the My Lai massacre. Ronald Ridenhour pieced
together the My Lai story with information from fellow soldiers in Vietnam. He disclosed the information
through extensive correspondence with Department of
Defense officials, members of the House Armed Services
Committee and other congressmen seven months before
the tragedy became public knowledge.

The results—the inquiries, charges, and trials of
Army personnel who were responsible—are well known.
One of those involved, General Samuel Koster, who
commanded the unit which participated in the massacre
and received a demotion for his failure to thoroughly
investigate the incident, commented later that the only
difference between My Lai and many other similar
tragedies in Vietnam was Ronald Ridenhour.

13. Oscar Hoffman and the Navy

Not all whistle blowers in the military fare so well as
the preceding ones. Oscar Hoffman, a pipe fitter assigned to inspect pipes on ships under construction
for the Navy, did not. While working at Todd Shipyards in Seattle, Hoffman submitted to his Navy supervisor several reports on unsatisfactory work by the
contractor. On several occasions these reports were
rejected. Then Hoffman was ordered to destroy some
fifty of his reports. He refused.

When Navy management learned that Hoffman was
planning to file a grievance to correct the conditions,
they retaliated with a reprimand. Despite a ruling by a
Navy hearing officer that the reprimand was improper,
the Navy did not return Hoffman to his former duties
but sent him to Tacoma, Washington, to monitor the
construction of a ferry boat. Having formally assigned
him to Tacoma, the Navy proceeded to abolish his job.
Hoffman was fired through a "reduction in force."

The Navy lieutenant who had rejected Hoffman's
reports and then improperly issued a reprimand was
promoted to lieutenant commander.

Stymied in his attempts to protect the taxpayer and
resolve his difficulties with the Navy, Hoffman informed
Senator Proxmire and the Joint Economic Committee
of the shoddy work he had observed. Then later events

proved that had his criticism been heeded earlier, the taxpayer could indeed have been saved huge sums and Navy personnel would have avoided unnecessary risks. One of the ships constructed by Todd Shipyards during the period when Hoffman was attempting to call attention to unsatisfactory welds suffered damage from fire while anchored in Hawaii. Investigation indicated that a number of welds in the piping were faulty.

Despite an (otherwise) unblemished record, Hoffman has been unable to find a position with any other Navy command. He is currently pursuing legal actions seeking reinstatement.[9]

14. Kenneth S. Cook and the Air Force

Kenneth S. Cook was an Air Force weapons analyst assigned to Holloman Air Force Base in New Mexico. A highly educated and competent physicist,[10] Cook complained in 1966 that Lieutenant Colonel Roderick W. Clarke, Acting Commanding Officer, was distorting scientific reports of the defense against intercontinental ballistic missiles and exaggerating claims for the effectiveness of defense systems. Cook was highly disturbed by what he saw as a lack of scientific honesty.

When Cook found that his pleas for incorporating the full pro-and-con analysis arguments in study reports were not heeded, he sent a confidential letter on November 2, 1966, to Brigadier General Ernest Pinson, Commanding General of the Office of Aerospace Research at the Pentagon. In the letter he stated his charges of information manipulation.

On November 22, 1966, Cook was called in by his commanding officer, who informed him that he had a copy of Cook's "confidential" letter to General Pinson. What followed was a Kafkaesque nightmare. Cook's top-secret security clearance was summarily removed without explanation. Then he was ordered to submit to an examination by military medical personnel. According to Cook, the most vehement of the latter was a psychologist who was deputy commander of the NASA "monkey lab." Then, before a military medical panel where he was not permitted legal counsel, he was found mentally and physically incapable of performing further service for the Air Force or elsewhere within the government.

Cook's attempts to alter the verdict or simply to present the testimony of his own doctors were futile. His only recourse from the Air Force's action was the Civil Service Commission, which upheld the decision in a hearing at which neither Cook nor his representatives were permitted to be present. Lieutenant Colonel Paul Grissom, consultant in psychiatry and neurology in the Office of the Surgeon General, stated that the action was an injustice. Two lieutenant colonels and colleagues of Cook at Holloman gave testimony to the Civil Service Commission that it was one of the worst examples of getting rid of an employee. Their efforts were to no avail.

Cook's case is now being pursued by the American Civil Liberties Union and may become a test case in protecting the rights of whistle blowers who simply appeal privately to their superior's superior.

Cook's suit was filed in August, 1969, against the Air Force and Civil Service Commission, challenging the finding of his incompetence and the procedure which allowed him no hearing or means of defending himself. One of the primary facets of the case, which Cook is trying to challenge, is a provision in the Civil Service Code that the authority of the Civil Service Commission is final in such mental disability retirement cases.

Having been declared incompetent, Cook cannot find work. Now residing in Alexandria, Virginia, he spends all of his time researching his case and offering help to Congress in exposing incompetence in military research and development studies.

15. Peter Gall and HEW

The firing of Leon Panetta, director of the Office of Civil Rights in the Department of Health, Education, and Welfare, was met with unprecedented protest within HEW.[11] One of those concerned was Peter Gall, a special assistant to Panetta for press relations. Gall had long been troubled by the administration's vacillation on civil rights policy. He admired Panetta, who he felt was attempting to follow firm guidelines in enforcing Title VI of the Civil Rights Act, and felt that his dismissal compromised the administration.

Shortly after Panetta's dismissal was announced on February 17, 1970, HEW employees began to let the administration know their views. Within a few weeks a petition with close to two thousand signatures was presented to Secretary Finch, protesting the government's position on school desegregation. As a result, Finch promised to meet with employees and discuss the department's position on civil rights.

Other employees felt that stronger measures were called for and were not content to let the matter rest with HEW. Gall joined with a number of HEW employees in drafting a letter to President Nixon expressing their dismay over the action. (The letter was signed by 125 employees.) But he soon concluded that he could not remain a spokesman for a civil rights policy —or nonpolicy—that he opposed. He would have to resign.

Gall and Paul Rilling, an HEW regional director in Atlanta who also felt he could not stay with the department, decided to coordinate their departures and publicize their protest by issuing their letters of resignation to the press. They did so on March 3, the same day that the employees' letter was delivered to the White House. In his letter to Secretary Finch, Gall said, "I cannot any longer try to justify to the public the actions of this Administration regarding either the subject of civil rights generally, or its treatment of your Office for Civil Rights in particular."

Writing later in the *Washington Monthly*, Gall noted that "the protests in HEW raise a crucially important— although perhaps ultimately unanswerable—question: What is the correct balance between a bureaucrat's right under the First Amendment to express his views as a citizen and his obligation to follow the policies of his seniors, especially that senior of seniors, the President?"

His own answer was that a direct protest—in this case an employee's letter addressed to the President— is entirely justifiable. To do it quietly, without press coverage, as some employees suggested, would "have been a waste of everyone's time. . . . There was every reason to believe that the letter would not even have come to the attention of the President if it had been dropped off quietly at the White House mail room."

In similar fashion, he felt that a statement to the press on his own resignation gave force and meaning to his dissent.

Gall is now writing a book with Panetta about civil rights in the Nixon administration.[12]

16. Interior Department Dissenters

The Environmental Quality Act of 1970 requires that every federal agency file a public "environmental impact statement" before taking or approving any action that might substantially affect the environment. The purpose of the statement is to encourage thorough agency consideration of the ecological consequences of a plan and to provide more thorough public scrutiny of agency actions.

When the Trans-Alaska oil pipeline was proposed, the Interior Department was required to prepare and file such a statement. The draft statement finally drawn up painted a glowing picture of the pipeline and downplayed or omitted references to some of the potential environmental risks of the pipeline construction and operation.

Certain employees in the department's Bureau of Land Management were outraged by the proposed statement, which they saw as seriously deficient, particularly in view of information which they knew was available to the department.

Washington columnist Jack Anderson received from environmentalist sources a copy of a Bureau of Land Management memorandum that clearly spelled out the risks to the Alaskan environment which Interior spokesmen had publicly discredited. Anderson published excerpts of the memorandum, but Interior refused to make it available until Congressman Les Aspin (D., Wis.) published a copy in the *Congressional Record*.

The Department of Interior now maintains that it is rethinking its position on the pipeline. The whistle blowers remain unidentified.

The "leaked" memo has become a time-honored tactic for Washington bureaucrats to express their dissatisfaction with the policies of an administration, and for an administration to float trial balloons to test public reaction without risking criticism. Syndicated columnists such as Jack Anderson, and before him Drew Pearson, rely heavily on this form of insider expression to give their readers insights into the functioning of government, though Anderson is rarely the instrument of an "official" leak. The pervasiveness of the phenomenon has led some commentators to suggest that the practice may play an accepted role in molding opinion and in shaping policy.[13]

17. Health Employees for Change and the Public Health Service

In December, 1970, President Nixon signed the Lead-based Poison Prevention Act, a measure his administration had vigorously opposed. He failed, however, to mention the act in his first health message to the Ninety-first Congress and also failed to request appropriations for implementation of the act in his budget message.

By May, 1971, it had become clear to many concerned doctors and medical professionals in the Public Health Service that the administration would seek little if any funding for the lead-poisoning prevention program. Many felt that an unprecedented public break with the administration was the only hope of heading off this move. On May 10, 1971, a group calling itself "Health Employees for Change" (HEC) released to the press a position paper criticizing their agency and the President for continued foot-dragging on the appropriations. Their statement began:

> In spite of the Administration's concern for prevention and health maintenance, there has been little support for action programs to deal with a clearly preventable disease that kills hundreds and leaves thousands of children with some form of measurable brain damage each year: Lead Poisoning.[14]

HEC was not merely an ad hoc attempt to meet the crisis of May, 1971. One hundred or more young

physicians and health professionals within the Public
Health Service had been holding open, informal meetings for several years to discuss various aspects of
administration and PHS health policy. All employees,
including superiors at every level, were welcomed.
Members of the group prepared discussion papers on
various topics for consideration at the open meetings.
Though discussions often involved sharp criticism of
the status quo within the agency, no attempt was made
to seek publicity or involve outsiders.

In the lead poisoning issue, HEC spokesmen tried to
elicit a response from the administration and the agency
to what they considered reasonable, nonemotional
criticism by professionals who had been hired to do
more than shuffle papers and follow orders. But their
efforts—like those by professionals and citizens outside the agency—proved futile. "Going public" was
their last resort.

By coincidence, the HEC statement was released
one day before the President announced a massive
federal commitment to seek a cure for cancer. The
administration proposed $330 million in the first year
for a separate cancer research organization. In contrast, the administration announced a month later that
it would request $2 million for lead poisoning preven-
tion for fiscal year 1972.[15] (New York City's existing
program alone is funded at $2.4 million.)

HEC members are by no means certain that their
efforts won even these paltry sums. But they believe
they were able to call attention to the situation to
powerful voices outside the administration who will
not remain silent on the issue in the future.

Asked whether their open criticism of the President's
health program has led to reprisals, one active member of Health Employees for Change commented,
"None at all. But worse, we had the strange feeling
that no one really cared." A number of high-level
administrators wrote off the criticism to a few "two-
year docs," commissioned Public Health Service officers
with only a two-year commitment to the agency, he
said. But this is not the case, according to HEC acti-
vists. Only about one-quarter to one-third of the professionals involved were "short-timers." Many were

older physicians and professionals with a clear career stake in what is happening at PHS.

It is too early to judge the ultimate effect of Health Employees for Change. One outsider—a doctor and former Public Health Service officer—believes that the service is one of the most exciting places in the federal health establishment because of their efforts. As for administration response to date, the only substantiated reaction has been a flurry of "memo-rattling" by mid-level managers who may be threatened by the new voices.

18. Dr. Robert S. McCleery and FDA

In December, 1968, the National Academy of Sciences completed a study of twenty-eight hundred drugs that had entered the market between 1932 and 1962. Its findings were startling. Medical experts agreed that certain drugs were dangerous and should be removed from the market immediately.

The study was commissioned by the Food and Drug Administration, which is responsible for protecting the public from hazardous and ineffective drugs. But instead of moving to follow the report's recommendations, the FDA began a long and tedious series of consultations—many of them with drug companies. It became obvious to some FDA staff members that it would be months or years before action was taken, even on drugs reportedly most hazardous.

Among the concerned staff was Dr. Robert S. McCleery, special assistant for medical communication. As he said later, "FDA's methods for getting drugs off the market were influenced by political and economic factors which, in my judgment, had no place in matters of such serious scientific and public concern."

In February, 1969, convinced that the agency needed prodding from the outside as well as from within, Dr. McCleery resigned.

He did not blow the whistle publicly—for the obvious reason that a one-day announcement by a little known government employee would have minimal effect. Instead, he chose to "try to make the system work."

First, he went to the House Intergovernmental Relations Subcommittee headed by Congressman L. H. Fountain (D., N. C.). The committee had long been aware of FDA's effectiveness, or lack of it. McCleery was able to give Congressman Fountain enough additional information to convince him to hold hearings on the question of removal of dangerous drugs.

McCleery helped organize the hearings as a member of the subcommittee staff from February to October, 1969. As a result, the FDA's methods for dealing with drug hazards, as well as the study by the National Academy of Sciences, became a matter of public record.

Unfortunately, according to McCleery, the FDA did not appreciably change its methods even after extensive congressional scrutiny. So McCleery went a step further. He helped prepare a law suit against the FDA, asking the court to order the agency to take antibiotic combinations, such as Parke-Davis's Panalba, off the market. Medical experts were virtually unanimous in judging these drugs to be hazards.

In June, 1970, a suit was filed in federal district court by the National Council of Senior Citizens and two public health officers. That suit is still pending.

McCleery also wrote a sharply critical report of quality control within the medical profession, *One Life —One Physician*, while working for the Center for Study of Responsive Law. The report was issued in the fall of 1970.

McCleery is a whistle blower through the system. Rather than take his case directly to the public, he went to the institutions that are supposed to check abuses of executive power, the Congress and the courts. As his experience suggests—and as he himself says—this kind of whistle blowing is often not enough by itself. The system in this case has gone nearly three years without responding fully to a disclosure of imminent public hazards.

19. Dr. Harvey Minchew and FDA

Another FDA staff member chose another route on the same issue. Dr. B. Harvey Minchew resigned as acting director of FDA's Bureau of Medicine in May, 1969, when he became convinced that the agency was not responding adequately to the drug hazards detailed in the National Academy of Sciences report. A memo he wrote to his superiors in March urging immediate action had been ignored, as had other informal efforts. Soon after his departure, he helped investigative reporters get the story to the public.

20. Philip I. Ryther and the FAA

Philip I. Ryther was a twenty-six-year veteran of government service when he was forced into early retirement as evaluation chief of the Federal Aviation Administration. The reprisal followed Ryther's efforts to establish stricter regulations of air charter planes.

Ryther had filed a report severely critical of air charter abuses and the applicable FAA regulations six months before the air crash of a chartered plane snuffed out the lives of the Wichita State University football team on October 2, 1970. His immediate superior held up the report for five weeks. Ryther then by-passed channels and contacted the deputy administrator, who indicated that he was unimpressed. The administrator of the agency refused to answer his inquiries and indicated through subordinates that he had no comment on the report.

Seven weeks after filing his report, Ryther was called on the carpet at a special meeting of his superiors for ignoring proper channels. Ryther responded that between the date of his report and the meeting at least 170 persons had been killed in accidents in general aviation, eventualities he had warned against in his report.

On August 19 eleven pages of "charges" were filed against him, including charges that he spent $5.25 for a dinner a year earlier, missed two hours of work (on a day when he was involved in a five-car accident on his way to work), and initialed his own time card rather than leaving it to the authorized clerk. He was subsequently promised that the charges would be dropped if he resigned.

Ryther's "retirement" was approved on October 2, 1970, the day of the Wichita State disaster. He insists that the plane would not have crashed had the recommendations of his report been adopted. Many of them were implemented three-and-a-half weeks after the crash. Ryther did not reveal his story to the press until after he left the FAA.

21. Dr. X

Dr. X is a government inspector, one of those "forgotten men of the consumer movement" who stand at the precise point where industry and bureaucratic pressures are likely to meet. A veterinarian, Dr. X was the inspector in charge of a federally inspected poultry plant. He had a reputation in the inspection service of being "tough on the plants" and of supporting the inspectors under him.

Conditions in the plant to which Dr. X was assigned were far from ideal. At one point he estimated that forty-eight percent of the birds leaving the plant were contaminated. Even his superiors referred to it as a problem plant. But when new plant management was installed, conditions began to deteriorate even further. The new management, inexperienced and openly hostile to the inspection service, began to threaten to oust Dr. X, who doggedly listed all violations and discrepancies and made every effort to have them corrected.

In the fall of 1970, Dr. X's immediate superior in the inspection force removed his right to control the speed of plant production, as unnecessary to insure a wholesome product. The move not only limited Dr. X's ability to improve conditions but also undermined his authority with plant managers. Dr. X felt his authority could not be maintained without the support of his superiors. He also believed that the production issue should be brought to the attention of Ralph Nader. He sent letters to Mr. Nader and Mrs. Virginia Knauer, the President's consumer advisor, describing conditions in the plant.

In December, 1970, grossly substandard conditions forced Dr. X to request that the plant slow the speed of the production line. The plant managers refused and proceeded to run several thousand pounds of birds they knew would be unsalable. Although the regional office of the Consumer and Marketing Service agreed that Dr. X had acted properly, they rewarded him with a notice in January, 1971, that he would be transferred.

The handling of Dr. X's letter to Mrs. Knauer is a classic illustration of bureaucratic response to criticism. After some delay, Mrs. Knauer's office forwarded the substance of Dr. X's charges (but not his name) to the administrator of the Consumer and Marketing Service of the Department of Agriculture. The administrator then referred the charges to the regional office with jurisdiction over Dr. X's plant. Early one morning Dr. X was visited by the USDA officer in charge who asked him to respond to (his own) charges about the plant! Dr. X restated the need for improvement in the plant and suggested that the way to accomplish this was to support inspectors in the field.

The final irony came when the administrator of the Consumer and Marketing Service replied to Mrs. Knauer's letter by informing her that the service had transferred the plant inspector—the very individual who had raised the issues. Later Mrs. Knauer's office sent the Consumer and Marketing Service a perfunctory letter informing them that the complaint had been lodged by the very plant inspector whose removal the service felt "solved" the problem.

The Public Interest Research Group of Washington is assisting Dr. X in challenging his transfer and has provided an attorney to represent the inspector in administrative procedures in the Department of Agriculture. The Group believes that Dr. X's case involves not only important issues of consumer protection and the integrity of USDA's meat and poultry inspection service, but also basic questions about the support to which whistle blowers are entitled when they insist on doing their job properly.

III

Prescriptions for Change

16

The Corporation

There is more law today running in favor of individual rights in the armed services than there is in any of our major corporate communities. I see no reason why the industrial army should not be at least as democratic as the other one. In fact, there is no good reason in the world why The People should not participate generally in the processes of our private governments.
—David Bazelon in *Paper Economy*, 1963

The men and women featured in this book are full-time citizens. When they went to work for large organizations they did not trade one set of responsibilities for another—they merely added their duties as employees to those they felt as citizens. And at critical moments under compelling circumstances, they chose to be citizens first and employees second. This is what whistle blowing is all about.

How should and how can our legal system, our corporations, and our government respond to the citizen-employee? One way, of course, is to ignore him; another, to suppress and punish him. But if the whistle blowers treated here have one thing in common, it is that they cannot—indeed, they will not—be ignored. Suppression must also be self-defeating in the long run for the organizations that practice it. It will make martyrs of its victims, it will enrage their allies within and outside the organization, it will discourage internal self-correction, and it will stifle the very qualities that make for an effective and loyal employee. Under such conditions, self-renewal for the organization itself becomes highly improbable.

The corporation and organizations of employees that represent or purport to represent corporate employees —professional societies and labor unions—are in the best position to respond to the challenge of citizen-employees. Each organization should freely experiment with different approaches consistent with its own needs and the needs of its members. Since professional societies frequently compete among themselves and with labor unions for members, and since corporations frequently compete with each other for the best talent, it is to the interest of each to develop wise and beneficial approaches. Finally, professional societies, unions, and corporations, if we are to believe their leaders and apologists, should be sufficiently flexible to make the kinds of changes necessary to accommodate this new type of citizen-employee.

Professional societies should reformulate their codes of ethics to make them relevant to the employment relationship as well as to the client-professional relationship. The Code of Professional Responsibility of the American Bar Association, for example, does not directly deal with the lawyer who is employed on a full-time basis by a corporation. The explanatory notes to the code do suggest that when he gives business advice, the lawyer who is "house counsel" is subject to different obligations. But it does not explain how business advice differs from legal advice, nor does it suggest what the lawyers' obligations are when business and legal advice are inextricably mixed together. And the two are often indivisible. The distinction is critical to the internal logic of the code, since *all* lawyers, whether serving one employer-client or a number of clients, are required to "exercise independent judgment". One resolution to this dilemma would be to impose duties on *employers* as well as on employed lawyers. The American Association of University Professors (AAUP) does precisely that to preserve academic tenure for its members. Institutions which do not provide procedures to protect or which do not in fact protect the academic independence of faculty members are subject to censure. AAUP can in turn significantly limit the ability of the institution to recruit the teachers it wants.[1] Professional societies could establish similar mechanisms to censure employers that ignore the ethical obligations of society members.

Professional societies should establish independent appeal procedures for corporately employed members who have exhausted whatever procedures are available in the corporation. Similarly, they could offer to arbitrate disputes when the corporation is unable or unwilling to provide any internal mechanism for dealing fairly with dissent. If a firm refuses arbitration, the society should nevertheless proceed to make a determination and to make its decision public. Independent appeals procedures could complement the type of internal due process that enlightened corporate managers should establish. Unfortunately too many of these societies are either so subservient[2] to industry or so involved in defining their own identity that it is unlikely that these changes will occur in the absence of vigorous efforts by individual members.

Societies should also intervene on behalf of members involved in controversies over the application of their professional ethics. Charles Pettis reports that the American Society of Civil Engineers, through its executive director, has attempted to clear his name with potential employers. When a professional's dispute becomes a matter of public concern, the society should intervene, whether or not it is requested to do so, at least to the extent of offering its services as a reasonably disinterested but expert referee. And societies should actively seek employment for members fired for behaving ethically.

Few societies have become involved in legislative controversies unless broad "pocketbook" interests of members are at stake. Of the major engineering societies, only the National Society of Professional Engineers engages in any extensive lobbying effort. The other societies could, if they chose, organize separate lobbying arms and still preserve their own preferred tax status. They could promote legislation to protect members from employer retaliation for obedience to the law. A scientist who refuses to file a false report with a federal regulatory agency should not be forced to pay for his employer's attempted misconduct by involuntarily giving up his livelihood. Likewise, an engineer who reports an employer's illegal conduct to "appropriate authorities," as he must under the NSPE code of ethics when that conduct threatens public health or safety, ought to be protected from retaliatory firing, demotion, or transfer. The government agency authorized to prevent the illegal conduct can also be given the power to penalize a vindictive employer and to order compensation for the employee. But agencies will not be given additional authority unless groups that purport to represent the interests of engineers and other professionals demand that legislatures grant it.

Societies could contribute to other legislative efforts as well. For example, those with members employed by large corporations ought to be leading the fight to require that pensions "vest"[3] early and that pension rights be transferable from one employer to another. The fear of losing a pension is one of the invisible chains that limit an employee's freedom to speak out or refuse to do work that might wantonly imperil others. The American Chemical Society (ACS) has been trying to organize a central pension fund for members much like the one that college teachers enjoy. They have met stiff opposition from large corporations that employ chemists and from the pension fund industry. Since employer participation (voluntary or not) is essential to the success of such a fund, the society could alternatively compel by statute the same result. At this writing the ACS has given no serious consideration to throwing down the gauntlet with such verve. If ACS continues to hesitate, older chemists, except those fortunate enough to be college teachers, will continue to be the indentured servants of their corporate masters, unable to dissent and unable to blow the whistle without fear of losing far more than current income.

Typical of the corporation's power to influence more than the salaries of its employees is its power to sever pension rights even after retirement. DuPont's pension plan, for example, allows the company to cancel a retired employee's rights to receive benefits if he has involved himself in "any activity harmful to the interest of the company." Such vague language cannot help but have a chilling effect on many forms of employee dissent and dissent by retired employees.

Finally, professional societies, especially those that have paid lip service to professional responsibility in the past, ought to investigate the extent of dissent and whistle blowing among their members. The American Society of Planning Officials (ASPO) recently published a study by staff member Earl Finkler entitled *Dissent and Independent Initiative in Planning Offices.*[4] Finkler surveyed planning office directors as well as staff members to come up with the first comprehensive inquiry into dissent in his profession. He explored attitudes, put together five case studies based on real controversies, and developed tentative guidelines for dissent for both employers and employees. ASPO is to be commended for sponsoring such a study. But its executive director, Israel Stollman, apparently tried to dissociate the society from Finkler's effort. In an unprecedented "dissent" to the report, he wrote, "The normal path of internal review for each PAS [Planning Advisory Service] report that we issue produces staff agreement on its content. The report remains an individual statement of the author but falls within a broad range of ASPO policies and views. This report by Earl Finkler does not entirely fall within this broad range." Whether ASPO uses the Finkler study as the basis for further inquiry and action is highly problematical. If it does not, it will have missed an opportunity that few other societies have had for concrete action to protect dissenters.

Labor unions are sometimes cited as the ideal alternative to both new legal protections for whistle blowers and to internal channels for free employee expression. In theory the union may, through the collective bargaining process, demand both substantive rights to protest work that threatens the public and procedural devices for a fair hearing when those rights are asserted. In practice, this potential has been neglected. First, according to union spokesmen, collective bargaining agreements today simply do not prohibit discharge and other forms of retaliation for protests directed against company policies and practices other than those traditionally associated with pay scales, work rules, retirement benefits, and job classification. Article 14, Section 1 of the United Auto Workers contract with

Ford, for example, specifically reserves all "designing" and "engineering" questions to management. Second, grievance procedures have not been considered appropriate forums for challenging the work product as well as working conditions. UAW officials, for example, agreed with Edward Gregory on the carbon monoxide leakage problem, but took action only on the issue of whether or not his transfer was authorized under the collective bargaining agreement. The *real* reason for his transfer, his persistent complaints about safety defects in the automobiles he was assigned to inspect, were considered by the union beyond its authority. Third, unions traditionally have been mesmerized by bread-and-butter issues to the exclusion of others. Some of the professional unions affiliated with the AFL-CIO, however, have recently expressed an interest in pursuing noneconomic concerns of professional employees. They have a significant self-interested motivation, of course, since professionals have resisted collective bargaining as a threat to their status as professionals. If professional societies continue to avoid the issue of professional independence for their employed members, unions will have a growing appeal, especially to younger professional employees. Several professional unions have successfully organized new bargaining units by convincing potential members that collective bargaining is the only effective means to make ethical norms and professional autonomy integral elements of the employment relationship. Representatives of the American Federation of State, County, and Municipal Employees told the authors that younger professionals in government service have been amazingly responsive to this approach.

Until the trade union movement rejects management's tendency to view employees—professional as well as nonprofessional—as obedient cogs and moral neuters rather than as responsible citizens, workers will be unable, for example, to object publicly to unsafe products, environmental hazards, and fraudulent sales practices without fear of retaliation. The experience of steelworker Gilbert Pugliese demonstrates that in the absence of strong pressures from the membership, unions, or at least their local leaders, are not likely to come to the immediate aid of a single embattled member.[5] On June 5, 1969, Pugliese refused to pump any more oil into the Cuyahoga River from the Cleveland plant of the Jones and Laughlin Steel Corporation. The Cuyahoga River, one of the most polluted rivers in America, has been officially described by the city of Cleveland as a "fire hazard." Jones and Laughlin was under pressure from pollution abatement officials at the time and declined to make an issue of Pugliese's refusal. He did not receive a similar order until July 14, 1971. Pugliese, fifty-nine years old with eighteen-year seniority and six years away from pensioned retirement, adamantly refused. The only union official nearby, the assistant chief grievance official, tried to persuade him to follow orders and file a protest later. But Pugliese refused and was suspended for five days for breach of discipline with the strong likelihood that he would be fired at the end of that period.

Pugliese then called everyone he could think of to get action. But he got no response from the pollution agencies nor from the local media. Finally, a former news reporter put in a few calls on his behalf. By the end of the next day he had become a *cause célèbre* in Cleveland and beyond. He was told by a fellow worker, "This puts the union on the spot and they've got to do something now after all the publicity." On the next day other workers were threatening a wildcat strike unless Pugliese received his job back. The union's chief grievance official immediately returned from Washington— he was attending the second week of industry-wide negotiations with the steel companies — and Pugliese's grievance began moving through regular channels. By the afternoon of the second day, Pugliese had been reinstated with pay. When he returned to work on Saturday, July 17, the company was installing drums and pumps to dispose of the oil. Ironically, this was precisely the method he had recommended when he first refused to pour the oil into the river in June, 1969.

Corporations, if they are as flexible, adaptive, and innovative as they purport to be, should be able to accommodate the citizen-employee. Mack Hanan, managing director of Hanan and Son, a New York City management consulting firm specializing in long-term corporate planning, recently recommended that corporations for compelling reasons of self-interest adopt their own "bill of rights for employees" to deal with what he describes as "the new organization man."[6] He writes that the best of the new organization men and women —"the very ones who are most able to help their companies grow—are being lost by businesses which appear reluctant to adjust to the new realities." In the meantime these men and women "see the corporation as having an arbitrary kind of power over individual employees that is unmatched in the rest of the real world because there is no recourse from its exercise and no appeal from its verdicts."

Hanan's proposed bill of rights would emphasize "the free expression of personal beliefs of a social, economic, or political nature within or without the confines of the corporation" rather than rights to object to company policy or action. Its adoption would represent a significant breach in the love-it-or-leave-it philosophy of employment. This would certainly be true if some of Hanan's other recommendations were also adopted. He suggests, for instance, the appointment of an internal ombudsman to whom employees can present complaints. Hanan's ombudsman would be authorized to intervene on behalf of the employee and, most importantly, to dramatize and publicize *outside the corporation* complaints that do not receive proper management attention. Given the present attitudes of top managers, it might also be necessary to adopt a special bill of rights, legally enforceable, for the truly committed ombudsman. No internal mechanism can operate unless last-resort appeals to the outside are explicitly recognized *and* protected.

The corporate ombudsman is not a new proposal. Isidore Silver, writing in the *Harvard Business Review* in 1967, provided a detailed plan for just such a company watchdog based on the experience of various countries with governmental ombudsmen. Silver's corporate ombudsman for employees would be on the staff of the president of the company but would have to be independent and not merely another management functionary. "In corporate terms," writes Silver, "he must have a long-term contract at substantial pay."[7] He points out that other forms of grievance review—for example, "open door" policies providing access to top executives and multi-step personnel office appeals—are totally inadequate to ensure justice or to serve even the corporation's interest.

Many of the proposals of Hanan and Silver are worthy of immediate adoption by giant corporations and by other large organizations, including labor unions, as initial steps in the right direction. They can not be passed off as stopgap public relations gimmicks to pacify restive managers and professionals. The concerns which manifest themselves in whistle blowing will not fade away. Organizations which ignore them or which attempt to suppress them will.

The Xerox Corporation recently announced a program to grant selected employees—28,500 of its 38,000 United States employees are eligible—leaves of absence to work on "social welfare projects."[8] This is a promising new approach which should be watched closely by other large corporations. The crunch will come, however, if one or more employees become involved in projects that Xerox management believes to be in conflict with company policy—or if, for instance, an employee who may have a reputation within the company for complaining about in-plant pollution at one of Xerox's manufacturing facilities seeks a sabbatical to join an occupational safety and health research group. Xerox may certainly assert the right to avoid such situations as a matter of policy. But if it does, it will severely limit one of the most imposing aspects of the program —its explicit recognition that citizenship is not something that can be held in abeyance during the work day or subordinated to the interests of a powerful employer.

17

The Government

Most of what has already been said about the interaction between employee organizations and corporations applies with equal force to the interaction of the
same organizations with government. Since government
employees do not generally have the right to strike,
however, and since the civil service system purports to
take the place of any need for militant unions or com-
bative professional societies, government employees
are in a different situation. Accordingly, their organizations would be expected to adopt slightly different
strategies. What changes are or should be forthcoming
in government employer-employee relationships?

The Pickering case, decided by the Supreme Court
in 1968,[1] validated the proposition that the government-
as-employer does not have the same freedom to control
employee behavior as the corporation-as-employer, even
when its employees act or speak in ways contrary to
certain governmental policies. The Court said that a
school board could not fire a teacher who had written
a letter critical of the board to a local newspaper. Even
Justice William H. Rehnquist, who feels that the "government is entitled to demand at least a large part of
the same personal loyalty owed by any employee to
his employer," has recognized that the Supreme Court's
opinion in the Pickering case requires that public employees be allowed to exercise at least part of their
First Amendment right of free speech against the government.[2] The still unresolved constitutional question
is no longer *whether* the public employee is free to
criticize his or her employer, but *how much* freedom he
has.

Any government agency, of course, can grant more freedom to its employees than the Constitution requires it to give as a minimum, whatever that minimum is finally determined to be. Congress, the state legislatures, the various civil service commissions, and government agencies are therefore free to move well beyond the Pickering case.

Ernest Fitzgerald had framed and hung on the wall of his office in the Department of the Air Force the following Code of Ethics for Government Service:

Any person in Governmental service should:

Put loyalty to the highest moral principles and to country above loyalty to persons, party, or Government department.

Uphold the Constitution, laws, and legal regulations of the United States and of all governments therein and never be a party to their evasion.

Give a full day's labor for a full day's pay, giving to the performance of his duties his earnest effort and best thought.

Seek to find and employ more efficient and economical ways of getting tasks accomplished.

Never discriminate unfairly by the dispensing of special favors or privileges to anyone, whether for remuneration or not; and never accept, for himself or his family, favors or benefits under circumstances which might be construed by reasonable persons as influencing the performance of his governmental duties.

Make no private promises of any kind binding upon the duties of office, since a Governmental employee has no private word which can be binding on public duty.

Engage in no business with the Government, either directly or indirectly, which is inconsistent with the conscientious performance of his governmental duties.

Never use any information coming to him confidentially in the performance of governmental duties as a means for making private profits.

Expose corruption wherever discovered.

Uphold these principles, ever conscious that public office is a public trust.

(This Code of Ethics was agreed to by the House of Representatives and the Senate as House Concurrent Resolution 175 in the Second Session of the 85th Congress. The Code applies to all Government Employees and Office Holders.)

As the notation indicates, this code is not the product of wishful thinking by malcontents in the bureaucracy. It expresses the will of Congress that civil servants be more than mindless and amoral automatons. Unfortunately the Congress did not provide penalties for violations of the code. It is merely a strong admonition to all concerned. But if it were applied vigorously and if it were accompanied by rigorous action on behalf of employees, the code would legitimize ethical whistle blowing as an instrument of policy influenced and directed by employees acting as citizens.

THE NEED FOR OMBUDSMEN

Government agencies should encourage internal dissent and internal whistle blowing up through the hierarchy as an early warning system for abuses and as a means of spotting operational deficiencies otherwise shielded by layers of bureaucracy. And they should go further: They should establish employee ombudsmen empowered to go public with an employee's protest if the agency fails to listen. The Code of Ethics for Government Service requires, in effect, that *each* civil servant serve as an ombudsman for the public interest. If he is blocked within the agency he has no choice—if he is to act consistently with the code—but to go outside the agency.

In April, 1971, Secretary of the Navy John H. Chafee wrote Admiral Bernard A. Clarey, president of the Flag Selection Board, which selects captains for promotion to rear admiral:

> I would hope that you would select a few iconoclasts—original, provocative thinkers who would stimulate the Navy to constantly re-examine its premises and whose selection would encourage those in the lower ranks to do likewise, with the realization that they are not just tolerated but in fact welcomed.[3]

The difficulty, perhaps not fully comprehended by the Secretary, is that candidates for these iconoclast slots are likely to have been weeded out in the lower ranks. Oscar Hoffman, whose tale is recounted in Chapter 15, was a civilian employee of the same Navy out of which Chafee expects his provocative admirals to emerge.

At least one federal agency, the Manpower Administration in the Department of Labor, has developed an internal whistle blowing mechanism for spotting "questionable activities" that may involve fraud, criminal malfeasance, gross mismanagement, and conflicts of interest. The Special Review Staff of the Assistant Secretary for Manpower solicits reports from any person within the agency, from top to bottom, and intervenes selectively to correct serious problems at any level. A spokesman for the staff told one of the authors, "We do our best to convince everyone that brownie points are gained by freely surfacing problems and requesting assistance in their solution, and not by trying to cover up and ending with a larger problem when the initial one erupts, as it almost inevitably does." The mandate of the Special Review Staff, which was created in a reorganization of the Manpower Administration in March, 1969,[4] does not extend to whistle blowing beyond the agency, nor is the staff in any sense independent of the assistant secretary, who also has line responsibility for the very situations the staff might uncover. It is still an important first step in assuring employee access to the highest levels within the agency.

An ideal internal agency ombudsman would include the following elements:

1) Its director and staff would be entirely independent of any other office or division within the agency.

2) Its director would report directly to the agency head and would be empowered to contact persons outside the agency, including those in other departments or branches of government, when the agency head refuses to listen or, without justification, takes no action.

3) The director and his staff should be insulated from the normal budgetary procedures. He should be able to go directly to Congress for his appropriations and he should be accountable solely to the legislature, much as the General Accounting Office today reports to and is accountable only to Congress.

4) The director should be appointed by Congress. Tenure should be protected and should be of suffi-

cient duration to insulate him or her from the partisan pressures of any one term of Congress. The director should be free to appoint his or her own staff.

5) The ombudsman should be empowered to intervene in any agency or civil service proceeding involving an employee of the agency against whom action has been taken in retaliation for communication with or support of the ombudsman's office.

6) The office should have complete access to all agency files and records with limitations on the disclosure of personnel or citizen files unless the individuals concerned consent to disclosure.

7) The ombudsman himself should be held accountable if he fails to perform his duty properly. Aggrieved employees might be given, for example, the right to seek judicial review if the ombudsman fails to act without just cause or if he acts in an arbitrary manner against the interests of the employee.

THE NEED FOR CIVIL SERVICE REFORM

Perhaps only a lawyer—or a civil servant who has been through the wringer—can appreciate the tortured logic of current civil service procedures. Originally designed to provide procedural safeguards for the employee, they make it difficult for the conscientious supervisor to discharge an incompetent and they unfairly burden the "troublemaker" who does his job too well and then tries to defend himself from harassment or worse.

The following is a rough outline of current procedures. Practices do differ from agency to agency, but these seem to be the predominant ones. An important distinction to keep in mind is the difference between "adverse" and "non-adverse" actions. "Non-adverse" actions involve agency actions that on paper at least are not directed against particular employees but rather involve reorganizations, staffing changes, office transfers, and the like that would theoretically apply to any person in the position. "Adverse" actions include the dismissal or demotion of particular individuals.

If the action taken against the employee is "non-adverse" under current regulations, he or she may request and will ordinarily be granted an informal meeting with the supervisor. At such an interview, and at most similar informal proceedings, the civil servant may or may not be accompanied by counsel or a witness, depending on the regulations of the particular agency or, in some cases, on the whim of the responsible official. If this meeting proves unsatisfactory, the employee may either seek a further informal meeting with the supervisor's superior or with some other higher official, or seek a formal consideration of his grievance. Ordinarily, at least one informal meeting is required before the grievance is considered by a grievance officer representing the head of the agency. Normally, an informal meeting is then arranged with the grievance officer, who, on the basis of this meeting, presents a formal recommendation to the agency head. If the grievance is denied in this recommendation, an appeal is usually open to the personnel officer of the full department under which the agency operates unless the agency is independent, in which case the appeal is to the agency's personnel officer.

The personnel officer may, at his discretion, grant a formal hearing, and may, again at his discretion, allow witnesses to testify and allow adverse witnesses to be cross-examined. The personnel officer then issues a final decision on the grievance under the signature of the agency head. The substance of this decision is *not* appealable to any other agency—including the Civil Service Commission—or to any court, though a "procedural" appeal is available to the Civil Service Commission if the employee feels his agency has failed to follow its own procedural rules.

In "adverse" action cases, the employee must be given thirty days notice of the action to be taken. He has the right to respond within five to ten days. His immediate supervisor can either reaffirm the proposed action, deny the merits of the response, or postpone the action for further consideration. The supervisor's original decision, which except in extraordinary cases is rarely modified at this early stage, may then be appealed to a higher level within the agency or to the Civil Service Commission. A specially designated hearing examiner presides at the agency hearing, and the employee has the right to counsel but does not have the right to an open hearing. If he has elected to appeal within the agency, he forfeits any appeal on the merits of his case to the Civil Service Commission, but may go directly to federal court if the agency action is upheld. Again, however, the Civil Service Commission, as in the case of "non-adverse" actions, may review procedural matters if the employee feels the agency has violated its own rules.

If he does decide to go to the Civil Service Commission rather than take his final appeal within the agency, he first goes to a hearing examiner, then to the Board of Appeals and Review, and finally, at their discretion, to the full commission. If the final decision at the commission is unsatisfactory he may then appeal to a federal district court.

These appeal processes appear to be unnecessarily complex and they are. They are time-consuming, expensive, and emotionally exhausting. And what is worse, in most agencies the original action—adverse or non-adverse—remains in effect until final disposition. Unless the employee has independent financial resources or the support of a wealthy private benefactor or organization while he is pursuing his remedies, his final victory will be a Pyrrhic one. Nevertheless, at any point in the process he may receive a favorable decision rendering further action unnecessary. And his opportunity for a fair hearing is immensely greater than that available to his corporately employed counterpart.

Under the Veterans Preference Act, veterans of the military services are entitled to special civil service review of certain "non-adverse" actions. Ernest Fitzgerald's is just such a case. Fitzgerald was not "fired"; rather, his job was abolished under an allegedly department-wide reorganization. This is not technically an adverse action, a consideration of little comfort to the person whose job is suddenly abolished in retaliation for speaking out. But Fitzgerald has already won an important legal victory which may be valuable in the more widely available appeal procedures. A federal district court has ordered that the hearing granted veterans under the Veterans Preference Act must be an open hearing to meet the due-process requirements of the Constitution.

In the absence of an unlikely revolution in the attitudes of the Civil Service Commission and the personnel management officials in the agencies of the federal government, the Civil Service Act should be amended and the commission reorganized. The reform should include safeguards for employees who are obliged for reasons of conscience or ethics to blow the whistle on agency action or inaction that threatens the health or safety of citizens or that involves fraud, corruption, gross mismanagement, or conflict of interest. Mechanisms to minimize potential abuses by whistle blowers would also be written into the law. A detailed discussion of the Civil Service System is beyond the scope of this book,[5] but a review of the experiences of employees whose stories are recounted here suggests a few of the needed reforms.

New legal rights. Civil servants should be given more substantive rights, and these rights should be written into law rather than left to the unlimited discretion of the various agencies. Under the present civil service regime, the few rights that employees have are "procedural": They have a right not to be fired without some form of appeal, but once into the appellate process management can defend almost any action on the grounds that it was "in the interest of the service." And management's own view of the interest of the service is not subject to serious challenge. The employee should have the right, for example, to complain about public health and safety hazards and to go outside established channels if those channels are closed or unavailing. Employees should likewise have the right, without fear of retaliation, to communicate with Senators and Representatives and with congressional committees. They should have the right to rely on the Code of Ethics for Government Service to justify their actions.

The widely held belief that government managers face insurmountable obstacles in discharging even incompetent personnel is a gross exaggeration. The procedural steps that must be taken to discharge someone are a deterrent to swift personnel actions in *routine* situations. Thus, if an incompetent or nonproductive employee can be ignored—if he does not pose a threat to the sovereignty of management—his work will often be assigned to someone else, or the manager will find some other way to work around him, and he will continue on the payroll. But the services of trouble-makers, especially those whose eagerness poses a personal threat to a supervisor or manager, can be and are easily terminated.

There is also a procedural gap in existing civil service law that tends to be of little or no concern to the ineffectual employee but that seriously hamstrings the defense of the employee who tries too hard and is discharged for it. Civil servants cannot subpoena witnesses to appear in any hearings that arise out of their discharge. They may thus be unable to get into the hearing record important matters bearing on their case. The lack of any subpoena power may also effectively prevent the appearance of favorable witnesses who would appear and testify if ordered but who might fear for their own jobs if they offered to appear voluntarily.

A special tribunal for employees. The Civil Service Commission and the personnel management offices of the various agencies should be divested of any responsibility for adjudicating disputes between employees and agency management. When these two responsibilities are placed in the same agency or office, conflicts of interest are inevitable. The commission or the personnel office must, in effect, represent the interests of management *and* see that the employee's rights against management are vindicated. All too often when the interests of management are weighed against the interests of a single employee the employee loses. This may be inevitable when the weighing is done by an agency or office that devotes substantial energy to representing the interests of management in personnel matters. One method of separating these two functions would be to establish an entirely separate administrative court for personnel matters. Its sole mission would be to investigate and decide issues arising between employees and agency management. Such a tribunal should be specifically empowered to challenge any assertion by management that a particular personnel action is in the interest of the service by requiring management to prove it.

Job protection during appeals. When an employee objects to a personnel action affecting his status, he should be privileged to continue in his current status pending a final decision on his case. Employees who attempt to overturn agency action against them either through the Civil Service Commission, through an agency's own employee appeals process, or in the courts may suffer the consequences of discharge during the entire appeals process. And all the steps of an appeal may take years. Thus even if an employee is reasonably certain he will someday be vindicated and receive all lost back pay, he may take no action because of the fear that he might not be able to support his family in the interim.

Reimbursement for costs. When an employee is ultimately vindicated, the Civil Service Commission or the court should be authorized to order an agency to reimburse the employee for all costs associated with his challenge of the agency's action, including an allowance for reasonable attorney's fees. Even if an employee is willing and able to survive an extended period of unemployment, he may not be willing to risk going deeply into debt to obtain satisfaction. Similarly, few attorneys are in a position to invest large amounts of time and money with little hope of receiving reasonable compensation. Ernest Fitzgerald has doggedly pursued every appeal open to him, but only because the American Civil Liberties Union was willing to underwrite the costs of the litigation.[6]

Intervention by citizens. Citizens directly interested in the disposition of cases involving civil servants should be permitted to intervene on their behalf both in administrative proceedings and in any judicial proceeding involving the employee. Victims or potential victims of the agency action that was the subject of the employee's disclosure or complaint would, of course, be directly interested.

Some of these proposals, if adopted, may cost us some of the stability we have come to expect from civil administration. But we are now paying a much higher price than this for a kind of well-oiled, imaginary efficiency in the operation of government that is in fact grossly inefficient. Too often, "stability" means ease of access for special interests, gross neglect of the will of Congress, and disregard of the interests of ordinary citizens. Nevertheless, some attention will have to be paid to resolving some very practical problems created by these suggestions.

Agency management will continue to have a strong interest in the loyalty and obedience of employees in circumstances other than those which may justify a protest or a public disclosure. After an employee has confronted his superiors in the procedures outlined in the reform proposal, it may be necessary that he move out of his particular office. In the Pickering case, the Supreme Court emphasized that had the teacher's letter to the editor created such tensions in his work situation that it would have been impossible for him to teach, the school board might have taken some action against him. Presumably he could have been reassigned to another school or given substantially different duties. Federal agencies should likewise be permitted to show the need for such transfers. But any new duties should be consistent with the experience and background of the employee.

The bureaucratic "Siberia treatment" should not be permitted. This is the tactic of moving a civil servant to an office with a telephone and perhaps even a secretary, but without any responsibility or with responsibilities totally inconsistent with his expertise and training. Ernest Fitzgerald spent his last year at the Air Force monitoring the performance of Air Force bowling alleys in Thailand.

Fitzgerald himself has suggested that an employee unwanted because he blew the whistle in the public interest should be granted "livelihood" rather than "job" security until he can find another position commensurate with his talents. In such a case, the employee should also be given the opportunity to present his side of the story in communications between the agency and any potential employer. He should also have the opportunity to examine any and all personnel files or data banks that contain information about him, and he should have the right to enter his comments and his own evidence into these records.

WHEN NOT TO BLOW THE WHISTLE

Any system of law or administration that protects whistle blowers must also deal with potential abuses. There are several obvious types of possible misconduct to control.

The whistle blower does not have the facts straight. If the whistle blower manufactures facts or falsifies evidence, he or she clearly deserves no protection whatsoever. But suppose he has access only to some of the facts but suspects that certain details, if disclosed, would reveal a serious threat to public health or safety? At the time of disclosure, he might reasonably be expected to indicate the limited state of his own knowledge in order to be entitled to protection later. Second, if the whistle blower's suspicions were totally irrational to the extent that no person with his background or training and in his position reasonably could have entertained them, it might also be undesirable to protect him. These kinds of determinations are made by judges and juries every day. There is no reason to believe that they would be any more difficult in whistle-blowing cases, if both sides have access to competent experts and other witnesses and if both are represented by competent counsel.

The whistle blower is a "disgruntled" employee, that is, he might be motivated by a desire to vindicate a personal dispute. The law does not generally take into account motives to determine guilt or innocence or to fix liability. This is because second-guessing someone's mental processes is a difficult if not impossible exercise. Suppose an employee, disgruntled because he has not been promoted, decides to reveal that the head of his agency has deliberately lied to a congressional committee about a serious public health menace? It may be difficult for the agency to prove, or for him to contradict, any allegation that he blew the whistle *because* he was disgruntled. And his true motives, the ones that no one can know with any degree of certainty, might have been mixed. So it might not be fair to deny this particular employee a protected status. On the other hand, the fact that he was disgruntled would still be relevant in judging the reliability of his information.

The whistle blower has disclosed confidential information in return for money or the promise of some other benefit. Though the law generally does not examine motives, there are important exceptions. A landowner, for example, may build a fence on his property for almost any reason, but if he does it to harass a neighbor, a court may order him to pull down the "spite fence." And someone who uses a legal process such as a subpoena for some ulterior and illegal purpose may be liable for damages. Suppose the hypothetical whistle blower just discussed releases the same information in return for a fee from a personal enemy of the agency head? Protection could and should be denied on the grounds that public policy should not encourage, indeed it should condemn, the sale of confidences.

The whistle blower decides to blow the whistle in order to save his job. An employee about to be discharged for a legitimate reason or an employee whose job is about to be abolished may try to protect himself by, for example, communicating with a congressional committee and then plead that he cannot be discharged for blowing the whistle in the public interest. Conversely, an agency might seek to justify the dismissal of a whistle blower on legitimate grounds purportedly unconnected with the fact that he spoke out or made damaging information public. In either case the problem is how to determine with reasonable certainty the causal relationship, if any, between these events. One possible solution is to shift to the employer the burden of proof to justify the discharge. The employer is, after all, in the best position to gather all the facts necessary to explain and to justify its decision.

Whether or not the burden is shifted, the employer is also in the best position to selectively marshal the facts to support its point of view. And it will be difficult for an outsider, no matter how objective or disinterested, to second-guess the agency's judgment that certain facts are sufficient grounds for dismissal, independent of the whistle blowing. So the employee

will have to be given the means to place additional
facts in the record as well as to challenge the decision-
making process that ended with the decision to discharge him. As already suggested, he should be
permitted to subpoena and examine under oath his superiors and his co-workers, including those who may
have transferred, changed jobs, or left the government
entirely. He should also be provided a transcript of
their testimony and any cross-examination. He should
also be permitted to subpoena relevant documents from
agency files, including his own personnel file. (Today in
many agencies employees are not even permitted to examine their own personnel file!) Finally, he should
also be allowed to introduce in evidence any facts
showing that his treatment was different from that of
other employees in cases not involving whistle blowing.
If he can show that other employees would have been
discharged had the criteria applied to him been applied
even-handedly, the court or administrative tribunal
considering his case might conclude that his discharge
was a reprisal.

These are not the only possible limitations on the
proposed rights of whistle blowers. Personnel files, for
example, should remain sacrosanct. Genuine national
security information should also be protected. But a
bureaucrat's decision to use a rubber stamp marked
"Confidential" or "Secret" should always be subject
to challenge.[7] A requirement that intra-agency or intra-
governmental channels of communication be explored
first might also be desirable, but should not apply when
even the use of those channels places the whistle
blower in jeopardy.

18

The Law

Professor Arthur S. Miller in his statement before the Conference on Professional Responsibility described the legal picture for potential whistle blowers as "a glum one." The simple fact is that a "love-it-or-leave-it" philosophy permeates the law of private employment relationships. Nevertheless, there have been a number of developments in related areas of the law that can form the basis for a repudiation of the old shibboleths. In addition, there are widely accepted principles which can be reshaped by creative lawyers, judges, and legislators into viable protections for the whistle blower. Many of these guideposts for change are indicated below. It is hoped that legal scholars, sympathetic legislators, and counsel for whistle blowers can build upon this list and expand the analysis of each item.

The First Amendment and the Corporation. In the Pickering case the Supreme Court said:

> teachers may [not] constitutionally be compelled to relinquish the First Amendment rights they would otherwise enjoy as citizens to comment on matters of public interest in connection with the operation of the public schools in which they work.[1]

Pickering had been fired for writing a letter to the editor of a local newspaper critical of school board policies. Had Pickering been a teacher at a private trade school and written to criticize the policies of a conglomerate which owned the school, the Supreme Court undoubtedly would have said that the First Amendment doesn't apply to action against free speech by nongovernmental bodies. Lawyers, of course, would have no difficulty understanding the logic of this distinction. The First Amendment, indeed the entire Bill of Rights, was written to curb the power of the federal government, and the Fourteenth Amendment to curb the power of state and local governments. A number of authorities, Professor Miller and Adolf Berle among them, have suggested that, short of formal amendment to the Constitution, constitutional protections could be extended to protect citizens from corporate as well as governmental action.[2]

Their theory is that since many corporations have the attributes of government—in terms of their size and wealth, and their ability to control the lives of employees and affect the lives of other citizens—citizens should reasonably enjoy the same protections against them that they enjoy against government. Furthermore, the very existence of a corporation is a manifestation of governmental power—the legislature's grant of a charter for corporate organization. The Supreme Court has not accepted this line of reasoning except, to a limited extent, in one case involving a "company town" and another involving a large regional shopping center.[3]

Even if the First Amendment were extended to limit corporate action abridging free speech, the problem of protecting the disclosure of certain confidential information would remain. Had Pickering supported his criticism of the school board with a document from the board's confidential files, the Court might have come to a very different conclusion on the propriety of his discharge. It might have said, for instance, that the release of confidential information is not itself "speech" within the First Amendment. But the line between disclosure and speech cannot be well defined. None of the whistle blowers discussed in this book appropriated documents, nor did they publish "trade secrets" which in themselves had economic value, nor did they publish classified information the release of which might threaten the national security. In most cases they simply "spoke the truth," or in Ernest Fitzgerald's phrase, "committed truth." Nevertheless, when purloined documents, trade secrets, or specifically classified information are involved, issues quite different from and more complicated than free speech arise. In these areas, too, old rules and new developments can form the basis for lifting the legal veil of secrecy.

"Just cause" provisions in collective bargaining agreements. Under the National Labor Relations Act, employees may not be discharged for engaging in legitimate unionization efforts, nor may they be dismissed for filing charges of violations of the act or testifying in proceedings of the National Labor Relations Board. The act does not, however, protect whistle blowing involving matters not covered by the act. Thus, the union member who complains about an unfair labor practice cannot be fired, but the member who complains about in-plant pollution (not an unfair labor practice) can be.

But the act does approve of and protect collective bargaining agreements, many of which contain "just cause" provisions stating that members cannot be fired "without just cause" but rarely indicating what is and what is not a proper cause for dismissal. Labor agreements generally establish a grievance mechanism through which members may complain about contract violations and other problems encountered on the job. Though the member files the grievance, the union represents him in the grievance procedures. If the union and the employer are unable to settle a grievance to their mutual satisfaction, the grievance may "go to arbitration." At that point an independent professional arbitrator is called in to make a decision binding on both parties.

There have been a number of arbitration decisions involving whistle-blowing situations. The arbitrators in these cases usually rely heavily on the old rule that disloyalty, in the words of a 1953 Supreme Court opinion, is "an elemental cause for discharge,"[4] but they sometimes find that a superior public interest intervenes to protect the employee.

In a case involving a cab driver who had reported that his employer was rigging meters to overcharge passengers, a California arbitrator eloquently explained:

> There is evidenced in this case a tension between an employee's private loyalty to his employer and his public loyalty to the community. Each citizen has a

duty of citizenship imposed and enforced by law to disclose criminal conduct of which he becomes aware. That duty never ceases as long as he has the knowledge and it remains undisclosed. The fact that his disclosure would be of "incalculable damage" to his employer can hardly be thought to reduce that duty of disclosure. When disclosure to management reasonably appears to the employee to be a futility because of their apparent involvement can it justly be held to constitute the "grossest misconduct" if public disclosure is assured and in fact results from disclosure to a competitor? . . . [The meter irregularities] quite clearly were contrary to the public interest and warranted disclosure.[5]

But there are a number of serious problems with "just cause" provisions. First, they apply to a relatively small percentage of the work force: union membership is down to twenty percent and an even smaller percentage have "just cause" provisions in their contracts. Second, the employee is almost totally at the mercy of the union, which can decide that his grievance has no merit. His only remedy if the union refuses to support his case is to sue the union for failing to fulfill its duty of fair representation. Needless to say, it is usually worth neither the effort nor the expense. Finally, contracts do not generally spell out "unjust" causes, so that arbitrators have very little to rely on except their own sense of what is right in a particular case.

The law of agency. In the law an employee is the "agent" of his or her employer. According to the Restatement of Agency, an agent has three primary obligations to his principal: the duty of obedience, the duty of loyalty, and the duty of confidentiality. But all of these duties are qualified. The "reasonable" directions of the employer must be obeyed, for example, but the employee can rely on business or professional ethics to determine what is reasonable. And the employee is under no duty to obey an order to perform an illegal or an unethical act. Likewise, an employee has a duty not to speak or act disloyally, except, in the words of the Restatement, "in the protection of his own interests and those of others." The Restatement then gives the following example:

A, employed by P, a life insurance company, in good faith advocates legislation which would require a change in the policies issued by the company. A has violated no duty to P.

Finally, even though an employee must keep his employer's secrets, he may reveal confidential information, according to the Restatement, "in the protection of a superior interest of himself or of a third person."

Whistle blowers cannot, however, take unrestrained comfort in these limitations on an agent's or an employee's duties. An employer's right to terminate the relationship at will is, unfortunately, not limited by agency principles. This is so because the employer has no legal duty to keep an employee on, regardless of any limitations on the *employee's* duties. Therefore, the discharged whistle blower cannot seek a court order to compel his or her reinstatement relying simply on the law of agency. But he can assert these limitations on his duties as one of his defenses to a legal action by his employer. Suppose, for example, a person resigns and then brings evidence of illegal activity by his employer to law enforcement authorities. Suppose further that while the authorities are deciding whether to take any action, the employer sues the former employee for violating the duty of confidentiality. This is precisely what happened in a recent English case.[6] The Court of Appeal refused to strike the employee's defense that he had no duty to keep confidential information about a price-fixing agreement and substantial deception. One of the judges wrote that "any misconduct of such a nature that it ought in the public interest to be disclosed to others" is not protected by the duty of confidentiality. The court was well aware of potential abuses. The same judge said that had the disclosures been made out of spite or malice or for a reward he might have decided differently. But the court clearly was not willing to sacrifice the principle of protecting the employee in this situation for fear of possible abuse in other cases.

Suits for malicious discharge. The legal principle which allows an employer to discharge his employees for any reason and without risking legal retaliation by his employee was succinctly stated by a Tennessee court in 1884: All employers "may dismiss their employees at will . . . for good cause, for no cause, or even for cause morally wrong, without being thereby guilty of legal wrong."[7] Until the National Labor Relations Law was upheld in 1937, the Supreme Court had said that state laws which limited the employer's freedom to fire for any reason were unconstitutional.[8]

Professor Lawrence E. Blades has written a pioneering assault on the doctrine of employment at will. In a 1967 *Columbia Law Review* article,[9] he forcefully argues that employees ought to be allowed to sue for "malicious discharge" and to receive compensation for lost wages, expenses, and other damages caused by improper action by an employer. Such a suit should be available, he argues, when a person is discharged for refusing to support the employer's political position, for declining to participate in immoral or unlawful activity, or for refusing to compromise professional ethics. This new remedy would grant the employer the right to discharge anyone for any reason (in the absence of a contract limiting that right), but would preserve at least part of the employee's livelihood by allowing him to recover damages.

The law of trade secrecy. Law protecting trade secrets arose in a variety of commercial settings. In the typical case, an employee or ex-employee revealed information to a competitor for a price or for new and perhaps more remunerative employment. Courts deciding these cases recognized that businesses have a legitimate interest in keeping certain information out of the hands of competitors. It is generally assumed by nonlawyers as well as nonexpert lawyers that "trade secrets" consist of certain specific classes of information. *Virtually any information,* however, can be protected as a trade secret if the possessor takes reasonable steps to keep it secret and if he claims it is valuable to him. In law suits against those who have disclosed trade secrets, the central issue is generally *not* whether the particular kind of information involved should be treated as a trade secret, but rather, whether it was taken "wrongfully." Thus, courts decide whether the employee or recipient obtained the information "unfairly," or whether a breach of confidence or breach of a contract was involved. And to decide these questions they rely on general notions of equity and fairness and on other areas of the law, such as the law of agency and the law of contracts.

This is not to say that the whistle blower who reveals confidential corporate information to the public is immune to law suits or does not run the risk of adverse court rulings. On the contrary, he is at the mercy of the court—and of the advocacy skills of his attorney. Counsel must argue that there can be no breach of confidence in revealing information the suppression of which might well be lethal to innocent victims. Or he must argue that there is a superior public interest in, for example, protecting the integrity of a regulatory scheme created to protect the public from the very predatory practices that the whistle blower revealed. Here is an example of the kind of "trade secret" that should not, and perhaps cannot, be protected: The Campbell Soup Company has developed a process to inspect for botulism in its products. The United States Department of Agriculture has the details of this process on file and at Campbell's request has refused to disclose it to the public and to other companies on the grounds that it is a trade secret. Mr. Samuel Cochran, Jr., of Bedford, New York, died fifteen hours after eating vichyssoise produced by one of Campbell's smaller competitors, the now bankrupt Bon Vivant Company. He died of botulism poisoning.

Government employees are prohibited from revealing "trade secrets" and other confidential business information by federal criminal statute.[10] And most of the regulatory laws contain provisions which prohibit such disclosures. Government agencies usually recognize without question an industry's claim that any particular information is a legitimate trade secret or otherwise deserves confidential treatment. For years, for example, the Department of the Interior recognized industry's claim that the amount and identity of pollutants entering our waterways from a particular plant was a trade secret. When the Corps of Engineers finally decided to enforce the Refuse Act of 1899 by requiring permits for discharges, the Environmental Protection Agency, under mounting congressional and public pressure, demanded and received from the Corps agreement that the information on permit applications would be public. Very few of the industries concerned complained. We must conclude that the information did not contain such valuable trade secrets after all. But had the environmental agency accepted the original position of industry—the position that Interior had blithely accepted the year before—federal civil servants might have faced criminal prosecution for any unauthorized disclosure!

Clearly, the concept of trade secrecy must be modified when the public has a superior interest or when the corporation is unable to justify the need for confidentiality. Section 208 (b) of the Clean Air Act as amended in 1970 is an example of one of the changes needed in regulatory laws as they apply to trade secrecy. Under this section, pollution data submitted to the Environmental Protection Agency is public *unless* an industry requests confidential treatment *and* submits its request to public scrutiny and comment. The administrator must then decide whether that class of data ought to be secret. His decision is based not only on bald assertions by industry, but also on comments from citizens, and his decision can be reviewed later by a court.

Recently, the National Commission on Reform of Federal Criminal Laws advanced a potentially far-reaching proposal for changing the criminal statute prohibiting disclosures by civil servants.[11] The commission's recommendation would in effect permit a civil servant to defend himself on the grounds that release of the information was in the public interest. The employee could not assert this defense if his agency had classified that particular class of information secret by formal regulation. This is a significant qualification, but the proposal is a substantial improvement over the uncertain prior law.

Criminal penalties against the corporation. Several states have made it a crime for corporations to coerce their employees in certain ways. In at least seven states, for example, it is illegal for an employer to interfere with an employee's political activity. But criminal statutes, even if they were to include additional prohibitions against coercion of whistle blowers, would have serious drawbacks. The most obvious is that the prosecutor can always choose not to pursue a matter for almost any reason. There have in fact been very few prosecutions under the existing laws, partly because the coerced employee is the only person in a position to file a complaint—and he may not want to risk losing his job. And as Professor Blades has pointed out, these particular laws do not provide for specific redress to employees. Thus, even if an employee files a complaint as a matter of principle and the employer is subsequently fined or jailed for his misdeeds, the employee will still have to suffer the consequences of the coercion without remedy.

Yet the criminal sanction should not be rejected completely. Counsel for the employee can argue that the criminal prohibition *implies* that persons harmed by a violation have the right to sue for damages. Generally, in our legal system, if the client is in the class of persons that the legislature intended to protect and if the harm that resulted is the very type the legislature sought to prevent, courts frequently grant relief. Unfortunately, no courts have apparently taken this position in suits brought under the anticoercion statutes.[12] These statutes could be amended to include a right to a private law suit against violators. Our federal antitrust laws include such multiple sanctions. But even without significant amendment—and even if courts refuse to grant the right to a suit for damages—criminal sanctions should still remain on the books as a fail-safe protection against the most severe instances of coercion or retaliation and for the highly visible cases.

Federal interference-with-witnesses laws. By federal statute it is a crime to coerce a witness giving testimony under subpoena in federal proceedings. A similar provision makes it a crime to coerce witnesses before congressional committees. But those laws have not helped whistle blowers in the past. In 1953 a United States Court of Appeals refused to allow employees to seek damages for discharge in retaliation for their testimony before a federal grand jury against their employer, the Humble Oil and Refining Company.[13] These employees were subpoenaed to testify. They would have risked citation for contempt of court had they refused and prosecutions for perjury had they lied, yet the court said that their employer could be compelled to answer only to a federal prosecutor, not to them, for punishing them for testifying truthfully. And Senator Proxmire has tried in vain to get the Justice Department to prosecute—or even to investigate—those persons responsible for Ernest Fitzgerald's discharge after he testified before the Joint Economic Committee. As Fitzgerald said at the Conference on Professional Responsibility, "Would John Mitchell put Melvin Laird in jail?"

Senator Richard M. Nixon of California introduced an amendment to this statute on April 26, 1951. He told the Senate:

> Mr. President. I have introduced in the Senate today a bill to make it a violation of law for any officer of the Federal Government to dismiss or otherwise discipline a Government employee for testifying before a committee of Congress. . . . There is too much at stake to permit foreign policy and military strategy to be established on the basis of half truths and the suppression of testimony.
>
> Unless protection is given to witnesses who are members of the armed services or employees of the Government, the scheduled hearings will amount to no more than a parade of yes men for administration policies as they exist.[14]

The Federal Fair Labor Standards Act. This statute prohibits the discharge of employees who complain of or testify about violations of federal wage and hour laws. The discretion to enforce the prohibition and to seek damages or reinstatement is left primarily with the Secretary of Labor. Under certain circumstances a complainant can sue the employer on his own behalf, but since there is no adequate provision for recovering attorney's fees, few attorneys are willing or able to commit substantial resources to law suits under the act. So unless the Secretary of Labor takes up his case or unless the employee has independent financial resources to support a law suit, he may be left with a right without a remedy.

But this provision and others like it, even if inadequate as presently drawn, are significant precedents for including employee protection provisions in other federal regulatory laws.

The Muskie amendments to existing federal water quality legislation. Amendments to federal water quality legislation currently under consideration by Congress contain just such a provision. Under the Senate version of the amendments—the so-called Muskie amendments, which have been approved by the Senate Public Works Committee and by the full Senate—an employee cannot be discharged, harassed, or discriminated against for reporting suspected violations of the federal water quality law to federal authorities. This proposal (reproduced in the Appendix), if approved by House and Senate conferees, will be a historic precedent for similar amendments to regulatory legislation in which employee cooperation can be an important element of law enforcement.

There are, however, imperfections in the Muskie version of employee protection. Only the Secretary of Labor, for example, is empowered to go to court on behalf of an aggrieved employee; and the proposed section allows him very wide discretion in making this decision. At the very least, any similar provision should authorize an employee to seek his own remedy in the event that the Secretary of Labor fails to act to protect his rights within a specified period of time. The ideal employee protection provision would also allow a court to award full attorney's fees and other costs incurred by an employee seeking a remedy.

The Universal Military Training and Service Act of 1948. The draft law may be an unlikely place to find an employee protection section, but it does prohibit discrimination in employment against returning veterans. Under its provisions, an ex-serviceman is entitled, with certain limited exceptions, to be reinstated in the job he held before entering the armed forces. To protect this right Congress provided that a reinstated veteran cannot be discharged except for "just cause" for a period of one year after his return. This is, of course, the same language generally used in collective bargaining agreements to protect members from retaliatory or malicious discharge. The provision is enforced by the local United States attorney, who may seek an order of reinstatement with back pay in federal court. If the employee fails to interest the United States attorney in acting on his behalf, he may personally petition a federal court for reinstatement with back pay. This is limited protection for a very limited class of persons, but it is one more breach in the wall of employer freedom to fire for any reason.

The Federal Automobile Dealer Franchise Act of 1956. The so-called Dealer's Day in Court Act in effect prohibits automobile manufacturers from terminating dealerships without just cause.[15] A massive lobbying effort by the National Association of Automobile Dealers was a significant factor in the adoption of the legislation. Two dealer–whistle blowers, however, persuaded many congressmen and senators that noneconomic issues—including the right to free speech —were involved.

Lee Anderson, a former General Motors dealer in Pontiac, Michigan, testified before Senator O'Mahoney's Antitrust and Monopoly Subcommittee that his dealership had been terminated for "disloyalty." Specifically, in a speech he delivered at a local Rotary Club meeting, he charged that the Pontiac Division executives bought cars from the factory at a discount. These "disloyal" utterances were reported in a trade paper, *Automotive News.* He lost his dealership shortly thereafter. Pontiac denied any connection between the two events.

J. E. Travis, a Buick dealer in St. Charles, Missouri, publicly argued for protected territories for established dealers. This point of view was very unpopular in Detroit, where rigorous competition among dealers in the same makes was then company policy. Travis was a former president of the state auto dealers association and had been in the business for thirty-five years. His franchise was canceled—for poor sales, according to General Motors. Travis's sales had in fact declined somewhat in the face of discount dealer competition in nearby St. Louis. But in view of his record his fellow dealers and a number of key senators were convinced that his outspoken position on protected territories was the real reason for his termination. Travis's only satisfaction was the support his testimony gave to the bill under consideration.

The Dealer's Day in Court Act is not a perfect model for employer-employee relations. But it does demonstrate that legislation can effectively redress "natural" imbalances in bargaining power between parties in a continuing economic relationship to one another. A relatively small number of suits have been filed under the act, and few have been entirely successful. But as Professor Stewart Macauley, of the University of Wisconsin Law School, has pointed out, the mere existence of the law—and the potential power of organized dealers reflected in its passage—has probably had more of an impact than the new legal rights it created.

Unconscionable contracts. A contract can be so unfair as a result of disparities in bargaining power between two parties that a court will nullify the whole agreement or parts of it, or even rewrite some of the terms of the agreement, to better protect the disadvantaged party. Whether or not there is a written agreement, the relationship between an employer and his employee is essentially contractual: one party pays salary or wages in return for work performed by the other. Though courts have traditionally been reluctant to interfere in any way with this or any other form of contract, they have increasingly done so when the terms are so favorable to one party as to "shock the conscience" or when one party has to accept excessively burdensome collateral terms to get what he really wants out of the bargain. Some courts, for example, have refused to enforce contracts in which a low-income purchaser must mortgage all of his personal possessions in order to purchase a single appliance on credit.

Often the same *type* of agreement that might be approved by a court if between two merchants or businessmen will not be tolerated between a merchant and a consumer, especially a poor consumer. Though they may not discuss it in their opinions, the judges in these cases are piercing legal formalisms with considerations of fairness and equity to base their decisions on such factors as the awareness of the consumer, the lack of any real bargaining between the parties, and society's interest in discouraging such practices.

A court could consider similar factors in examining
employment agreements the terms of which can be
dictated by a single employer or by all employers
with the same interest in muzzling employees. In a
few cases judges have invalidated agreements in which
the employee was forced to give up important rights
that he or she already had, but none have apparently
gone so far as to give the employee new rights. To
protect a whistle blower on a contract theory a court
would clearly have to read into the contract some very
significant new terms. In reaction to such a suggestion
a judge might say that it would be more proper for a
legislature than for a court to take such a giant step
or that the employee should turn to collective bargaining
rather than to the courts to exact such terms from an
employer. But the issue cannot be so easily avoided.
Judges have been and can be persuaded that they ought
not "pass the buck" to others whenever tough policy
questions underlie the decision in a case before them.

Retaliatory eviction. Recently some courts have said
that a landlord cannot evict a tenant for reporting
housing code violation to government authorities.[16]
They reason that although a landlord generally has the
right to evict for any reason, he cannot do so in order
to frustrate the public policy of requiring that all
housing meet certain minimum standards. Of course
there are significant differences between a landlord's
relationship to his tenants and an employee's relationship to his employees. But in either case there may be
superior, legislatively defined public policies making
it reasonable, if not necessary, for a court to interfere
in the relationship.

There is also a First Amendment aspect to these
cases. If a court or other public agency, the police for
example, aids a landlord by ordering the eviction of a
tenant for reporting a law violation, it supports the
suppression of a form of speech. Thus, even though the
First Amendment might not directly limit the landlord,
it would still limit any arm of government that inhibited
speech by making it possible for the landlord to retaliate. This approach has not yet been accepted by the
high courts. Many jurists believe that it would set a
precedent for vastly expanding the First Amendment to

limit virtually any private action affecting speech or expression. Whether these fears are justified or not, the fact is that the Supreme Court has used precisely this kind of reasoning to extend *other* constitutional guarantees and to limit libel and slander suits by public figures against their critics. For example, in *Shelly* v. *Kramer* the Supreme Court ruled that state courts could not enforce racially restrictive covenants. The Court's reasoning: Although the subdivider's action in writing the anti-Negro provisions into land conveyances was *not* a violation of the equal protection clause, any court that *applied* the restriction in a private law suit would violate that clause of the Bill of Rights. And in the libel and slander area the Court reasoned that although a public figure, like a corporation, suing for libel would *not* violate the First Amendment, a court which entertained the suit might be doing so under certain circumstances.

Equal Employment Opportunity Laws. Title VII of the Civil Rights Act of 1964 outlaws discrimination in employment for reasons of race, color, religion, sex, or national origin. The Equal Employment Opportunity Commission (EEOC) has certain limited powers to prevent all of these forms of discrimination. But it does not have the power to intervene on behalf of persons discriminated against for speaking out against the practices or policies of their employer or for releasing information critical to the protection of the public health or safety. Giving the EEOC jurisdiction in such cases would be a logical extension of its present authority—or a new agency or commission could be created and given this responsibility.

The task of the new commission, or of the EEOC were its jurisdiction expanded, would be somewhat more complicated than finding discrimination under present law. Under the Civil Rights Act, it is *never* proper to single out employees for special treatment on the basis of race, color, religion, sex, or national origin. But it may or may not be proper for an employer to take some action against the employee who blows the whistle. This is so because whistle blowing may or may not itself be proper, depending on such factors as the magnitude of the alleged evil, the validity of the charge made by the whistle blower, and the motives of the whistle blower. The EEOC or other agency will have to make these and other determinations in every case. It will have to guard against abuses as well as protect justifiable whistle blowing.

Conclusion. Existing laws thus provide a framework for protecting whistle blowers, though they are far from satisfactory at present. Still, the tools are available. It remains for courageous and innovative lawyers, judges, and legislators to reshape old laws, to apply the precedents at hand to new circumstances, and to develop new doctrines and laws to defend the ethical whistle blower.

Whatever legal mechanisms emerge—and there is clearly a wide variety of possibilities—they should, as a minimum

—extend First Amendment guarantees to prohibit interference with expression within private as well as public organizations;

—create guarantees of due process, including open hearings, the right to subpoena and cross-examine witnesses, the right to obtain all relevant documentary evidence, the right to counsel, and the right to appeal to independent authority;

—distinguish sharply between individual privacy and organizational secrecy, but recognize that individual privacy *within* organizations is also entitled to protection; and

—establish legal standards to balance an institution's interest in secrecy against the public's interest in disclosure.

We have included in the Appendix a draft proposal for reform of the federal civil service system incorporating these and other elements. The proposal should be applicable to state civil service systems with minor changes, and any private organization should be able to use it as a guide in establishing its own system for dealing fairly with potential whistle blowers. Congress could, of course, enact an extensive reform of the employee-employer relationship to include unorganized as well as organized workers in private and public institutions. A better approach might be to establish as a matter of law a number of new rights which could then be applied by organizations and ultimately by the courts to individual cases. The series of rights written into our proposal for civil service reform could be adapted to serve this purpose.

No new system of law will develop without the active intervention of citizens concerned with the issues raised by the whistle blowers of the last few years. And no system of law will be meaningful unless the ethic of professional and individual responsibility is embraced by organizations and the persons who serve them. It is a tall order, but it is far closer to being filled than any would have dreamed possible a short time ago.

IV

Strategies for Whistle Blowers

19

To Blow the Whistle

There is no tried and true formula for blowing the whistle effectively and safely. Every person is unique and every situation is different; that which has proved successful in one instance may be totally inappropriate in another. Still, it is imperative that a person considering such a bold action do so with as much forethought as he can muster. We have attempted in the following pages to set down some of the more important questions that a person contemplating blowing the whistle will have to resolve before he puts together his own strategy. Our suggestions are drawn primarily from the experiences of the men and women in this book and from common sense. They are necessarily tentative and form only an outline for action. They are intended merely to help the potential whistle blower organize his thoughts and review all the options.

1) PRECISELY IDENTIFY NOT ONLY THE OBJECTIONABLE ACTIVITY OR PRACTICE, BUT ALSO THE PUBLIC INTEREST OR INTERESTS THAT ARE THREATENED AND THE MAGNITUDE OF THE HARM THAT WILL RESULT FROM NONDISCLOSURE. As a potential whistle blower you must clearly define the issue for yourself before you can hope to enlist the support of others within your organization or on the outside. The nature of the issue in turn will largely determine the succeeding steps to be taken. The practice or activity, for example, might be covered by existing regulatory legislation or it might be the subject of intensive legislative scrutiny by a committee of Congress. If similar practices are the subject of intense pub-

lic debate, citizens' groups may be willing and able to
follow up on your information. And the more widespread the abuse which you can document the better,
for the electorate and the elected consider one complaint a peccadillo, but many of them an issue. You
must identify the threatened interest in order to determine which outside group or authority, if any, should
be contacted. Is it a health or safety interest? And if so,
does it involve an immediate threat of the sort that can
be removed only by quick and effective action? Clearly,
where imminent hazards to health are involved, you
have a strong case for blowing the whistle loud and
clear to outside authorities.

You have to identify the interest to help you decide
whether or not to blow the whistle within the organization. In some cases both the public and corporate
managers share a strong interest in the same corrective
action. George Geary objected to selling what he considered to be inadequately tested oilfield tubing for
United States Steel. He followed his immediate superior's order to sell the pipe despite his reservations, but
appealed to top management to recall the pipe pending
further tests. Management's review substantially confirmed Geary's position. The pipe was then recalled,
perhaps saving the lives and property of purchasers and
other citizens, and incidentally saving U.S. Steel from
the law suits and unfavorable publicity that might have
resulted.

You can never be certain that your disclosure will
have any effect. But you must be convinced that without disclosure there is little hope that significant damage
to health, safety, or some other well-defined public interest can be avoided. The greater the harm that is sure
to result if you remain silent, the more reason you have
to speak out and the likelier you are to find support.
Blowing the whistle on trivia is never justified. It ex-
poses you and your family and your organization to
unnecessary risks, and it may make it more difficult
for others to speak to reveal important matters.

2) VERIFY THE ACCURACY OF YOUR KNOWLEDGE OF THE
SITUATION. In a sense, the burden of proof is on the
whistle blower from the outset. And it is a heavy bur-

den. An error of fact, even if it involves a minor point or a collateral issue, may seriously undermine the integrity of other information you provide authorities and the public. Accurate and complete information is also a precondition to obtaining the assistance of any outside organization. Public interest groups, law enforcement and regulatory agencies, legislators, and even newspaper reporters have limited resources and little spare time. You must provide them with reliable information to expect fast and effective action on your behalf. Ideally, it should be possible for the outside party—or for higher authorities within the organization—to verify your position without merely relying on your word. You should be able, for example, to refer them to other individuals or to available documents which will confirm key facts supporting your position.

Accuracy is also important for anticipating the response of the organization and its allies. Anticipate the worst. If your motives are impugned, for example, your case should be able to stand on its own merit. Ronald Ostrander was described by Procter and Gamble as a "disgruntled employee." In fact, Ostrander left the company not in protest or even out of disenchantment, but rather to take over the operation of a family business which he had inherited. But Procter and Gamble did not effectively contradict the fact that package directions recommended the use of eight to ten times more detergent than necessary for the best cleaning results.

3) IDENTIFY ETHICAL STANDARDS AS WELL AS LAWS, RULES, AND REGULATIONS THAT SUPPORT YOUR DECISION TO BLOW THE WHISTLE. Government employees and members of organized professional groups are subject, at least nominally, to formal, written ethical codes. They are rarely enforced, but they provide important guidelines for a potential whistle blower. These codes, with varying degrees of specificity, dedicate one's primary allegiance to the public interest. The code of ethics for United States government employees is quite clear: "Put loyalty to the highest moral principles and to country above loyalty to persons, party, or government," and "expose corruption wherever discovered." The government code was adopted by the Eighty-fifth Congress as

House Concurrent Resolution 175. It is therefore an expression of the highest legislative authority in the country and not merely a codification of the personal ethical preferences of civil servants.

In the preamble to its code of ethics, the National Society of Professional Engineers recognizes that the individual must serve more than one master: "The Engineer will serve with devotion his employer, his clients, and the public. . . ." Section 2 of the code is quite explicit:

> The Engineer will have proper regard for the safety, health, and welfare of the public in the performance of his professional duties. If his engineering judgment is overruled by nontechnical authority, he will clearly point out the consequences. He will notify the proper authority of any observed conditions which endanger public safety and health.
>
> a. He will regard his duty to the public welfare as paramount.
>
> b. He shall seek opportunities to be of constructive service in civic affairs and work for the advancement of the safety, health and well-being of his community.
>
> c. He will not complete, sign, or seal plans and/or specifications that are not of a design safe to the public health and welfare and in conformity with accepted engineering standards. If the client or employer insists on such unprofessional conduct, he shall notify the proper authorities and withdraw from further service on the project.

Other sections of the NSPE code buttress this commitment. Section 13, for example, warns members not to associate with "enterprises of questionable character" and not to become professionally associated with "engineers who do not conform to ethical practices."

These ethical maxims not only condemn wrongful conduct, they inveigh against the failure to act responsibly. Thus, under the NSPE code, the failure to report "observed conditions which endanger public safety and health" to proper authorities is as unacceptable as creating those conditions through incompetence or the misapplication of professional know-how.

Even lawyers are permitted to report clients' plans for future criminal conduct by Disciplinary Rule 4-

101(c) of the American Bar Association's Code of Professional Responsibility.

Our criminal law has long imposed on all citizens the obligation to report criminal misconduct. The failure to do so, at least where some effort is made to conceal knowledge of the crime,[1] is itself a crime called "misprision." The person guilty of misprision may have had absolutely nothing to do with the commission of the crime or preparations leading up to the crime.

Many federal laws encourage citizens to report misconduct by providing monetary rewards for doing so. For example:

—The Secretary of the Treasury is authorized to pay a reward for information on violation of the internal revenue laws.[2] 26 U.S.C. §7623

—He may also pay informers twenty-five percent of the recovery for information leading to the collection of customs revenue from smugglers.[3] 19 U.S.C. § 1619

—The Secretary of Agriculture may be required by a federal court to pay one-half of any civil penalties collected for falsified reports filed by cotton dealers to persons who reveal the misrepresentations.[4] 26 U.S.C. § 7263

—The Commissioner of Narcotics is authorized to pay rewards for information leading to the seizure of contraband narcotics.[5] 21 U.S.C. § 199

—The Commandant of the Coast Guard is required to divide the fifty-dollar fine that may be collected from seamen found to possess sheath knives between the informer and a "fund for the relief of sick and disabled seamen." 46 U.S.C. § 710

The last example may provide no great incentive to the modern merchant mariner, but it demonstrates that Congress has from early times considered citizen cooperation an important instrument of law enforcement. The recently rediscovered reward provision in the Refuse Act of 1899 is now widely recognized by conservationists and environmental groups, if not by the Justice Department, as a valuable incentive to encourage ordinary citizens to spot water polluters.

None of these provisions draw any distinction be-

tween employees and other persons who might seek
rewards but, as a practical matter, employees or former
employees of an offender are likely to have access to
the kinds of information necessary for conviction.

4) DEVELOP A PLAN OF ACTION: CONSIDER THE PER-
SONAL COSTS AND THE LIKELY RESPONSE OF ALLIES AND
ANTAGONISTS WITHIN AND OUTSIDE THE ORGANIZATION.
There is obviously no single plan of action that will be
effective in all circumstances. Indeed some of the men
and women whose experiences are recounted in this book
have said that they did not really plan to blow the whistle. Ernest Fitzgerald, for example, says that he merely
candidly answered Senator Proxmire's questions at a
public hearing. Dr. Jacqueline Verrett did the same
when interviewed by television newsmen.

Whistle blowers have acted in a number of distinctly
different ways. We have set down some of these in the
hope that others can use them to decide whether, when,
and how to blow the whistle. Our list is not complete,
nor is any one plan necessarily exclusive of the others.
Above all, they must be read with the understanding
that every situation that might require such a heavy
investment of personal courage is unique and not subject to simple analysis.

Blowing the whistle within the organization. Formal
channels for bringing a situation to the attention of top
management should be pursued first, if such channels
exist. In the law there is an analogous principle called
"exhaustion of remedies," by which a person wishing
to file suit must try to obtain satisfaction from the responsible governmental agency before his case will be
heard in court. One reason courts usually apply this
principle is to avoid, if possible, the high costs of litigation to both parties and to the legal system. Would-be
whistle blowers should pursue internal remedies first
for parallel reasons, if they can.

Going to management first minimizes the risk of retaliatory dismissal, as you may not have to go public
with your demands if the corporation or government
agency takes action to correct the situation. It may also
strengthen your case if you ultimately go outside the
organization, since the managers are likely to point out

any weaknesses in your arguments and any factual deficiencies in your evidence in order to persuade you that there is really no problem. Before the public accepts your position they will want to have some assurance that you are responsible and likely to be accurate. One indication that you are a responsible person—and one test of the strength of your convictions—is your willingness to submit your evidence to those who purport to be in the best position to act on it, the organization's top managers. Giving your employer a chance to respond not only enhances your credibility; it tends to minimize the effect of later efforts to impugn your motives or to accuse you of unfairness and disloyalty.

Officers David Durk and Frank Serpico of the New York Police Department discovered first hand the efficacy of pursuing internal avenues first. They went to the *New York Times* with their story of massive corruption in the department *after* trying for several years to get through to Mayor Lindsay. Police corruption might not have been big news, but their repeated failures to get action clearly was. And their credibility with the newspaper was enhanced immeasurably by the fact that they had tried literally every recourse within the department and within the city government before reaching outside.

Blowing the whistle within the organization is not, however, appropriate in every case. As George Geary discovered at United States Steel, it may cost you your job even if your position is completely vindicated by the company. Geary never spoke to an outsider until he sought counsel for his legal challenge to the company's action against him. The pipe he complained about was recalled for testing in line with his recommendation—but he was fired. So there are situations— Geary's may have been one of them—in which seeking relief inside the organization may be too costly to the employee or may be just as costly as going outside. In other circumstances "exhausting one's remedies" may unnecessarily jeopardize the very interests the whistle blower wants to protect. If, for example, a newly discovered defect in a consumer product poses such an imminent hazard to human life that any delay might result in death or serious injury, you should contact authorities who can act immediately to remove the product from the retail market. The legal doctrine of exhaustion has a related limitation: You are not required to exhaust other remedies before seeking relief from a court if to do so would result in a denial of justice.

Resignation with a strong public statement of the reasons. Neither John Gardner when he resigned as Secretary of Health, Education, and Welfare under President Johnson, nor Walter Hickel when he resigned as Secretary of the Interior under President Nixon used the opportunity to protest policies with which they disagreed and which may have led to their departures. There was speculation in the press that Gardner was either unhappy with his department's budget or upset with the Vietnam war. Hickel's private letter to the President concerning youthful protests and the war received a lot of attention, but it apparently reached the press by mistake.[6] He had no intention of resigning at the time. When he did leave months later he did not mount a platform to try to vindicate his position.

Gardner and Hickel may in fact have left for totally personal reasons, or, more likely perhaps, they may have felt that a public protest would be improper or inappropriate. Silence seems to have become an unwritten rule for many departing top officials. James Reston, commenting on this pattern, wrote:

> One thing that is fairly clear from the record is that the art of resigning on principle from positions close to the top of the American Government has almost disappeared. Nobody quits now, as Anthony Eden and Duff Cooper left Neville Chamberlain's Cabinet, with a clear and detailed explanation of why they couldn't be identified with the policy any longer. . . . Most of those who stayed on at the critical period of escalation gave to the President the loyalty they owed to the country. Some . . . are now wondering in private life whether this was in the national interest.[7]

But there are signs that the pattern is changing. On three occasions in the winter of 1969–70, key government employees, including an agency head, resigned or were asked to resign and then publicly articulated their disagreements with the Nixon administration.

In August, 1969, Gary Greenberg, a senior trial attorney in the Civil Rights Division of the Justice Department and sixty-four of his colleagues — almost ninety percent of all nonsupervisory lawyers in the division—signed a written protest against the administration decision to delay the enforcement of desegregation orders in Southern schools. They maintained that further delay was clearly contrary to the Constitution they had sworn to uphold and that it could not be supported by any legal argument. Greenberg was asked to resign when, at the request of several judges, he stated his personal views in the course of a proceeding before the United States Court of Appeals in St. Louis. Though Greenberg did not technically resign in protest, he clearly did not leave the department quietly.

Terry Lenzner, former director of the Office of Legal Services in the Office of Economic Opportunity (OEO) publicly rebuked the Nixon Administration for subordinating the legal services program to local political powers. Lenzner and Frank Jones, another top Legal Services official, held a press conference on November 20, 1971, the day after their dismissal. Shortly thereafter all ten regional Legal Services directors signed and submitted a statement protesting the firings and supporting the Lenzner-Jones criticism of political influence in Legal Services. Since then key senators and congressmen, as well as the American Bar Association, have sought to block efforts to fracture the Legal Services program or to subordinate it to local or bureaucratic interests.

In June, 1970, Peter Gall, a special assistant to the director of the Office of Civil Rights at HEW, resigned to protest the forced resignation of the director, Leon Panetta. Gall and the Atlanta regional director, Paul Rilling, who also resigned, circulated statements to the press outlining the real reasons for Panetta's dismissal. Gall's story is presented in some detail in Chapter 15.[8]

Resignation followed by a reasonable period of silence. Dr. A. Dale Console, one-time medical director for E. R. Squibb and Sons, and a participant in the Conference on Professional Responsibility, chose this course of action. He did not express his concern about what he considered unethical and highly deceptive prescription drug marketing practices until a number of years after he left Squibb. This was no strategy decision, but a delayed realization of the implications of silence. In some cases the whistle blower may not realize the significance of his knowledge until later developments reveal it to him. Ronald Ostrander, for example, knew that Procter and Gamble and other detergent manufacturers recommended the use of excessive quantities of their products, but no one knew the significance of phosphate pollution until many years later.

Primarily, of course, delayed whistle blowing gives the individual an opportunity to start a new career or otherwise secure a livelihood for his family before his employer has any opportunity to retaliate. Dr. Console argues that it also tends to reduce the persuasiveness of charges that the individual is acting out of spite or to satisfy some other personal grievance. Procter and Gamble's charge, for example, that Ostrander was a disgruntled employee sounded somewhat foolish, since he had left the company twenty years earlier. But unless the whistle blower can tie his revelations to a *current* issue, he may have no impact whatsoever.

There are two serious problems with this approach. First, many of the situations which demand action by insiders are of such a magnitude or require such immediate attention that comfortable delays are intolerable. Charles Pettis blew the whistle on the trans-Andean highway while he continued to serve as chief consulting engineer because to do otherwise would have cost both the Peruvian and United States governments millions of dollars and perhaps the lives of many more workmen. Second, the drama and poignancy of the disclosure may be lost unless the whistle blower has a well-established reputation or speaks out at a time when other circumstances have made his information vital, as, for example, during an important Congressional hearing or an important public controversy.

Blowing the whistle outside the organization. This is the classic form of whistle blowing. It is often the most effective, but it can also be the most difficult. It certainly involves the greatest risk to the whistle blower, who may lose his job or destroy his career in the process. There are at least three variations of blowing the whistle outside the organization: remaining totally anonymous; revealing your identity only to those who will then, in effect, blow the whistle for you; or identifying yourself openly.

Ernest Fitzgerald has called anonymous whistle blowers "secret patriots." But anonymity, though it may be a means of protection from retaliatory dismissal or harassment, has serious drawbacks. Those who receive information from an anonymous insider have a heavy burden of substantiating and cross-checking the data. And the "secret patriot's" motives are immediately suspect, and there may be no way of allaying these suspicions. If he is later identified, he is far more likely to be vilified as a "rat fink" or a "spy" than his counterpart who openly confesses the reasons for his concern. Finally, anonymity tends to weaken the significance of the disclosure, since the whistle blower is unwilling to put his job on the line, or to subject himself to the public scrutiny he directs on his organization.

There are, however, certain circumstances in which anonymity may be justified: if the whistle blower is able to provide information which is independently verifiable, if he would be unable to support his family except in his present job, *and* if there is no other reasonable means to assure the confidentiality of his communication.

Recently, an anonymous whistle blower (or perhaps one who revealed his or her identity only to an outside contact) provided columnist Jack Anderson with an internal memorandum allegedly written by Dita Beard, Washington lobbyist for the International Telephone and Telegraph Corporation (ITT), to a high company official. The memo suggested that the corporation's pledge to provide substantial financial support for the 1972 Republican National Convention had a significant impact on negotiations between ITT and the Antitrust Division of the Justice Department concerning an out-of-court settlement of a suit to divest ITT of the recently acquired Hartford Fire Insurance Company.

Anderson printed excerpts of the memo in his nationally syndicated column the day after the Senate Judiciary Committee had completed its consideration of the nomination of Richard Kleindienst to be Attorney General. The publication of the memo and the subsequent investigation by Anderson and his associate Brit Hume led Kleindienst to request that the hearing be reconvened to clear up the cloud created by his participation in the alleged "deal." The hearings, which are continuing at this writing, have given the American public a rare insight into the relationship between giant corporations and high government officials. Both Kleindienst and former Antitrust Division chief Richard McLaren, in attempting to disprove the existence of a bargain, have spread across the public record evidence of private informal meetings between various ITT officials and representatives of the Justice Department as well as the White House and of interference by White House political operatives in the antitrust law enforcement process. McLaren, an outspoken critic of conglomerate mergers who had developed a series of challenges against conglomerates under existing laws, though still believing his position would be vindicated by the Supreme Court, was persuaded to settle the case on the basis of flimsy, politically backed evidence.

The "confidential whistle blower"—one who reveals himself to a third party with the understanding that his name will not be used without his consent—may, like the anonymous whistle blower, be protecting himself while sacrificing the chances of generating effective action. Like his anonymous counterpart he acts in the face of a strongly held belief that persons or organizations ought to be able to face their accusers. Underlying this belief is the notion that the veracity and even the integrity of those who claim to speak the truth should be subject to challenge. Those who use information from a confidential whistle blower must challenge him as relentlessly and thoroughly as he would be challenged were his identity revealed. They must play the role of the devil's advocate and play it well. They must insure that the whistle blower's disclosures will stand alone and that they can be thoroughly supported by an independent examination of the underlying facts.

Until our organizations and our laws make significant concessions to the need to recognize and protect individual and professional responsibility of employees, confidential appeals to those independent of the organization will remain absolutely necessary. Ultimately, of course, blowing the whistle is not easy. There is no perfect shield against firing, transfer, demotion, or any other form of retaliation. There is likewise no method that will guarantee curing the situation that threatens the public. Ernest Fitzgerald, for example, feels that he has barely dented the Defense Department's massive giveaways to the defense industry. And despite engineer Carl Thelin's revelations, all Corvairs have not been re-called.

Yet each initiative has made a significant first step by generating broader awareness, facilitating the participation of others in the cause, and building citizen pressure on authorities to act in the public interest. Perhaps it will compel more bystanders to ask themselves the question, if one person accomplished this much, how much more could be done if a few more people bent their arms to the oars?

5) SELECT AN APPROPRIATE OUTSIDE CONTACT. Suppose the decision is made to contact someone outside the organization. Where should you go? You should first consider contacting one or more government agencies that may have jurisdiction in the area of your concern. Even if you are a civil servant, there may be another agency with a direct interest in the matter. Under the National Environmental Policy Act of 1969, for example, all agencies considering major actions that might have a significant effect on the environment must file a draft "environmental impact statement" with the Council on Environmental Quality. The council in turn must circulate draft statements for comment to all other agencies who may have an interest in the proposal. Under the Air Quality Amendments of 1970 the Environmental Protection Agency (EPA) must comment on the draft. When a final statement is issued, any citizen may sue to block a project on the basis that the statement is inadequate. It was during this very process that employees within the Interior Department released a memorandum charging that Interior's draft impact statement on the proposed Alaska pipeline was

incomplete. EPA then severely criticized the draft statement, and citizens groups have blocked the project in
court pending a redraft of the statement.

The procedures established by agencies to receive
reports and complaints from citizens vary greatly. Some
simply refuse to act on anonymous complaints, but
will consider action on the basis of information provided by an identified person who wishes his name with-
held from third parties. The Occupational Safety and
Health Administration, for example, will not act on
anonymous complaints, but does guarantee confidentiality to workers who complain of unsafe or unhealthy
working conditions and identify themselves. Under the
1899 Refuse Act, one-half of the fine collected in the
successful prosecution of a water polluter is to be paid
to persons who give the information leading to conviction. Employees or former employees are, of course,
entitled to collect the reward. And some courts have
said that under the "qui tam" doctrine, a citizen can
sue the polluter on behalf of the government for the
fine and still collect his reward if the United States
attorney fails to act. Clearly, the Refuse Act—which
was largely ignored for the first seventy years it was
on the books—contemplates citizen involvement in the
enforcement process.

In many communities, citizens' groups and police
departments encourage citizens to report drug traffick-
ing, anonymously if they desire, to a special address
or telephone number.[9] Few communities have set up
similar mechanisms for citizens to report polluting industries or corruption. One exception is New York
City, where United States attorney Whitney North Seymour recently announced a post office address to which
citizens can send reports of possible corruption in government. Seymour's office will accept anonymous communications and will guarantee confidentiality if
requested. Whether or not there is a special procedure
like the one in New York City, you should communicate with the state or United States prosecutor's office
or a law enforcement agency if criminal activity might
be involved.

Remember, however, that prosecutors have virtually
unlimited discretion to press a case or to drop it. They

can select what goes before a grand jury and they can settle a case without trial. So when you contact a United States attorney or a district attorney, be prepared to persuade him that he ought to act by showing that there is or will be substantial evidence available and that significant damage will be done to an identifiable group or interest if he fails to prosecute.

You should also consider contacting state or federal legislators. Your United States senator or representative usually has several staff members assigned to "casework." They can act as informal ombudsmen for you in your relations with agencies in the executive branch. More importantly, you may have an issue of political significance to your representative. The best way to find out is to contact his or her office. Finally, your senator or representative may be a member of a committee that deals with issues related to the matter you are bringing to his attention.

Do not limit your contacts to your own legislators. Others may have a strong interest in the matter because of their committee assignments. Henry Durham, the former Lockheed employee who publicly supported Ernest Fitzgerald's charges of mismanagement, did not contact his own congressman or senator. Instead, he brought his evidence to Senator Proxmire, who had already shown a deep interest in military procurement generally and in Lockheed's C–5A air transport contract in particular.

Durham also believed that the senators and representatives from Georgia might have ignored him for political reasons. Lockheed is a major employer in the state and one of the largest employers in the Atlanta area. In fact, you should always consider political implications before contacting persons in political office. Officers Durkin and Serpico attempted to contact Mayor Lindsay just before an election about an issue—police corruption—that might have damaged his chances of reelection. On another occasion they were told by a Lindsay aide that the city administration would delay action to avoid angering policemen on the eve of a "long hot summer."

If government agencies and legislators are unresponsive, you may be forced to contact a citizens' group, the press, or some other unofficial action group. You may even have to organize your own group. One Weyerhauser employee did just that to protest his company's plan to build a logging road through the area where he lived. He organized his neighbors and together they generated enough unfavorable publicity to convince the company to reverse itself. The Weyerhauser executive who told the story to one of the authors of this book said that the company seriously considered firing the employee, but decided he was too valuable. They also may have admired his courage.

If you cannot organize your own constituency or if you prefer to try other unofficial means first, you should proceed with considerable thought and some caution. Which citizens' group, which newsman, which interested outsider you contact will depend on a host of factors, such as the nature of the situation which must be reported; the geographic scope of the problem (i.e., whether it is of local, state or national significance); the type of organization you work for; the accessibility of the citizens' group or of a key newsman who can be trusted to keep your confidence. Here are a few practical suggestions:

—Try to be selective. Even if you have no interest in confidentiality and wish to alert the whole world to a problem, scatter-shot salvos are usually ineffective. Mimeographed barrages are easily discounted by those who receive them as products of crackpots. And you may unnecessarily affront potential listeners. An investigative reporter, for example, is interested in an exclusive story. If he knows or has reason to believe that his colleagues in competing media have the same story at the same time, he may be less interested in dedicating the necessary time to pursuing the matter. And it may be tactically disadvantageous to bring in the whole world before you have seen the response of your initial outside contact. He may point out weak points in your case; he may demand that you cross-check or find further support or evidence for a particular contention. He may prevent integrity and credibility from being destroyed if you are about to make unsubstantiated or poorly thought out allegations.

—Contact local groups or media first, unless they are likely to be biased against you or unless the situation clearly has national significance. If you decide to contact a national organization, try to select one with the strongest interest in developments in your locale. The National Wildlife Federation, 1412 Sixteenth Street NW, Washington, D.C. 20036, publishes a directory of environmental and conservation groups in the United States. The Clearinghouse for Professional Responsibility, P.O. Box 486, Washington, D.C. 20044, maintains a file on local, state, and national citizens' groups active in many areas of public concern.

—Do your homework on the media, and help them with their homework. Investigative reporters are assigned to stories which require development and analysis. They are not limited to crisis-oriented, single-event reporting that newspapermen call "spot news." Rather, they are expected to develop stories too complex or too important to be treated routinely. Consequently, if you decide to tell your story to the media, try to interest an investigative reporter. Unfortunately, finding such a reporter, especially outside the very large metropolitan areas, may be a serious problem, and once you do find one you may have a difficult time interesting him or her in your situation. They are typically burdened with many assignments, face an endless series of deadlines, and, if they have established reputations, have a number of stories as important as yours from which to choose. You must come to the reporter fully prepared: develop a complete picture of the situation you wish to disclose and write it down beforehand. If you plan to submit a lengthy explanation, summarize or outline it separately so the reporter can get the essence of what you have to say without having to read page after page of supporting material and elaboration. This technique is equally applicable to any communication with an outside group or person you might wish to interest in taking some action. If the daily newspapers or broadcast media are not interested, consider approaching the more specialized journals like the *New Republic,* the *Nation,* the *Progressive, Washington Monthly, Environment,* or the *Texas Observer.* Frequently, once a smaller periodical has developed a story, the mass media will pick it up.

—Contact the Clearinghouse for Professional Responsibility, P.O. Box 486, Washington, D.C. 20044. The Clearinghouse was established to receive and disseminate information from professional and non-professional employees of large public and private organizations whose activity might imperil or endanger the public health, safety, or welfare.

The Clearinghouse strictly protects the mail sent to P.O. Box 486 in order to insure that any correspondent who so desires may have his letter held in confidence. The Clearinghouse does not act directly on the reports it receives. Instead, the writer is advised of the possible courses of action that may be available to him. He is told, for example, how to get in touch with a government agency, private group, or individual who might be interested in taking action on his information or complaint. The Clearinghouse may offer to communicate with an agency or group in his behalf. If he risks placing himself in some form of legal jeopardy, the Clearinghouse will warn him of the possibility. In some cases it may be necessary for the potential whistle blower to seek legal advice before taking any further action. When unsupported or poorly substantiated allegations are made, the correspondent will be asked to develop his position more fully or will be referred to someone who can help him strengthen his case. The Clearinghouse does not provide legal counsel to employees discharged or otherwise harassed for acting as their consciences dictate, but it will attempt to find legal counsel, attempt to enlist the aid of professional societies or other employee organizations, and suggest employment alternatives.

Underlying the struggle of persons within organizations and those without is the Nuremberg principle. Whatever the particular violation and wherever ultimate responsibility rests, this principle and those articulated by all the whistle blowers in this book have one common denominator: no organization, not even an army which demands discipline of the highest order or a nation which makes punishment for treason the price of disloyalty, can be the final arbiter of the rightness or wrongness of its actions. The individuals within the organization are on notice that the defense of "following orders" is fundamentally defective because there exists with respect to every organization a higher law, a higher principle, a higher morality. Organizations and those who direct them are on notice that subordinates— and this generation of whistle blowers should serve as conclusive evidence of the fact—will no longer remain serfs. The challenge for both the individual and the organization is to develop personal and institutional responses to accommodate these principles.

Notes

4. Whistle Blowing and the Law

1. "Power to the Corporation," *Industry Week*, January 4, 1971.

5. A. Ernest Fitzgerald

1. "The Dismissal of A. Ernest Fitzgerald by the Department of Defense," Hearings before the Subcommittee on Economy in Government of the Joint Economic Committee, Congress of the United States, November 17–18, 1969, p. 161.
2. Ibid., p. 12.
3. Ibid., p. 18.
4. Ibid., p. 150.
5. Ibid., p. 159.
6. Ibid., p. 45.
7. Ibid., p. 8.
8. Ibid.
9. Ibid., p. 10.
10. Ibid.
11. Ibid., p. 11.
12. Ibid., pp. 777–78.
13. *Congressional Record*, January 22, 1970.
14. Hearings, p. 11.
15. Ibid., pp. 130–131.
16. "Hearings on Military Posture," Armed Services Committee, May 7, 1969, p. 2693.
17. Hearings, Subcommittee on Economy in Government, p. 113.
18. Whistle Blowers Conference, January 30, 1971.
19. *Washington Post*, November 3, 1971, p. A-3.
20. *Washington Post*, November 23, 1971, p. A-2.
21. Conference.
22. Conference.
23. Conference.

6. Dr. John W. Gofman and Dr. Arthur R. Tamplin

1. Ralph E. Lapp, *New Republic*, January 23, 1971, p. 21. See also *New York Times Magazine*, February 7, 1971, p. 16.

2. The Federal Radiation Council was composed of the Secretaries of Health, Education, and Welfare (chairman), Labor, Defense, Commerce, and Agriculture, the Chairman of the Atomic Energy Commission, and the Special Assistant to the President for Science and Technology. The actual formulation of the standards, however, was accomplished by a special committee of the National Academy of Sciences which "relied heavily on data and information and standards of the National Council on Radiation Protection and the International Commission on Radiological Protection," according to the press office of the Atomic Energy Commission. See also Philip M. Boffey, "Radiation Standards: Are the Right People Making Decisions?" *Science*, vol. 171, February 26, 1971, p. 780.

3. "Epidemiologic Aspects of Cancer," *Ca—A Cancer Journal for Clinicians 19*, 1, pp. 27–35, 1969.

4. "Unanticipated Environmental Hazards Resulting from Technological Intrusions," reprinted in *Environment*, vol. 11, no. 2, March, 1969, pp. 9–28.

5. "Low Dose Radiation, Chromosomes, and Cancer," 1969 IEEE Nuclear Science Symposium, Sheraton-Palace Hotel, San Francisco, October 29, 1969.

6. Hearings, Senate Subcommittee on Air and Water Pollution, November, 1969.

7. Ibid.

8. Speech at Pitzer College, Claremont Colleges, January 14, 1971.

9. Dr. John Totter told William Hines of the *Chicago Sun-Times* in a taped interview on May 4, 1970: "Gofman, for example, has accused me of never reading it [the handbook]. Well, I'd like to know how many handbooks he has read. They're not for that purpose."

10. Letter from Dr. John Totter to Dr. Arthur Tamplin, August 21, 1969.

11. "AEC Staff Comments on Papers and Congressional Testimony by Dr. John W. Gofman and Dr. Arthur R. Tamplin."

12. "Staff Report on Allegations Made by Drs. Tamplin and Gofman of Censorship and Reprisal by the Atomic Energy Commission and the Lawrence Radiation Laboratory at Livermore," July 21, 1970, Atomic Energy Commission.

13. Interview with William Hines.

14. Bob Potter of the AAAS.

15. Philip M. Boffey, "Radiation Standards: Are the Right People Making Decisions?" *Science*, vol. 171, February 26, 1971, p. 780.

16. *Washington Post*, June 8, 1971, p. A-20.

17. Dr. James T. Brennan (NCRP), Department of Radiology, University of Pennsylvania Hospital, October 15, 1970, over TV Channel 16, Scranton, Pa.; also Dr. Richard M. Chamberlain (NRCP), Department of Radiology, University of Pennsylvania Hospital, August 20, 1970, to the Pennsylvania Senate, transcript p. 248.

18. "Government is the Most Dangerous of Genetic Engineers," *Washington Post*, Sunday, July 19, 1970 (based on Professor

Lederberg's testimony before Rep. Flood's House Appropriations Subcommittee).

19. *Bulletin of Atomic Scientists*, September, 1970.
20. Egan O'Connor quotes from "Health Implications of Fallout from Nuclear Weapons Testing through 1961," Report no. 3 of the Federal Radiation Council, May, 1962, Appendix B.
21. *Bulletin of Atomic Scientists*, September, 1970, p. 10.
22. Whistle Blowers Conference, January 30, 1971.
23. Egan O'Connor quotes Gofman in a review of the Gofman-Tamplin book in *Environmental Action*, February 8, 1971.
24. See Lauriston Taylor, AEC Commissioner, and H. J. Dunster, former chairman of the ICRP committee on radiation standards, who reviewed Gofman and Tamplin's book in *Nuclear Engineering*, a United Kingdom publication. Congressman Chet Holifield has publicly called them "irresponsible," as has Dr. John Totter of the AEC. Ralph Lapp refers to them as "overnight converts to a radiation religion," *New Republic*, January 23, 1971.
25. *Nuclear Engineering* (United Kingdom).
26. Dr. John W. Gofman, speech at Pitzer College, Claremont Colleges, January 14, 1971.

7. Edward Gregory

1. Statement at Whistle Blowers Conference, January 30, 1971.
2. Ibid.
3. Interview.
4. *Detroit News*, February 27, 1969.
5. *Newsweek*, March 10, 1969.
6. *Detroit News*, March 2, 1969.
7. No. 70 00394 06 23.
8. No. 71 00189 01 25.
9. No. 71 00177 01 25.
10. No. 71 00181 01 25.
11. Interview.
12. Conference.
13. Interview.

8. Jacqueline Verrett

1. Whistle Blowers Conference, January 30, 1971.
2. James S. Turner, *The Chemical Feast* (New York: Grossman Publishers, 1970), pp. 12–13.
3. Ibid., p. 13.
4. Ibid.
5. Conference.
6. Conference.
7. Conference.
8. Conference.
9. *The Chemical Feast*, p. 16.
10. Ibid., p. 25.

11. Ibid., p. 26.
12. Conference.
13. Conference.
14. Conference.

9. William I. Stieglitz

1. *Washington Post*, February 3, 1967, p. 11.
2. *New York Times*, February 3, 1967, pp. 1, 15.
3. Whistle Blowers Conference, January 30, 1971.
4. *Technology Review* (MIT alumni journal), February, 1971, pp. 30–31.
5. "Motor Vehicle Safety," Hearings of the House Subcommittee on Health and Safety, Committee on Interstate and Foreign Commerce, July, 1959, p. 234.
6. Ibid., p. 227.
7. Conference.
8. Conference.
9. "HR 13229 and Other Bills Relating to Safety," Hearings of the House Committee on Interstate and Foreign Commerce, April, 1966, p. 898.
10. Conference.
11. *New York Times*, February 3, 1967, pp. 1, 15.
12. Conference.
13. *New York Times*, February 3, 1967, pp. 1, 15.
14. "The Implementation of the National Traffic and Motor Vehicle Safety Act of 1966," Hearings of the Senate Committee on Commerce, March, 1967, p. 158.
15. Conference.
16. Conference.
17. Conference.
18. Conference.
19. Conference.
20. Conference.

10. Fumio Matsuda

1. According to family legend, the people who lived on the slopes of the mountain were irate. They surrounded the family's house with burning torches, but the family did not yield.
2. There was some publicity in the spring of 1971 about an infiltrator who attempted to learn the names of the secret backers and to discredit Matsuda and the Users Union.

11. A. Dale Console

1. "Competitive Problems in the Drug Industry," Hearings of the U.S. Senate Monopoly Subcommittee of the Select Committee on Small Business, March 14, 1969, p. 4501.
2. Ibid., p. 4501.

3. Ibid., p. 4503.
4. Ibid., p. 4501.
5. Ibid., p. 4503.
6. Ibid., pp. 4493–4.
7. Ibid., p. 4496.
8. Ibid., p. 4501.
9. Ibid., p. 4479.
10. Ibid., p. 4480.
11. Whistle Blowers Conference, January 30, 1971.
12. Conference.
13. Conference.
14. Conference.
15. Conference.

12. Christopher Pyle and Ralph Stein

1. Whistle Blowers Conference, January 30, 1971.
2. Conference.
3. *Washington Post*, March 3, 1971.
4. Conference.
5. "CONUS Revisited: The Army Covers Up," *Washington Monthly*, August, 1970, p. 50.
6. Ibid.
7. Ibid.
8. Ibid., p. 51.
9. Ibid.
10. Conference.
11. "CONUS Revisited," p. 51.
12. Conference.
13. *Washington Post*, March 25, 1971.
14. *Washington Post*, February 26, 1971.
15. Ibid.
16. Conference.

13. Charles Pettis

1. "Allegations of Mismanagement of a Peruvian Highway Project Financed with U.S. Assistance Funds," by the Comptroller General of the United States, December 2, 1971.
2. Ibid., p. 47.
3. Ibid., p. 53.
4. *Washington Monthly*, May, 1971, pp. 24–27.

14. The Colt Workers

1. The report is reproduced in 117 *Congressional Record* (daily ed.), November 5, 1971, p. E-11894.
2. Affidavit of Richard J. Welch, 117 *Congressional Record* (daily ed.), November 10, 1971, p. E-12051.
3. Affidavit of Victor L. Martinez, 117 *Congressional Record* (daily ed.), November 10, 1971, p. E-12051.

4. Affidavit of Robert J. Gregoire, 117 *Congressional Record* (daily ed.), November 10, 1971, p. E-12052.
5. Affidavit of Victor L. Martinez, 117 *Congressional Record* (daily ed.), November 10, 1971, p. E-12051.
6. 117 *Congressional Record* (daily ed.), November 22, 1971, p. S-19403.
7. *Hartford Times*, December 4, 1971, p. 1.

15. Whistle Blowers Beyond the Headlines

1. Paul C. Edwards, "A-Power Plant Near Completion," *Washington Post*, August 19, 1971, p. G-1–3.
2. *New York Times*, March 12, 1972, p. 64.
3. Ralph E. Lapp, *A Citizen's Guide to Nuclear Power* (Washington: The New Republic, 1971), a New Republic Pamphlet.
4. Thomas O'Toole, *Washington Post*, May 28, 1971, p. A-4.
5. Morton Mintz, *Washington Post*, July 18, 1971, pp. 1, 8.
6. Based on discussions with Gary Sellers and on Morton Mintz's article in *Washington Post*, September 27, 1970.
7. From Durk's testimony before the Knapp Commission reprinted in the *Washington Post*, December 20, 1971, p. A-18.
8. See *Washington Monthly*, May, 1971, pp. 34–35.
9. "The Acquisition of Weapons Systems," Hearings before the Subcommittee on Economy in Government of the Joint Economic Committee, 91st Congress, 2d Session, 1969, pp. 544–555.
10. See *American Men of Science,* 1954, 1960, and 1964. See also *Congressional Record*, February 28, 1969, p. S-2184.
11. Panetta's "resignation" was announced simultaneously to the public and to him.
12. *Washington Monthly*, June, 1970, pp. 75–83.
13. See, for example, Blumberg, "Corporate Responsibility and the Employee's Duty of Loyalty and Obedience," 24 *Oklahoma Law Review*, August, 1971, p. 306.
14. An estimated 400,000 children are poisoned each year, including 12,000 to 16,000 who require medical treatment and 3,200 who suffer moderate to severe brain damage from ingesting lead-based paints. *Congressional Record* (daily ed.), May 10, 1971, p. E-4177.
15. *Congressional Record* (daily ed.), June 4, 1971, p. E-5453.

16. The Corporation

1. This is not to suggest that the AAUP is a perfect model. It is in fact reluctant to get into what it considers local disputes unless it deems the threat to academic freedom to be of sufficient magnitude. It likewise grants wide discretion to institutions and to local faculty committees in dealing with individual cases.
2. Societies such as the Society of Automotive Engineers (SAE) and the American Society of Mechanical Engineers (ASME) rely so heavily on company-paid membership and facilities

and company-defined roles and meetings that the working committees and procedures are dominated by professional employees who are on company missions. Independence of decision is seriously lacking.

3. When a pension "vests," the employee will receive all or part of it at age sixty-five, for example, even if he retires immediately after vesting.

4. Available from ASPO, 1313 E. 16th St., Chicago, Ill. 60637, $6 prepaid.

5. Barbara and John Ehrenreich recount the Pugliese story in "Conscience of a Steelworker," *The Nation*, September 27, 1971, p. 268.

6. *Harvard Business Review*, July–August, 1971.

7. "The Corporate Ombudsman," *Harvard Business Review*, May–June, 1967.

8. *Wall Street Journal*, September 9, 1971.

17. The Government

1. *Pickering* v. *Board of Education*, 391 U.S. 563 (1968).

2. Remarks of William H. Rehnquist, "Public Dissent and the Public Employee" (speech before the Federal Bar Association, Washington, D.C., September 18, 1970).

3. *Washington Post*, April 17, 1971.

4. Secretary's Order No. 14-69, U.S. Dept. of Labor, March 14, 1969.

5. These reforms and others will be discussed at length in *The New Spoils System*, a study of the civil service and the Civil Service Commission by Robert Vaughn, scheduled for release in the summer of 1972. See also Appendix D of this book.

6. ACLU attorneys are volunteers, but the ACLU underwrites out-of-pocket expenses for cases its members undertake.

7. Daniel Ellsberg's disclosure of the Pentagon Papers sharply focuses the need to reform the current system of classification and to define any exception for national defense information so that the classification of any piece of information can be challenged in the proceeding in which the employee appeals his or her discharge. The former deputy assistant for security in the Air Force, William C. Florence, wrote, "Literally millions of documents are needlessly classified alongside of the relatively few—I would estimate from 1 to 5 percent in the Pentagon—which must legitimately be guarded in the national interest." *Washington Post*, December 12, 1971, p. C-1.

President Eisenhower's former press secretary, James Hagerty, dramatically confirmed Florence's analysis in testimony before Congressman William Moorhead's Government Information subcommittee. Hagerty reported that he would often have the President declassify documents personally to avoid red tape. "And the only thing that was Top Secret about that was what he [the President] would say when he had to go through such nonsense." *Washington Post*, March 7, 1972, p. A-8.

18. The Law

1. *Pickering* v. *Board of Education*, 391 U.S. 563 (1968).
2. See, for example, Adolf Berle, *Twentieth Century American Capitalism*, 1954, and his *Three Faces of Power*, 1967; Arthur S. Miller, "The Corporation as a Private Government in the World Community," 46 *Virginia Law Review*, 1960, p. 1539.
3. Respectively, *Marsh* v. *Alabama*, 360 U.S. 501 (1946) and *Amalgamated Food Employees Union* v. *Logan Valley Plaza*, 391 U.S. 308 (1968).
4. *NLRB* v. *Local 1229, IBEW*, 346 U.S. 464 (1953).
5. *Yellow Cab of California*, 65-1 ARB Par. 8256,44 LA 174,-445 (164) (Edgar A. Jones, Arbitrator).
6. *Initial Services, Ltd.* v. *Putterill*, 1967, *Wisconsin Law Review* 1032 (1968). For a discussion of this case and other legal aspects of whistle blowing, see Philip I. Blumberg, "Corporate Responsibility and the Employee's Duty of Loyalty and Obedience: A Preliminary Inquiry," *Oklahoma Law Review*, vol. 24, no. 3, August, 1971, pp. 279–318.
7. *Payne* v. *Western & A.R.R.*, 81 Tenn. 507 (1884).
8. State anti–yellow dog contract laws were overturned in *Adair* v. *United States*, 208 U.S. 161 (1908) and in *Coppage* v. *Kansas*, 236 U.S. 1 (1915). The NLRA was upheld in *NLRB* v. *Jones & Laughlin*, 301 U.S. 1 (1937).
9. Lawrence E. Blades, "Employment at Will vs. Individual Freedom: On Limiting the Abusive Exercise of Employer Power," 67 *Columbia Law Review* 1404 (1967).
10. Section 1905 of Title 18 of the U.S. Code.
11. See Working Papers of the Commission, Vol. I, p. 723, July, 1970.
12. See Professor Blades's article cited in Note 9.
13. *Odell* v. *Humble Oil & Refining Co.*, 201 F2d 123 (10th Cir. 1953).
14. *Congressional Record*, April 26, 1951.
15. The most exhaustive study of this act and the factors involved in its passage is Professor Stewart Macaulay's "Changing a Continuing Relationship Between a Large Corporation and Those Who Deal with It: Automobile Manufacturers, Their Dealers, and the Legal System, Parts I and II," in *Wisconsin Law Review*, Summer and Fall issues, 1965.
16. *Edwards* v. *Habib*, 397 F2d 687 (D.C. Cir. 1968). See also Note, 3 *Harvard Civil Rights—Civil Liberties Law Review* 193 (discussion of the lower court's treatment of the case).

IV. Strategies for Whistle Blowers

1. In the relatively infrequent prosecutions for the crime of misprision, most courts require that there be some evidence that the defendant concealed something from the authorities. See the case of *Lancey* v. *U.S.*, 356 F2d 407 (9th Cir. 1967) interpreting the federal crime, "misprision of a felony," 18 U.S.C. Section 4.

2. 26 U.S.C. Section 7623.
3. 19 U.S.C. Section 1619.
4. 26 U.S.C. Section 7263.
5. 21 U.S.C. Section 199.
6. Or so Hickel explained in his book, *Who Owns America.*
7. *New York Times*, March 9, 1969.
8. The experiences of Greenberg, Lenzner, and Gall are also treated at length in the *Washington Monthly* of December, 1969; June, 1970; and January, 1971, respectively.
9. For example, Blackman's Development Center in Washington, D.C., solicits confidential and anonymous reports on narcotics peddlers, and *Chicago Today*, a newspaper, has established a Secret Witness Bureau to "receive, pass on, and reward information that will help police to solve any of five major crimes." *Chicago Today*, May 26, 1971, p. 26.

Program of the Conference on Professional Responsibility

Mayflower Hotel—Colonial Room
Washington, D.C.
Saturday, January 30, 1971

9:00–9:10 AM	Peter Petkas: Introductions and Welcome
9:10–9:30	Ralph Nader: The Principles of Whistle Blowing
9:30–9:45	Questions and Answers
9:45–10:15	Professor Arthur S. Miller, George Washington Law School: "Whistle Blowing and the Law"
10:15–10:30	Questions and Answers
10:30–11:00	Robert Townsend: Whistle Blowing and the Corporation
11:00–11:15	Questions and Answers
11:15–11:45	Senator Proxmire: his views and experiences
11:45–Noon	Questions and Answers
Noon–12:45 PM	Lunch
12:45–1:30	First Panel Presentations

1. A. Ernest Fitzgerald (formerly with Air Force): C-5A and cost overruns
2. Ralph Stein (former Army enlisted man): Army intelligence operations against civilians
3. Edward Gregory (inspector at Fisher Body Plant, St. Louis): 2.5 million Chevrolets recalled with defective exhaust systems
4. William Stieglitz (former director, Motor Vehicle Performance Services, National Traffic Safety Agency)

1:30–1:45	First Panel Q&A
1:45–2:30	Second Panel Presentations

1. Dr. John Gofman and Dr. Arthur Tamplin (Lawrence Radiation Lab): AEC radiation guidelines
2. Dr. Dale Console (former medical director, E. R. Squibb Co.): AMA and the pharmaceutical industry
3. Dr. Jacqueline Verrett (FDA): cyclamates

2:30–2:45	Second Panel Q&A
2:45–3:00	Coffee Break
3:00–4:00	First Panel Roundtable: Discussion and audience participation
4:00–5:00	Second Panel Roundtable: Discussion and audience participation
5:00–5:45	Peter Petkas: Summation and Prospectus

Appendix B

Codes of Ethics

The following are taken from the codes of ethics or other official statements on professional responsibility of some of the leading professional societies in the United States.

The Engineer's Code*

Preamble

The Engineer, to uphold and advance the honor and dignity of the engineering profession and in keeping with high standards of ethical conduct:

—*Will be honest and impartial, and will serve with devotion his employer, his clients, and the public;*

—*Will strive to increase the competence and prestige of the engineering profession;*

—*Will use his knowledge and skill for the advancement of human welfare.*

Section 2—The Engineer will have proper regard for the safety, health, and welfare of the public in the performance of his professional duties. If his engineering judgment is overruled by non-technical authority, he will clearly point out the consequences. He will notify the proper authority of any observed conditions which endanger public safety and health.

a. He will regard his duty to the public welfare as paramount.

b. He shall seek opportunities to be of constructive service in civic affairs and work for the advancement of the safety, health and well-being of his community.

c. He will not complete, sign, or seal plans and/or specifications that are not of a design safe to the public health and welfare and in conformity with accepted engineering standards. If the client or employer insists on such unprofessional conduct, he shall notify the proper authorities and withdraw from further service on the project.

Section 7—The Engineer will not disclose confidential information concerning the business affairs or technical processes of any present or former client or employer without his consent.

a. While in the employ of others, he will not enter promotional efforts or negotiations for work or make arrangements for other employment as a principal or to practice in connection with a specific project for which he has gained particular and specialized knowledge without the consent of all interested parties.

Section 13—The Engineer will not associate with or allow the use of his name by an enterprise of questionable character, nor will he become professionally associated with engineers who do not conform to ethical practices, or with

* From the Code of Ethics for Engineers of the National Society of Professional Engineers, NSPE Publication No. 1102, as revised, January, 1971

persons not legally qualified to render the professional services for which the association is intended.

a. He will conform with registration laws in his practice of engineering.

b. He will not use association with a nonengineer, a corporation, or partnership, as a "cloak" for unethical acts, but must accept personal responsibility for his professional acts. Note: In regard to the question of application of the Code to corporations vis-a-vis real persons, business form or type should not negate nor influence conformance of individuals to the Code. The Code deals with professional services, which services must be performed by real persons. Real persons in turn establish and implement policies within business structures. The Code is clearly written to apply to the Engineer and it is incumbent on a member of NSPE to endeavor to live up to its provisions. This applies to all pertinent sections of the Code.

The Civil Engineer's Code*

For attainment of the broad goal of quality living, the American Society of Civil Engineers recommends that the individual civil engineer dedicate himself to the following objectives in relation to his work, to his clients and to his professional affiliations, and to his role as citizen in a democratic society.

1) In relation to his work, the civil engineer must recognize the effect his efforts will have on the environment. He is, therefore, obligated to increase his knowledge and competence in incorporating ecological considerations in his design.

2) In relation to his client, the civil engineer must inform the latter of the environmental consequences compared with the benefits of the services requested and the design selected, recommending only responsible courses of action. He must be prepared to relinquish his services in the event the client insists on a course of action which can be demonstrated to have undesirable consequences to the environment. The engineer must also seriously weigh social and national considerations and alternatives when appropriate, in addition to the apparent lowest-cost and technical aspects of a project.

3) In relation to ASCE, the civil engineer must fully utilize mechanisms within the Society which lend support to his own individual efforts to implement environmental considerations. Active support by the Society will enable him to deal more effectively with clients reluctant to accept such factors in their projects.

4) In his role as a citizen, the civil engineer must recognize the urgent need for adequate legislation and enforcement to protect the environment. He must, therefore, take the lead in development, modification and support of government programs, to insure adequate environmental protection.

* From a position paper of the American Society of Civil Engineers' Council on Environmental Systems published in the Society's magazine, *Civil Engineering*, September, 1971

The Chemist's Creed*

AS A CHEMIST, I HAVE A RESPONSIBILITY:

to the public
to propagate a true understanding of chemical science, avoiding premature, false, or exaggerated statements, to discourage enterprises or practices inimical to the public interest or welfare, and to share with other citizens a responsibility for the right and beneficent use of scientific discoveries.

to my science
to search for its truths by use of the scientific method, and to enrich it by my own contributions for the good of humanity.

to my profession
to uphold its dignity as a foremost branch of learning and practice, to exchange ideas and information through its societies and publications, to give generous recognition to the work of others, and to refrain from undue advertising.

to my employer
to serve him undividedly and zealously in mutual interest, guarding his concerns and dealing with them as I would my own.

to myself
to maintain my professional integrity as an individual, to strive to keep abreast of my profession, to hold the highest ideals of personal honor, and to live an active, well-rounded, and useful life.

to my employees
to treat them as associates, being ever mindful of their physical and mental well-being, giving them encouragement in their work, as much freedom for personal development as is consistent with the proper conduct of work, and compensating them fairly, both financially and by acknowledgment of their scientific contributions.

to my students and associates
to be a fellow learner with them, to strive for clarity and directness of approach, to exhibit patience and encouragement, and to lose no opportunity for stimulating them to carry on the great tradition.

to my clients
to be a faithful and incorruptible agent, respecting confidence, advising honesty, and charging fairly.

* Approved by the Council of the American Chemical Society, September 14, 1965

Excerpts from the
Code of Professional Responsibility
of the American Bar Association

Disciplinary Rule 1–102   Misconduct
(A) A lawyer shall not:
  (1) Violate a Disciplinary Rule.
  (2) Circumvent a Disciplinary Rule through actions of another.
  (3) Engage in illegal conduct involving moral turpitude.
  (4) Engage in conduct involving dishonesty, fraud, deceit, or misrepresentation.
  (5) Engage in conduct that is prejudicial to the administration of justice.

Disciplinary Rule 2–110   Withdrawal from Employment
(B) Mandatory withdrawal.
  A lawyer representing a client before a tribunal, with its permission if required by its rules, shall withdraw from employment, and a lawyer representing a client in other matters shall withdraw from employment if:
  (1) He knows or it is obvious that his client is bringing the legal action, conducting the defense, or asserting a position in the litigation, or is otherwise having steps taken for him, merely for the purpose of harassing or maliciously injuring any person.
  (2) He knows or it is obvious that his continued employment will result in violation of a Disciplinary Rule.
(C) Permissive withdrawal.
  If DR 2–110 (B) is not applicable, a lawyer may not request permission to withdraw in matters pending before a tribunal, and may not withdraw in other matters, unless such request or such withdrawal is because:
  (1) His client:
    (a) Insists upon presenting a claim or defense that is not warranted under existing law and cannot be supported by good faith argument for an extension, modification, or reversal of existing law.
    (b) Personally seeks to pursue an illegal course of conduct.
    (c) Insists that the lawyer pursue a course of conduct that is illegal or that is prohibited under the Disciplinary Rules.
    (d) By other conduct renders it unreasonably diffi-

cult for the lawyer to carry out his employment effectively.

   (e) Insists, in a matter not pending before a tribunal, that the lawyer engage in conduct that is contrary to the judgment and advice of the lawyer but not prohibited under the Disciplinary Rules.

(2) His continued employment is likely to result in a violation of a Disciplinary Rule.

CANON 4
A Lawyer Should Preserve the Confidences and Secrets of a Client

Disciplinary Rule 4–101   Preservation of Confidences and Secrets of a Client

(A) "Confidence" refers to information protected by the attorney-client privilege under applicable law, and "secret" refers to other information gained in the professional relationship that the client has requested be held inviolate or the disclosure of which would be embarrassing or would be likely to be detrimental to the client.

(B) Except when permitted under DR 4–101 (C), a lawyer shall not knowingly:

   (1) Reveal a confidence or secret of his client.

   (2) Use a confidence or secret of his client to the disadvantage of the client.

   (3) Use a confidence or secret of his client for the advantage of himself or of a third person, unless the client consents after full disclosure.

(C) A lawyer may reveal:

   (1) Confidences or secrets with the consent of the client or clients affected, but only after a full disclosure to them.

   (2) Confidences or secrets when permitted under Disciplinary Rules or required by law or court order.

   (3) The intention of his client to commit a crime and the information necessary to prevent the crime.

   (4) Confidences or secrets necessary to establish or collect his fee or to defend himself or his employees or associates against an accusation of wrongful conduct.

(D) A lawyer shall exercise reasonable care to prevent his employees, associates, and others whose services are utilized by him from disclosing or using confidences or secrets of a client, except that a lawyer may reveal the information allowed by DR 4–101 (C) through an employee.

CANON 5
A Lawyer Shoud Exercise Independent
Professional Judgment on Behalf of a Client

Ethical Consideration 5–24
. . . Although a lawyer may be employed by a business corporation with non-lawyers serving as directors or officers and they necessarily have the right to make decisions of business policy, a lawyer must decline to accept direction of his professional judgment from any layman.

CANON 7
A Lawyer Should Represent a Client
Zealously Within the Bounds of the Law

Ethical Consideration 7–3
Where the bounds of the law are uncertain, the action of a lawyer may depend on whether he is serving as advocate or adviser. A lawyer may serve simultaneously as both advocate and adviser, but the two roles are essentially different. In asserting a position on behalf of his client, an advocate for the most part deals with past conduct and must take the facts as he finds them. By contrast, a lawyer serving as adviser primarily assists his client in determining the course of future conduct and relationships. While serving as advocate, a lawyer should resolve in favor of his client doubts as to the bounds of the law. In serving a client as adviser, a lawyer in appropriate circumstances should give his professional opinion as to what the ultimate decisions of the courts would likely be as to the applicable law.

Ethical Consideration 7–5
A lawyer as adviser furthers the interest of his client by giving his professional opinion as to what he believes would likely be the ultimate decision of the courts on the matter at hand and by informing his client of the practical effect of such decision. He may continue in the representation of his client even though his client has elected to pursue a course of conduct contrary to the advice of the lawyer so long as he does not thereby knowingly assist the client to engage in illegal conduct or to take a frivolous legal position. A lawyer should never encourage or aid his client to commit criminal acts or counsel his client on how to violate the law and avoid punishment therefor.

Ethical Consideration 7–8
A lawyer should exert his best efforts to insure that decisions of his client are made only after the client has been in-

formed of relevant considerations. A lawyer ought to initiate this decision-making process if the client does not do so. Advice of a lawyer to his client need not be confined to purely legal considerations. A lawyer should advise his client of the possible effect of each legal alternative. A lawyer should bring to bear upon this decision-making process the fullness of his experience as well as his objective viewpoint. In assisting his client to reach a proper decision, it is often desirable for a lawyer to point out those factors which may lead to a decision that is morally just as well as legally permissible. He may emphasize the possibility of harsh consequences that might result from assertion of legally permissible positions. In the final analysis, however, the lawyer should always remember that the decision whether to forgo legally available objectives or methods because of non-legal factors is ultimately for the client and not for himself. In the event that the client in a non-adjudicatory matter insists upon a course of conduct that is contrary to the judgment and advice of the lawyer but not prohibited by Disciplinary Rules, the lawyer may withdraw from the employment.

Ethical Consideration 7–10
The duty of a lawyer to represent his client with zeal does not militate against his concurrent obligation to treat with consideration all persons involved in the legal process and to avoid the infliction of needless harm.

Ethical Consideration 7–17
The obligation of loyalty to his client applies only to a lawyer in the discharge of his professional duties and implies no obligation to adopt a personal viewpoint favorable to the interests or desires of his client. While a lawyer must act always with circumspection in order that his conduct will not adversely affect the rights of a client in a matter he is then handling, he may take positions on public issues and espouse legal reforms he favors without regard to the individual views of any client.

Ethical Consideration 7–27
Because it interferes with the proper administration of justice, a lawyer should not suppress evidence that he or his client has a legal obligation to reveal or produce. In like manner, a lawyer should not advise or cause a person to secrete himself or to leave the jurisdiction of a tribunal for the purpose of making him unavailable as a witness therein.

Disciplinary Rule 7–102   Representing a Client Within the Bounds of the Law
(A) In his representation of a client, a lawyer shall not:

(3) Conceal or knowingly fail to disclose that which he is required by law to reveal.

(4) Knowingly use perjured testimony or false evidence.

(5) Knowingly make a false statement of law or fact.

(6) Participate in the creation or preservation of evidence when he knows or it is obvious that the evidence is false.

(7) Counsel or assist his client in conduct that the lawyer knows to be illegal or fraudulent.

(8) Knowingly engage in other illegal conduct or conduct contrary to a Disciplinary Rule.

(B) A lawyer who receives information clearly establishing that:

(1) His client has, in the course of the representation, perpetrated a fraud upon a person or tribunal shall promptly call upon his client to rectify the same, and if his client refuses or is unable to do so, he shall reveal the fraud to the affected person or tribunal.

(2) A person other than his client has perpetrated a fraud upon a tribunal shall promptly reveal the fraud to the tribunal.

Principles of Medical Ethics*

Preamble
These principles are intended to aid physicians individually and collectively in maintaining a high level of ethical conduct. They are not laws but standards by which a physician may determine the propriety of his conduct in his relationship with patients, with colleagues, with members of allied professions, and with the public.
Section 1
The principal objective of the medical profession is to render service to humanity with full respect for the dignity of man. Physicians should merit the confidence of patients entrusted to their care, rendering to each a full measure of service and devotion.
Section 2
Physicians should strive continually to improve medical knowledge and skill, and should make available to their patients and colleagues the benefits of their professional attainments.
Section 3
A physician should practice a method of healing founded on a scientific basis; and he should not voluntarily associate professionally with anyone who violates this principle.
Section 4
The medical profession should safeguard the public and itself against physicians deficient in moral character or professional competence. Physicians should observe all laws, uphold the dignity and honor of the profession and accept its self-imposed disciplines. They should expose, without hesitation, illegal or unethical conduct of fellow members of the profession.
Section 5
A physician may choose whom he will serve. In an emergency, however, he should render service to the best of his ability. Having undertaken the care of a patient, he may not neglect him; and unless he has been discharged he may discontinue his services only after giving adequate notice. He should not solicit patients.
Section 6
A physician should not dispose of his services under terms or conditions which tend to interfere with or impair the free and complete exercise of his medical judgment and skill

* Adopted by the American Medical Association in 1957

or tend to cause a deterioration of the quality of medical care.

Section 7

In the practice of medicine a physician should limit the source of his professional income to medical services actually rendered by him, or under his supervision, to his patients. His fee should be commensurate with the services rendered and the patient's ability to pay. He should neither pay nor receive a commission for referral of patients. Drugs, remedies or appliances may be dispensed or supplied by the physician provided it is in the best interest of the patient.

Section 8

A physician should seek consultation upon request; in doubtful or difficult cases; or whenever it appears that the quality of medical services may be enhanced thereby.

Section 9

A physician may not reveal the confidences entrusted to him in the course of medical attendance, or the deficiencies he may observe in the character of patients, unless he is required to do so by law or unless it becomes necessary in order to protect the welfare of the individual or of the community.

Section 10

The honored ideals of the medical profession imply that the responsibilities of the physician extend not only to the individual, but also to society where these responsibilities deserve his interest and participation in activities which have the purpose of improving both the health and the well-being of the individual and the community.

Appendix C

*The Muskie Amendments**

* From S.2770, an act to amend the Federal Water Pollution Control Act (the so-called Muskie amendments), passed unanimously (86–0) by the Senate, November 2, 1971. A similar, somewhat stronger, provision appears in the Coal Mine Safety Act, Public Law 91–173, signed into law, December 30, 1969.

Employee Protection

Sec. 507(a) No person shall discharge, or in any other way discriminate against, or cause to be discharged or discriminated against any employee or any authorized representative of employees by reason of the fact that such employee or representative of any alleged violator has filed, instituted, or caused to be filed or instituted any proceeding under this Act, or has testified or is about to testify in any proceeding resulting from the administration or enforcement of the provisions of this Act.

(b) Any employee or a representative of employees who believes that he has been discharged or otherwise discriminated against by any person in violation of subsection (a) of this section may within thirty days after such violation occurs, apply to the Secretary of Labor for a review of such alleged discharge or discrimination. A copy of the application shall be sent to such person who shall be the respondent. Upon receipt of such application, the Secretary of Labor shall cause such investigation to be made as he deems appropriate. Such investigation shall provide an opportunity for a public hearing at the request of any party to enable the parties to present information relating to such violation. The parties shall be given written notice of the time and place of the hearing at least five days prior to the hearing. Any such hearing shall be of record and shall be subject to section 554 of title 5 of the United States Code. Upon receiving the report of such investigation, the Secretary of Labor shall make findings of fact. If he finds that such violation did occur, he shall issue a decision, incorporating an order therein and his findings, requiring the party committing such violation to take such affirmative action to abate the violation as the Secretary of Labor deems appropriate, including, but not limited to, the rehiring or reinstatement of the employees or representative of employees to his former position with compensation. If he finds that there was no such violation, he shall issue an order denying the application. Such order issued by the Secretary of Labor under this subparagraph shall be subject to judicial review in the same manner as orders and decisions of the Administrator are subject to judicial review under this Act.

(c) Whenever an order is issued under this section to abate such violation, at the request of the applicant, a sum equal to the aggregate amount of all costs and expenses (including the attorney's fees) as determined by the Secretary of Labor to have been reasonably incurred by the applicant for, or in connection with, the institution and prosecution of such proceedings, shall be assessed against the person committing such violation.

Comments on the Muskie Proposal

The Muskie proposal is deficient in a number of ways:

1) Protection should also be extended to employees who report violations directly to the Administrator of the Act and to those who respond by testimony or otherwise to Congressional inquiries.

2) The employee must notify the Secretary within 30 days of the discharge or other act of discrimination. This gives him very little leeway in which to consider alternative courses of action or to negotiate a settlement directly with his employer. Also, since there is no provision for notifying employees of their rights under the Act, 30 days may pass before an employee even knows of his remedy.

3) The Secretary should be required to complete his investigation and make a decision within a limited period of time, perhaps 90 days. And he should be required to explain the reasons for any decisions against the employee, as he is required to do when he finds *for* the employee.

4) Courts reviewing the actions of the Secretary should have the *express* power of reviewing the adequacy of any remedy granted by the Secretary.

5) In another section of the Muskie bill (Section 505) provision is made for citizen suits against the Administrator for failure to carry out his responsibilities under the Act. But this provision does not expressly permit suits against the Secretary of Labor for failure to carry out the employee protection section. The employee should be given this additional assurance of his rights.

—The Authors

Draft of an Employee Rights and Accountability Act*

A BILL TO expand the rights of federal employees and to insure the accountability of such employees to the citizens of the United States.

Be it enacted by the Senate and House of Representatives of the United States of America in Congress assembled, That this Act may be cited as the "Federal Employee Rights and Accountability Act of 19—."

TITLE I.—FINDINGS AND DECLARATION OF PURPOSE

Sec. 101. Findings.

The Congress hereby finds that:

(a) Employees of the Federal government risk substantial damage to their careers, possible loss of their livelihoods, and other forms of harassment if they express their views about

    (1) the management of their agencies;

    (2) the failure of their agencies to serve their statutory functions;

    (3) the direction of agency policy;

    (4) conflicts of public and private interest within their agencies; or

    (5) illegal conduct by the agency or its employees.

(b) These risks exist to a large extent without regard to whether views are expressed through appropriate channels within the agency, to committees of Congress which have jurisdiction over the subject matter involved, through the fulfillment of lawful obligations of employees, or to the public at large;

(c) Existing laws, rules, and regulations of the separate

---

* This draft of a proposed Employee Rights and Accountability Act is a result of a request made to Ralph Nader by Senator Proxmire at the Conference on Professional Responsibility. It is keyed to present laws relating to federal government employees, but can be easily modified for adoption by state legislatures. It would *not* affect the rights of nongovernment employees, but many of the ideas contained within it—for example, an employee bill of rights, expanded access for citizen complainants, and expanded personal responsibility—could be incorporated into laws intended to increase the protection of unorganized employees. Senator Proxmire plans to introduce a version of this proposal in Congress in 1972. The principal draftsmen were Peter Petkas and Robert Vaughn, attorneys with Ralph Nader's Corporate Accountability Research Group and Public Interest Research Group, respectively.

agencies and of the Civil Service Commission have proven seriously deficient both for employees and for citizens;

(d) Similarly, citizens, under present laws, rules, and regulations do not have adequate access to the courts to seek the removal of employees and officials who fail to discharge their duties either under the laws which prescribe the responsibilities of federal agencies or those which regulate the conduct of federal employees;

(e) The failure of agencies and their employees to fully implement Congressional enactments is frequently due to the inability of knowledgeable employees to communicate to the Congress and to the public information vital to the oversight functions of Congress and to the public's right to know.

Sec. 102. Declaration of Purpose.

The Congress finds the purpose of this Act to be

(a) To enhance the rights of Federal employees to challenge the actions or failures of their agencies and to express their views, without fear of retaliation, through appropriate channels within the agency, through complete and frank responses to Congressional inquiry, through free access to law enforcement officials, through oversight agencies of both the executive and legislative branches of Government, and through appropriate communication with the public.

(b) To broaden remedies available to citizens to hold government employees accountable for the performance of their duties;

(c) To insure that Acts of Congress enacted to protect individual citizens are properly enforced;

(d) To provide new rights and remedies to guarantee that citizens can have confidence in their government and to insure that public offices are truly public trusts.

TITLE II.—PROTECTION OF EMPLOYEES AND OF CONGRESSIONAL ACCESS TO INFORMATION

Sec. 201. Definitions.

(a) For the purposes of the Act, "employee" (except as otherwise provided by this Act or when specifically modified) is defined as in 5 USC §2105 except that

(1) an employee paid from nonappropriated funds of the Army and Air Force Exchange Service, Army and Air Force Motion Picture Service, Navy Ship's Stores Ashore, Navy exchanges, Marine Corps exchanges, Coast Guard exchanges, and other instrumentalities of the armed forces conducted for the comfort, pleasure, contentment and mental and physical improvement of personnel of the armed forces is deemed an employee for the purposes of this Act; and

(2) an employee appointed by the President with the

advice and consent of the Senate or an employee in a confidential or policy-determining character as enumerated in 5 CFR §213.3276 is not an employee for purposes of this title.

(b) For purposes of this Act, "dismissed" (except as otherwise provided by this Act or when specifically modified) shall mean any personnel or manpower action which separates an employee or abolishes his position.

(c) For purposes of this Act, "agency" shall include every authority of the United States subject to the Administrative Procedure Act and shall also include any organization which has one or more corporate directors, commissioners, chief executive officers, or members of a governing body appointed by the President or an appointee of the President.

Sec. 202. Employee Bill of Rights.

Employees shall have the following rights which the Employee Rights and Accountability Board established in Title IV of this Act and its agents shall have the duty to defend, protect, and enforce:

1. The right to freely express their opinions on all public issues, including those related to the duties they are assigned to perform, *provided, however*, that any agency may promulgate reasonable rules and regulations requiring that any such opinions be clearly dissociated from agency or administration policy.

2. The right to disclose information unlawfully suppressed; information concerning illegal or unethical conduct which threatens or which is likely to threaten public health or safety or which involves the unlawful appropriation or use of public funds; information which would tend to impeach the testimony of officers or employees of the government before committees of Congress or the responses of such officers or employees to inquiries from members of the Senate or House of Representatives concerning the implementation of programs, the expenditure of public funds, and the protection of the constitutional rights of citizens and the rights of government employees under this Act and under any other laws, rules, or regulations for the protection of the rights of employees; *provided, however*, that nothing in this section shall be construed to permit the disclosure of the contents of personnel files, personal medical reports, or the disclosure of any other information in such a manner as to invade the individual privacy of an employee or citizen of the United States.

3. The right to communicate freely and openly with members of Congress and to respond fully and with candor to inquiries from committees of Congress and from members of Congress, *provided, however*, that nothing in this section

shall be construed to permit the invasion of the individual privacy of other employees or of citizens of the United States.

4. The right to assemble in public places for the free discussion of matters of interest to themselves and to the public and the right to notify fellow employees and the public of such meetings.

5. The right to due process in the resolution of grievances and appeals including, but not limited to:

—the right to counsel,

—the right to a public hearing and a copy of the transcript of such hearing,

—the right to cross examine witnesses and to compel the attendance and testimony of witnesses and to compel the production of all relevant documents in the course of such a hearing or other similar proceeding,

—the right to testify and submit evidence on behalf of other employees and of other citizens seeking redress in the courts or in the administrative process.

6. The right to humane, dignified, and reasonable conditions of employment which allow for personal growth and self-fulfillment, and for the unhindered discharge of job and civic responsibilities.

7. The right to individual privacy, *provided, however*, that nothing in this section shall limit in any manner an employee's access to his own personnel file, medical report file or any other file or document concerning his status or performance within his agency.

Sec. 203. Complaints of criminal harassment for Congressional testimony.

(a) Any complaint alleging violation of 18 USC §1505 (which prohibits coercion and harassment of Congressional witnesses) shall be promptly investigated by the Justice Department. Within six months after the filing of a complaint, the Justice Department shall render a decision on whether or not prosecution under that section is warranted. If the Department decides prosecution is not warranted, it shall state with specificity the facts and reasons upon which such decision is based.

(b) If the Justice Department renders a decision pursuant to this section that prosecution is not warranted or if it fails to render a decision as required by this section, any citizen may petition the United States district court for the district in which the alleged violation took place or the United States District Court for the District of Columbia for an order to compel prosecution. If the court finds, after an independent review of the evidence, that a prima facie case exists, it shall order prosecution to be commenced.

(c) In its independent review of evidence the court shall have access to the enforcement file of the Justice Department and to all other relevant documents or files within that department or any agency thereof.

TITLE III.—ACCOUNTABILITY OF EMPLOYEES
Sec. 301. Definitions.

(a) For purposes of this Title, "conflicts of interest" shall include behavior proscribed by 18 USC §§201–224. In addition, "conflicts of interest" may include behavior which the court in the exercise of sound discretion proscribes. In the exercise of its discretion, the court may consider Executive Orders addressed to the subject, rules and regulations governing employee conduct and principles of fiduciary law.

(b) For purposes of this Title, "employee" shall be defined as in section 201 of this Act, except that an employee appointed by the President with the advice and consent of the Senate or an employee in a position of a confidential or policy-determining character as enumerated in 5 CFR §213.3276 shall be an employee for purposes of this Title.

(c) For purposes of this Title, an "employee responsible" is one to whom Congress has delegated authority and any employee to whom such authority has been redelegated.

(d) For purposes of this Title, "consumer protection law" shall include any law intended to protect or which does in fact protect individual consumers from unfair, deceptive, or misleading acts or practices; anticompetitive acts or practices; or non-disclosure or inadequate disclosure of product quality, weight, size, or performance.

Sec. 302. Public employees as fiduciaries.

(a) Any employee who administers, enforces, or implements any health, safety, environmental, or consumer protection law or any rules or regulations promulgated for the enforcement of such laws, is a fiduciary to any individual or class of individuals intended to be protected or who are in fact protected from injury or harm or risk of injury or harm by such laws, rules, or regulations, and, as a fiduciary, is obligated to protect such individuals or class of individuals.

(b) Any individual or class of individuals may commence a civil action on his or its own behalf against any employee or employees in any agency for breach of a fiduciary duty upon a showing that said employee or employees by their acts or omissions have exposed said individual or class of individuals to injury or harm, or risk of injury or harm, from which they are to be protected by the employee or employees. Such action may be brought in the United States district court for the district in which the employee or any one of the employees resides or in the United States District for the District of Columbia. The district court shall have jurisdiction to entertain such action without regard to the amount in controversy or the diversity of citizenship of the parties. The United States through the Attorney General shall defend any employee or employees against whom such action is commenced. Such employee or employees may, however, at his or their option provide for his or their own defense.

(c) If the court finds that any employee or employees have breached their fiduciary duty by any act or omission or by any series of acts or omissions, the court—

(1) shall order performance or cessation of performance, as appropriate;

(2) may temporarily suspend any person or persons without pay from the agency for a period not exceeding three months;

(3) may remove an individual or individuals from the agency; or

(4) may take any other appropriate action against any employee or employees within the agency who have breached the duties of the fiduciary relationship.

Sec. 303. Curbing fraud and conflicts of interest.

(a)(1) Any citizen shall have a right to commence a suit in the United States district court of the district in which he resides or in United States District Court for the District of Columbia on behalf of the United States to recover funds which have been improperly paid by the United States while there exists any conflict of interest on the part of the employee responsible for such payment.

(2) It shall be an affirmative defense to any action under this section that the defendant did not know or have reason to know of the conflict of interest.

(b) Any citizen who commences a suit under this section shall be entitled to 30% of the amount recovered for the government plus attorney's fees and other costs incidental to the action.

(c) The right of a citizen to commence and maintain a suit under this section shall continue notwithstanding any action taken by the Justice Department or any United States attorney, *provided, however*, that if the United States shall first commence suit, a citizen may not commence a suit under this section, *provided further, however*, that if the United States shall fail to carry on such suit with due diligence within a period of six months or within such additional time as the court may allow, a citizen may commence a suit under this section and such suit shall continue notwithstanding any action taken by the Justice Department or any United States attorney.

Sec. 304. Intent of Congress in Section 303.

In Section 303 of this Title, it is the intent of Congress to create a right of citizens to commence and maintain suits under the provisions of this Title.

TITLE IV.—EMPLOYEE RIGHTS AND ACCOUNTABILITY BOARD

Sec. 401. Definition.

For purposes of this Title, "employee" shall be defined as in section 201 of this Act, except that an employee appointed by the President with the advice and consent of the Senate or an employee in a position of a confidential or policy-determining character as enumerated in 5 CFR §213.3276 shall be an employee for purposes of this Title.

Sec. 402. Establishment of the Employee Rights and Accountability Board.

(a) There is hereby established an Employee Rights and Accountability Board (hereinafter referred to as the "Board"). The Board shall be composed of five members, to be appointed as hereinafter directed. No more than three members of the Board may be of the same political party. No more than two members of the Board may have ever served in personnel, management, or administrative positions in any agency. Three members of the Board shall be attorneys admitted to practice before the bar of any jurisdiction in the United States for three years at the time of appointment. No member shall be eligible for reappointment.

(b) The term of office of each member of the Board shall be six years, except that, (1) of those members first appointed, two shall serve for two years and two shall serve for four years, respectively, from the date of appointment, and (2) any member appointed to fill a vacany occurring prior to the expiration of the term for which his or her predecessor was appointed shall be appointed for the remainder of such term.

(c) The Chairman of the Board shall be elected by the Board to serve a two-year term. The Chairman shall be the chief executive and administrative office of the Board.

(d) All members of the Board shall be compensated at the rate provided for in Executive Level 2 as set out in section 5313 of Title 5 of the United States Code.

(e) Three members of the Board shall constitute a quorum for the transaction of business.

(f) The Board may appoint and fix the compensations of such officers, attorneys, and employees, and make such expenditures as may be necessary to carry out its functions.

(g) Notwithstanding section 206 of the Budget and Accounting Act of 1921 (31 USC §15), the Board shall transmit its estimates and requests for appropriations (including any requests for increases therein) directly to the Senate and House of Representatives.

(h) One member of the Board shall be appointed by the President with the advice and consent of the Senate, two members shall be appointed by the president pro tempore of the Senate, and two members shall be appointed by the Speaker of the House of Representatives; *provided that* the first member appointed by the President shall serve six years, the first members appointed by the president pro tempore of the Senate shall serve two and four years respectively, and the first members appointed by the Speaker of the House of Representatives shall serve four and two years respectively.

Sec. 403. Office of Inspection and Complaint.

(a) The Board shall establish an Office of Inspection and Complaint which shall perform the following functions:

(1) Conduct inspections of all agencies to insure compliance with orders of the Board;

(2) Conduct inspections to provide information on the implementation of rules and regulations of the Board;

(3) Conduct inspections to discover violations of rules and regulations of the Board;

(4) Investigate complaints filed with the Board by citizens and employees pursuant to this Title;

(5) Initiate actions against employees for violations of this Title or rules and regulations promulgated hereunder; and

(6) Perform such other investigative functions as the Board may prescribe.

(b) The Office of Inspection and Complaint shall be administered by an Inspector General, who shall be appointed by the Board for a term of seven years and who shall be removable only for good cause.

Sec. 404. Office of Trial Examiners.

(a) The Board shall establish an Office of Trial Examiners which shall hear and adjudicate complaints filed under this Title.

(b) No person may serve as a trial examiner or perform any of the duties of a trial examiner, who is not admitted to practice before the bar of any jurisdiction in the United States.

(c) The Office of Trial Examiners shall be administered by a Chief Examiner appointed by the Board for a six-year term.

(d) The Office of Trial Examiners shall not be subordinate to any other office under the Board, but shall receive its authority and direction directly from the Board.

Sec. 405. Powers of the Board.

The Employee Rights and Accountability Board shall have, in addition to the authority necessary and proper for carrying out its duties and the duties of its subordinate agencies and officers as specified elsewhere in this Title, the authority to—

(1) Inspect and investigate all aspects of the Federal personnel system, including but not limited to the effectiveness of disciplinary procedures and violations of employee rights;

(2) Appoint and remove all subordinate officials and employees, subject to the rules and regulations of the Board applicable to all civil servants; *provided, however,* that the Inspector General and the Chief Examiner shall be removable only for good cause;

(3) Hear and adjudicate complaints received from Federal agencies and departments, from employees, and from citizens, including employee complaints alleging wrongful dismissal;

(4) Reprimand, suspend, fine, or remove any employee, or take other appropriate disciplinary action, *provided, however,* that any such action shall be taken pursuant to duly promulgated regulations of the Board and shall not be inconsistent with the rights of employees granted by the Act, *provided further, however,* that the Board shall have the power to order any fines or portion thereof assessed pursuant to this section paid to the person, persons, or agency damaged by the employee hereunder fined, upon application and proof of loss;

(5) Establish standards of conduct for all employees pertaining to the performance of duties, conflicts of interests, and improper use of personnel management authority;

(6) Conduct and manage its own litigation without review, clearance, or participation by any agency of the Executive branch, including the Department of Justice;

(7) Review employee complaints filed with the office of Inspection and Complaint which allege that a transfer, reassignment, or manpower separation or readjustment was motivated by malice or taken in retaliation for the exercise of any employee's rights as an employee or as a citizen; and

(8) Promulgate any rules or regulations necessary for the fulfillment of its duties under this Act.

Sec. 406. Complaint procedures.

(a) The Board shall establish a citizen complaint procedure and shall receive and consider complaints from any citizen alleging violation by an employee of any Federal law or any rule or regulation promulgated under any Federal law; violation of any employee code of conduct or standard, including but not limited to those promulgated pursuant to this Act, or any rules or regulations promulgated by the Board; failure of any employee to carry out his duty under any Federal law, rule, or regulation; negligent or improper performance of duty by any employee of the United States.

The citizen complaint procedure established under this section shall include the following provisions:

(1) Complaints shall be filed with the Office of Inspection and Complaint, which shall within 60 days of the receipt of the complaint render a written decision setting forth findings of fact and including either an order dismissing the complaint or initiating prosecution before the Office of Trial Examiners; *provided, however*, that an order of dismissal under this section shall not bar or otherwise limit any other rights of the complainant to raise the same or similar issue before the Board or before any other agency; *provided further, however,* that any order of dismissal shall refer the complainant to any other appropriate Federal, state, or local agency.

(2) If the Office of Inspection and Complaint orders the complaint dismissed, the citizen complainant or any other citizen may appeal the order to the Board within 30 days of the entry of such order.

(3) If upon review of any order of dismissal appealed under this subsection, the Board upholds the order of dismissal, the citizen complainant or any citizen may appeal the order of the Board upholding such dismissal to the United States Court of Appeals of the District of Columbia or the United States Court of Appeals for the district in which the complainant resides.

(4) The Office of Inspection and Complaint shall prosecute all complaints which a trial examiner finds meritorious or which the Board has found meritorious, or which an appropriate appellate court has found meritorious. All such complaints shall be adjudicated as set out in sections 407 and 408.

(b) The Board shall establish an employee complaint procedure and shall receive and consider employee complaints alleging any misconduct enumerated in section 406(a) of this Title as well as violations of any rules or regulations of the Board relating to the rights of employees and an action against an employee or against the interests of any employee by his employer agency motivated by malice.

The complaint procedure established under this subsection shall include the same provisions enumerated in subsection (a) of this section for citizen complaints.

(c) The Board shall establish an agency complaint procedure and shall receive and consider complaints from agencies alleging any misconduct enumerated in section 406(a) of this Title or cause for removal or discipline as specified in the rules and regulations of the Board.

The complaint procedures established under this subsection shall include the following provisions:

(1) Agency complaints against an employee shall be presented directly to the Office of Trial Examiners and shall not be subject to review or consideration by the Office of Inspection and Complaint.

(2) Before any complaint is accepted by the Office of Trial Examiners under this subsection the agency shall

[a] Give advance notice 10 days prior to filing the proposed complaint stating specifically and in detail any and all reasons for the proposed action;

[b] At the time of notice thus required, inform the employee of his right to answer personally and in writing and to submit affidavits in support of his answer;

[c] Provide the employee with a decision on whether or not a complaint will be filed, stating the reasons which have been sustained and informing the employee of his rights before the Office of Trial Examiners, which notice and statement of rights shall have been approved by the Board; and

[d] File the complaint within five days of notification of the employee of the decision to file;

Provided, however, that the employee against whom a complaint has been filed may be suspended with pay during the period herein provided for agency action and such additional time as may be necessary for the agency to obtain a ruling from the trial examiner as prescribed in paragraph (3) of this subsection for suspension pending a final decision on the merits, if his continued presence poses a substantial risk of harm to himself, to his fellow employees, or to the public.

(3) If the employee does not object to the Office of Trial Examiners within 15 days of receiving a decision that a complaint will be filed, the trial examiner to whom the complaint has been assigned shall order the action sought by the agency complainant.

(4) If the employee objects to the action requested by the agency, the trial examiner to whom the complaint has been assigned shall order a hearing; *provided, however, that,* if he finds that the facts alleged in the complaint would, if true, support the conclusion that the employee's continued presence poses a substantial risk of harm to himself, to his fellow employees, or to the

public, the trial examiner may also order that the employee be suspended with pay pending final decision on the merits by the trial examiner.

Sec. 407. Hearing Procedures.

(a) Hearings on any complaints prosecuted by the Office of Inspection and Complaint or by any agency shall be conducted by a trial examiner provided by the Office of Trial Examiners.

(b) Complaint hearings shall conform to the requirements of 5 USC §554 as in effect at the time of approval of this Act.

(c) Any hearing conducted by a trial examiner pursuant to this Title shall be open to the public.

(d) For the purpose of any hearing under this Title, any trial examiner is empowered to administer oaths and affirmations, subpoena witnesses, compel their attendance, take evidence, and require the production of any books, papers, correspondence, memoranda, contracts, agreements, or other records which he deems relevant or material to the inquiry. Such attendance of witnesses and the production of any such records may be required from any place in any State or in any Territory or other place subject to the jurisdiction of the United States at any designated place of hearing.

(e) In case of contumacy by, or refusal to obey a subpoena issued to any person, the Board may invoke the aid of any court of the United States within the jurisdiction in which such hearing is held, or where such person resides or carries on business, in requiring the attendance and testimony of witnesses and the production of books, papers, correspondence, memoranda, contracts, agreements, and other records. And such court may issue an order requiring such person to appear before the trial examiner, there to produce records, if so ordered, or to give testimony touching the matter under investigation or in question; and any failure to obey such order of the court may be punished by such court as a contempt thereof. All process in any such case may be served in the judicial district whereof such person is an inhabitant or wherever he may be found. Any person who, without just cause, shall fail or refuse to attend and testify or to answer any lawful inquiry or to produce any records, if in his or its power to do so, in obedience to the subpoena of the trial examiner, shall be guilty of a misdemeanor and, upon conviction, shall be subject to a fine of not more than $10,000, or to imprisonment for a term of not more than one year, or both.

(f) At least three members of the Board must participate in the deliberation preceding a decision and the decision of any appeal brought before the Board pursuant to this Title.

(g) All decisions of the Board, of trial examiners, and of any other official or employee of the Board required to issue findings of fact or written decisions under this Act or under the rules or regulations of the Board shall be published in a convenient form and made available to the public at reasonable cost.

(h) Any person against whom a complaint has been brought under this section may be represented by counsel or by his agency or both.

Sec. 408. Appeal Procedures.

(a) Any employee or agency party to an action before the Office of Trial Examiners, or any complainant, may appeal the decision of a trial examiner to the Board, *provided, however,* that, with respect to citizen complaints, any citizen who is a member of a class of individuals intended to be protected by the law, rule, or regulation on which the complaint is based and who is affected by the alleged violation, omission, or negligent act, or any employee affected by the alleged violation, omission, or negligent act, may appeal a decision to the Board.

(b) In any appeal taken pursuant to this section, the Board shall review the record and uphold, reverse, or modify the decision of the trial examiner. The Board may order oral argument, on its own motion or on motion timely filed by any party, and provide such other procedures or rules as it deems practicable or desirable in any appeal under this section and consistent with the Employee Bill of Rights in Title II of this Act.

(c) Any employee or agency party to an appeal to the Board, any complainant, any citizen or employee affected by an alleged violation who appealed the decision of the trial examiner, and any other citizen or employee affected by an alleged violation, may appeal the decision of the Board to the United States Court of Appeals for the District of Columbia or the United States Court of Appeals for the district in which the appellant resides, *provided, however,* that the venue for such appeals shall not be such as to cause undue hardship to any employee or citizen.

(d) In any appeal in which official dereliction that may threaten public safety has been alleged, the court may remand the appeal to an appropriate district court for a hearing on the facts.

Sec. 409. Congressional Intent.

It is the intent of Congress that the Board effectuate the following policy through its regulations and decisions:

1. That public employees be made personally accountable for failure to enforce the laws and for negligence, incompetence, or improper performance of their public duties;

2. That the rights of employees to expose corruption, dishonesty, incompetence, or administrative failure be protected;

3. That the rights of employees to contact and communicate with Congress be protected;

4. That employees be protected from reprisal or retaliation for the performance of their duties; and

5. That civil servants be motivated to do their duties justly and efficiently.

Index